Other Books
by Susan Sheehan

*Is There No Place on Earth for Me?**

Ten Vietnamese

A Welfare Mother

A Prison and a Prisoner

Kate Quinton's Days

A Missing Plane

Life for Me Ain't Been No Crystal Stair

The Banana Sculptor, the Purple Lady, and the All-Night Swimmer: Hobbies, Collecting, and Other Passionate Pursuits (co-written with Howard Means)

*Winner of the 1983 Pulitzer Prize for General Nonfiction

More from The Sager Group

Our Washington, DC

America's Hometown in Transition

Edited by

Susan Sheehan

Winner of the Pulitzer Prize

Our Washington, DC: America's Hometown in Transition

Cover and interior design by Siori Kitajima, PatternBased.com

Cataloging-in-Publication data for this book is available from the Library of Congress.
ISBN-13:
eBook: 978-1-958861-57-8
Paperback: 978-1-958861-58-5

Published by The Sager Group LLC
(TheSagerGroup.net)

Our Washington, DC

America's Hometown in Transition

Edited by

Susan Sheehan
Winner of the Pulitzer Prize

THE SAGER GROUP

Artifex Te Adiuva

Contents

Foreword.. xiii

Publisher's Note xvii

A Word on Style xxi

Contributors... xxiii

"I Have a Dream . . . "...1

Peroration by Dr. King Sums Up A Day the Capital Will Remember

By James Reston, *The New York Times*, August 29, 1963

The Saving of the President..5

It was one of the most dramatic stories in the city's history. Here is what really happened—plus what doctors and nurses remember from that fateful day that President Ronald Reagan was shot outside a hotel near Dupont Circle.

By John Pekkanen, *Washingtonian*, August 1981

Prisoners of Overachievement.......................................45

The residents of Washington have a work ethic like no other town. They looooove their work. Just ask them.

By Walt Harrington, *The Washington Post Magazine*, November 12, 1988

L'Enfant Terrible...57

Brilliant and Unbearable, Pierre L'Enfant Made Washington Much of What it is Today

By Howard Means, *Washingtonian*, January 1990

Street on the Hill 87

The residents of Acker Street like to think of their street as a micro-cosm of Capitol Hill, and of Washington in general. In some ways it is a microcosm of the future, as well.

By David Finkel, *The Washington Post Magazine*, February 27, 1993

Gary Hart In Exile 115

The personal and political lessons of Gary Hart's career paved the way for Bill Clinton's victory, but the former Senator is still paying for his own defeat.

By David Remnick, *The New Yorker*, April 19, 1993

Rosetta's Legacy 135

For four years Dash, a reporter at *The Washington Post*, followed the lives of DC resident Rosa Lee Cunningham, her children, and five of her grandchildren, in an effort to understand the persistence of poverty and pathology within America's Black underclass. An excerpt from the book that grew out of the story, winner of the Pulitzer Prize and the Robert F. Kennedy Journalism Award.

By Leon Dash | excerpted from *Rosa Lee*, Basic Books, 1996

The Heiress and the Gaucho 159

She was the daughter of a Monaco billionaire. He was the son of an Argentine farmhand. They met in Virginia horse country and became passionate teammates on and off the polo field. Now she's been charged with his murder.

By Eddie Dean, *Washington City Paper*, October 31, 1997

He began his teaching stint with idealism.
And ended it in jail. 185

A pupil points a finger. A teacher is fired, his life rerouted. Now can
they be buddies?

By Marc Fisher, *The Washington Post Magazine*, April 6, 2003 and
January 30, 2015

City Hall, and Step On It 217
Stumping for a D.C. Council Seat, Marion Barry Is Covering Familiar
Ground. And in the Distance—Is That His Old Job?

By Wil Haygood, *The Washington Post Magazine*, September 11, 2004

When Washington Was Fun...233
The grand hostesses are history, the president would rather be in
bed, and there's a price tag on every evening these days. Who killed
Washington society? Ask a few of the local experts.

By Maureen Orth, *Vanity Fair*, December 2007

A Walk Through Congressional Cemetery 255
The 60,000 graves at Congressional Cemetery reveal stories about
our past that you won't find anywhere else

By Josh Swiller, *Washingtonian*, May 19, 2011

Inside DC's Secret Covid Morgue..263
During the Covid Pandemic, the District built a secret disaster
morgue, assembled an army of volunteers to staff it, and trained
people who had never previously seen a dead body to care for the
dead. This is the story of the Covid morgue—and the quiet force of
civil servants tending to everyone lost to Covid.

By Luke Mullins, *Washingtonian*, February 22, 2021

Requiem for the Supreme Court **279**

With the stroke of a pen, Justice Samuel Alito and four other justices, all chosen by Republican presidents running on successive party platforms committed to overturning Roe v. Wade, erased the constitutional right to reproductive autonomy that the Supreme Court recognized more than 49 years ago. The end of an era? Or the beginning of a new one?

By Linda Greenhouse, *The New York Times*, June 24/26 (digital/daily), 2022

Maya Lin's Vietnam memorial blazed a path in 1982, but no one followed. **285**

Architects and designers have avoided grappling with Maya Lin's genius.

By Philip Kennicott, *The Washington Post*, November 16, 2022

The Golden Age of the White House Correspondents' Dinner (Yes, there was one.) **291**

The annual gala had a great run of giddy, glamorous years—exactly 24 years, in fact. Let us explain.

By Amy Argetsinger; Roxanne Roberts, *The Washington Post*, April 28, 2023

Acknowledgements 299

Permissions 301

About the Editor 303

About the Publisher 305

Foreword

Like a lot of us, Susan Sheehan is an accidental Washingtonian. Born in Vienna, Austria, in 1937, she survived the Blitz in London as a very young girl and then settled with her parents into a rent-controlled apartment on the Upper East Side of Manhattan, where she was educated through junior and senior high at the highly selective Hunter College schools. (She failed the test for Hunter's elementary school when she botched the question "If you are walking on the sidewalk and hear a loud siren, what should you do?" Susan's "Hurry to the bomb shelter!" wasn't the answer the school was looking for.) College was Wellesley.

"My generation at Wellesley," she recalls, "often got pinned junior year, engaged senior year, and married the Saturday after gradua- tion. If you worked, you were apt to go into teaching. A significant number of my classmates had children in their early twenties. It didn't happen that way for me. I believe I was lucky."

Maybe, more accurately, she made her own luck. After a three- month stint with a Manhattan ad agency, Susan landed a position as a fact-checker with *Esquire* magazine. A year and a half later, she went out on her own as a freelancer, and two months after that she sold her first piece to *The New Yorker*. By 1961, she was a staff writer for the magazine, migrating from short, humorous "casuals" to long factual articles on subjects such as welfare, imprisonment, and foster care.

Within a very few years, Susan had become part of the New York literary scene, which led—as happens in storybooks and some- times in real life—to a blind date arranged by (the now legendary journalists) Gay Talese and David Halberstam with Neil Sheehan, a young reporter just back from covering the war in Vietnam for United Press International. The *Times* hired him in June 1964; the providential date took place in September; the newspaper dispatched Neil to Indonesia in January 1965. The two had fallen in love quickly and Susan flew out to be married to Neil in March 1965. After a few months in Djakarta, Neil was transferred to Saigon, where the paper had a one-year limit on war zone reporting.

"By the summer of 1966, Neil needed another assignment, and the *Times* offered him nothing he liked. There was something in South America, which he had no interest in—he'd been a Middle Eastern history major at Harvard—and a couple of other places that didn't inspire him."

This is where Washington finally enters the story. "Someone was good enough to tell Neil to contact the Washington bureau. Neil had planned to stay abroad, as a foreign correspondent, but in the summer of 1966 Scotty Reston [James B. Reston, of *The New York Times*, collected here also], and Tom Wicker [the bureau chief], convinced him to take the job as Pentagon correspondent, which was open. Maria, our first daughter, was born in January 1967. Catherine, our second daughter, was born in July 1969."

In some ways, the rest is history. Neil would go on to fame for his role in surfacing the Pentagon Papers and to literary renown for his monumental history of the War in Vietnam: *A Bright Shining Lie: John Paul Vann and America in Vietnam*, winner of the 1989 National Book Award for Nonfiction and the Pulitzer Prize for General Nonfiction. Susan would continue writing for *The New Yorker* over the decades to come and publish seven books, including *Is There No Place on Earth for Me?*, awarded the 1983 Pulitzer Prize for Nonfiction. Rarely in reportorial or literary history has a couple been more honored.

These honors have been hard won. *A Bright Shining Lie* was sixteen (sometimes tortured) years in the writing. Susan couldn't financially afford to abandon her career, and much of the time felt that she had landed in an alien land.

The transition to Washington from New York was, she says, "a serious adjustment," not helped by the fact that they bought a house in Wesley Heights, near American University, rather than someplace closer in and better served by public transportation.

"Everyone told us to go directly to Cleveland Park, but Neil didn't like the stucco houses on the market at the time. He'd grown up in a family of modest means, but they owned a small, pleasant brick house in Massachusetts. So, we bought this brick house that was way beyond our incomes and our imaginations, and the $35,000 mortgage kept me awake at night."

The location also left her feeling isolated. "I have no peripheral vision, so I've never driven a car. That was fine in New York, but not so fine in this section of Northwest Washington. I'd always been a real subway and bus rider. I could go almost anywhere in Manhattan and other parts of the city on its frequent and round-the-clock subways. There was no Metro in Washington then, and the bus service was far more limited than New York's."

For half a century, Susan avoided her transportation issues by commuting every third week—by air or rail—to New York, where she would stay with her parents while researching her articles and books. Maria and Catherine spent virtually every school holiday with her and have fond memories of helping to run *The New Yorker*'s switchboard. She kept up this two-city life until recently. Neil died in 2021, but Susan is still in the house the Sheehans bought almost sixty years ago. Maria and Catherine and her teenage grandsons, Nicholas and Andrew, live nearby.

Twenty years ago, Susan and I co-authored a collection of profiles of forty people whose passionate pursuits—hobbies, collections, and avocations—bordered on (and sometimes crossed into) the obsessive. I confess to worrying a bit that the author of highly researched books, primarily about the disadvantaged, might turn our book toward a more somber examination than the material merited. But Susan, who is a little singular herself, dove into the project with a glee that belied both our years. In the end, *The Banana Sculptor, the Purple Lady, and the All-Night Swimmer*—among the longest titles Simon & Schuster has ever published—was sheer joy to work on.

Thanks to Susan's long-time friendship with Evelyn Lauder, a Hunter High classmate, and her husband, Leonard, the cosmetics heir and famed art collector, the book also got one of the great launch parties of all time, held in the Lauders' Fifth Avenue penthouse. I had slipped away from the living room and was studying an Edvard Munch painting hanging, as I recall, in the dining room, when another man wandered into the room, gazed up at the Munch, and said, "It holds the eye, doesn't it?" The other man, I soon realized, was Kurt Vonnegut. Susan existed unchanged and unfazed in multiple worlds.

Susan grew up reading *The New York Times* and became a devoted reader of *The Washington Post*, though it would take time to consider DC her home. In this collection she shares some of the writing of other great journalists that has made the nation's capital, its people, places, and events come alive for her during the nearly sixty years of her residence.

—Howard Means

Publisher's Note

A little more than a year ago, I received an email from my friend Patsy Sims—a pioneering female journalist and former director of Goucher College's well-regarded Creative Nonfiction Program—asking if The Sager Group might be interested in publishing an anthology of nonfiction stories about Washington, DC, written by well-known literary journalists, edited by the Pulitzer Prize-winning journalist Susan Sheehan.

Of course, I knew Sheehan and her work. We'd emailed several times when TSG featured one of her pieces in an anthology of memorable articles by great women journalists, *The Stories We Tell*, edited by Sims, published in 2017.

Sheehan is a long-time correspondent for *The New Yorker* and the author of eight books. She was married for 56 years to the late Neil Sheehan, who would be written into the history of the free press for his role in surfacing the Pentagon Papers, and also for his monumental history of the war in Vietnam: *A Bright Shining Lie*.

Both Susan and Neil were part of what I like to think of as The Greatest Generation . . . of journalists. Men and women like Gay Talese, David Halberstam, James R. "Scotty" Reston, Bob Woodward, Walter Cronkite, Barbara Walters, Martha Gellhorn, Edna Buchanan, Teresa Carpenter, Joan Didion, Janet Malcolm, others. During this era, pretty much everyone agreed that the order of the day was verifiable, fact-based journalism, guided by ethical standards and a steadfast commitment to finding the truth. People trusted the news because it was trustworthy.

My response to Sims: "Hell yeah!"

Sheehan, who would turn out to be a joy to work with, always humble and enthusiastic, would later write in an email: "Let your enthusiasm be contagious," "'Hell yeah!' are two words I already cherish."

At 87, Sheehan—Vienna born and New York City raised—was interested in putting together a collection of diverse stories that together portrayed some of the many facets of DC, the city that became her adopted hometown some sixty years ago.

Once we got on the same page with our digital tools, the Google list of stories Susan delivered was in turns bright, focused, and eclectic; humorous and weighty; surprising and dead on. Like the many ingredients in a good stew, all blended together, these stories bring forth the rich and complex aromas of America's hometown over the past half century.

I have learned by practice that building an anthology takes patience—you must decide upon and hunt copies of the pieces you want, and after that, you have to hunt down the rights holders.

In the case of *Our Washington, DC*, the rights to most of the stories were owned by news organizations. Though I encountered (mostly) nothing but kindness along the way, cutting through red tape and negotiating reasonable fees takes time. I'm still smarting from the loss of two stories from *Politico*—including a great piece on pandas!—but their price was too rich for our budget.

Regardless, here we are, 13 months after Sims' first email, finally ready to go to formatting and then to press. Earlier this year, in January, Sheehan (may I break the rules of good newswriting and refer to her Susan from here out?) wrote to me, in a somewhat offhand tone, with the sobering news that she has "an illness that is not going away, so there really is a deadline . . . It means a lot to me to see the book published this year."

And so we have proceeded, full speed ahead.

In another email, Susan noted that she was proud to emphasize that this collection will be her first digital book (it will be paperback as well) and it will also be her first book about "the city it took me so long to consider home."

From the earliest age, she told me, Susan was a "print junkie." As a youngster she had few children's books, but *The New York Times* landed on her parents' doormat seven days a week, and thus she learned to read: the movie section and the sports section were her first primers, she said.

Once she moved to Washington, she naturally subscribed to *The Washington Post*, "as much for local news—supermarket ads, romantic liaisons, and real-estate prices—as for international and national coverage." Through her years in residence, she has also been a great reader of local magazines and alternative weeklies, including *Washingtonian*, *City Paper*, and later *The Atlantic* and *Politico*.

Susan has always interacted with the world through the filter of great reporting and writing. From this point of view comes her idea of painting a portrait of her adopted hometown with a collection of the stories that left strong enough impressions to stick with her through the years.

I am proud to say we have assembled a wonderful lineup of amazing writers, some of whom I know personally from my own 19-year stint as a newsperson living in Washington, DC; all of whom I have read and enjoyed as wonderful stylists and trusted voices. When you live in DC, of course, it's not all about politics. As a local resident, you have a life to live, places to go, things to do. Your backdrop just happens to be the most powerful city on earth. In describing their hometown, all of these fine writers bring their residency and feelings to bear.

While it was statedly not Susan's idea to write a political book, it has been my experience that a random sample can often yield universal truths.

Published in chronological order, *Our Washington, DC* begins with James R. Reston's eyewitness account of Martin Luther King's historic and hopeful "I Have a Dream" speech on the National Mall in 1963 . . . and features antepenultimately a Linda Greenhouse *Times* column from 2022 decrying the Supreme Court's decision to strike down Roe v. Wade.

Washington, DC, America's hometown, is today in a period of rapid transition. As I write this, it feels that time is not marching but sprinting along. The future is yet to be seen. A free press will always be the best window.

—Mike Sager, April 2025

A Word on Style

The stories collected in this book may include words, attitudes, and sensibilities about gender, race, body-image, socio-economic class, and politics that reflect the time and place in which they were written, researched, and published. Some elements may be potentially triggering to modern readers. The stories have been left in their original form as befits historical writings.

"History is not the past, but a map of the past, drawn from a particular point of view, to be useful to the modern traveler."

—*Henry H. Glassie*

Contributors

Amy Argetsinger is an editor for the Style section of *The Washington Post*. A staff writer with *The Post* since 1995, she covered the Maryland suburbs, higher education, and later the West Coast as an L.A.-based reporter before serving eight years as the "Reliable Source," the paper's daily chronicle of Washington DC's notables and society events, which she co-wrote with Roxanne Roberts. The two appeared regularly on Friday evening segments of MSNBC's *Tucker* before the show was cancelled.

Leon Dash was born March 16, 1944 in New Bedford, Massachusetts, and grew up in New York City's Harlem and The Bronx. Dash is a 1968 graduate of Howard University with a BA in history. Dash was one of 44 journalists who founded the National Association of Black Journalists on December 12, 1975. Dash first worked as a reporter at *The Washington Post* from 1966 to 1968. He took a two-year leave of absence and worked as a Peace Corps volunteer high school teacher in rural Kenya, East Africa, in 1969 and 1970.

Dash returned to *The Post* in 1971. He lived with and reported on Angolan guerrillas on two occasions: June-September 1973 and October 1976-May 1977, and hiked 2,100 miles on foot through war-torn Angola on the second trip. Dash left *The Post* in 1998 to teach journalism at the University of Illinois Urbana-Champaign, where he taught until retirement in July 2025.

Eddie Dean is a journalist based in the Washington, DC area. He has written for *The Wall Street Journal*, *Spin*, *The Washington Post*, *Harper's*, *Washington City Paper*, *Men's Journal*, and *Washingtonian*, among other publications. He is the author of *Pure Country: The Leon Kagarise Archives 1961-1971*, and co-author of *Man of Constant Sorrow: My Life and Times by Dr Ralph Stanley*. His weekly radio show on American roots music,

Roadside Attraction, is broadcast Saturdays on WOWD-LP (94.3 FM), Takoma Park, MD, takomaradio.org.

David Finkel is a journalist and author whose honors include a Pulitzer Prize and a MacArthur Foundation genius grant. A graduate of the University of Florida, he lives in the Washington, DC area.

Marc Fisher is a columnist and associate editor at *The Washington Post*. His op-ed column covers Washington and its federal and local faces. His reporting has taken him from the Arab Spring revolutions to the presidential campaign trail. In 2016, he co-authored a biography of Donald Trump, *Trump Revealed: An American Journey of Ambition, Ego, Money, and Power* (Scribner), which was a *New York Times* bestseller.

He has won two Pulitzer Prizes for his reporting: the Public Service award in 2014 for his stories on government surveillance of Americans, as part of *The Post's* coverage of the Edward Snowden case; and the National Reporting award in 2016 for his articles on police shootings.

Fisher's history of radio since the advent of television, *Something in the Air: Radio, Rock and the Revolution that Shaped a Generation*, was published by Random House in 2007. Fisher also wrote *After the Wall: Germany, the Germans and the Burdens of History*, published by Simon and Schuster in 1995. He has also written for many magazines, including *The New Yorker*, *The Atlantic*, *GQ*, *Moment*, *Columbia Journalism Review*, and *American Journalism Review*.

Linda Greenhouse is a senior research scholar in law at Yale Law School, where she taught from 2009 to 2023. For the previous thirty years, she was the Supreme Court correspondent for *The New York Times* and won a Pulitzer Prize in 1998 for her coverage of the Court. Her commentary on the Court appears frequently in the *Times'* opinion pages, as well as in *The New York Review of Books* and other publications. Linda is a graduate of Radcliffe College (Harvard) and earned a Master of Studies in Law degree from Yale Law School.

In her extracurricular life, she has served on a number of nonprofit boards, including the Harvard Board of Overseers and the National Senate of Phi Beta Kappa. She served from 2017 to 2023 as president of the American Philosophical Society, the country's oldest learned society, founded by Benjamin Franklin in 1743. She is an elected member of the American Academy of Arts & Sciences, where she served on the Council for more than 20 years, and an honorary member of the American Law Institute. She is the author of six books, including *Becoming Justice Blackmun*, a biography of the Supreme Court Justice; *The U.S. Supreme Court: A Very Short Introduction*; and a memoir, *Just a Journalist*. *Justice on the Brink: A Requiem for the Supreme Court* was published by Random House in 2021. She has received 13 honorary degrees.

Linda and her husband, Eugene Fidell, live in Stockbridge, MA, and Pasadena, CA. Their daughter, Hannah Fidell, is a film director and writer in Los Angeles.

Walt Harrington is a former staff writer at *The Washington Post Magazine*, an Emeritus Professor of Journalism at the University of Illinois, and the author or editor of eleven books, including *The Detective: And Other Stories* and *The Everlasting Stream: A True Story of Rabbits, Guns, Friendship, and Family*.

Wil Haygood has worked as a journalist at *The Boston Globe*, where he was a Pulitzer Prize finalist, and *The Washington Post*, where he won many national awards. His *Washington Post* article about White House butler Eugene Allen was adapted into the major motion picture, *The Butler*, directed by Lee Daniels and starring, among others, Forest Whitaker, Oprah Winfrey, Colman Domingo, Jane Fonda, and Vanessa Redgrave. Haygood is also the author of biographies of Sammy Davis Jr., Sugar Ray Robinson, Adam Clayton Powell Jr., and Thurgood Marshall.

Philip Kennicott is the Pulitzer Prize-winning art and architecture critic of *The Washington Post*. He has been on staff at *The Post* since 1999, first as classical music critic, then as culture critic. In 2011, he combined art and architecture into a beat focused on visual culture and public space. Kennicott is the author of *Counterpoint: A Memoir of Bach and Mourning* (Norton 2020) and has also been a finalist for the Pulitzer Prize in editorial writing and the National Magazine Award, and an Emmy Award nominee.

Howard Means is a former senior editor at *Washingtonian* magazine. He is the author or co-author of eleven books including, most recently, *67 Shots: Kent State and the End of American Innocence* and *Splash! 10,000 Years of Swimming*. He and his wife, Candy, live in Millwood, Virginia, in the Northern Shenandoah Valley.

Luke Mullins is a contributing writer at *Politico* and co-author of *The Wolves of K Street: The Secret History of How Big Money Took Over Big Government*, published by Simon & Schuster. He has been a senior writer at *Washingtonian*, and he's also written for *The Atlantic*, *The New York Times*, *The Washington Post*, *Esquire*, and *Outside*, among other publications. He lives in Washington, DC, with his wife and son.

Maureen Orth first observed the Washington social scene after completing Peace Corps training for Colombia in the 60s when, as a recent graduate of UC Berkeley, she was invited to a dinner on the presidential yacht Sequoia. It was there she asked Bobby Kennedy whether he would run for vice president or senator. After her Peace Corps service in Medellin, where she helped build a school the community named for her, she began her first job in Washington. While on Capitol Hill in 1970, Orth organized House hearings for the first Earth Day. She moved permanently to Washington in 1989, as a special correspondent for *Vanity Fair*, and has been observing the mores of "cave dwellers," politicos, and presidents ever since.

Orth was one of *Newsweek*'s first female writers and produced covers on icons like Bob Dylan, Stevie Wonder, and Bruce Springsteen. Her groundbreaking pieces in *Vanity Fair* have included both profiles on Vladimir Putin and Margaret Thatcher as well as investigative scoops on Michael Jackson's and Woody Allen's child abuse charges. Orth's book *Vulgar Favors: the Assassination of Gianni Versace* was the basis of the FX Emmy-winning series. She founded the Marina Orth Foundation in Colombia in 2004 for underserved students who today win international robotics competitions and graduate from top universities. For her efforts and leadership in educational opportunities, Orth was honored with Colombian citizenship in 2022. She is currently writing her memoir.

John Pekkanen (born February 11, 1939, in Lyme, Connecticut) is an author, two-time National Magazine Award-winning American journalist, and the winner of ten other national journalism awards, including the National Headliner Award, the Penney-Missouri Award for medical journalism, and the Award of Excellence from the American College of Emergency Physicians.

A former correspondent and bureau chief for *Life* magazine and a senior writer for *Washingtonian*, Pekkanen has written for *The New Republic*, *The Atlantic Monthly*, and *Town and Country*. He is the author of *Donor: How One Girl's Death Gave Life to Others*; *The Best Doctors in the U.S.*; *Victims: An Account of a Rape*; *The American Connection - Profiteering and Politicking in the "Ethical" Drug Industry*; *M.D.: Doctors Talk about Themselves*; and *My Father, My Son* with Admiral Elmo Zumwalt and Lieutenant Elmo Zumwalt. He is also a published poet. Pekkanen has been a Nieman Fellow at Harvard University. He lives in the Washington, DC area.

David Remnick has been the editor of *The New Yorker* since 1998 and a staff writer since 1992. He has written hundreds of pieces for the magazine; under his leadership, *The New Yorker* has become the country's most honored magazine, the first magazine to receive a Pulitzer Prize for its writing. He also serves as the host of the magazine's national radio program and podcast, "The New Yorker Radio Hour."

Remnick began his reporting career in 1982, as a staff writer at *The Washington Post*, where he covered stories for the Metro, Sports, and Style sections. In 1988, he started a four-year assignment as a *Washington Post* Moscow correspondent, an experience that formed the basis of his 1993 book, *Lenin's Tomb: The Last Days of the Soviet Empire*. In 1994, "Lenin's Tomb" received both the Pulitzer Prize for nonfiction and a George Polk Award for excellence in journalism. He is the author of seven books.

James "Scotty" Barrett Reston (November 3, 1909 – December 6, 1995) was an American journalist whose career spanned the mid-1930s to the early 1990s. He was associated for many years with *The New York Times*, for which he interviewed many of the world's leaders and wrote extensively about the leading events and issues of his time. A two-time winner of the Pulitzer Prize. He is the author of numerous books, including *Deadline: A Memoir*, published in 1991.

Reston was also awarded the Presidential Medal of Freedom, the chevalier of the Légion d'honneur from France, the Order of St. Olav from Norway, the Order of Merit from Chile, the Order of Leopold from Belgium, and honorary degrees from 28 universities.

Roxanne Roberts is a reporter covering Washington's social, political, and philanthropic power brokers. She has been at *The Washington Post* since 1988, working for the Style section as a feature writer and columnist. Roberts is the co-author of "The Reliable Source" column with Amy Argetsinger, the paper's daily chronicle of Washington DC's notables and society events. She is a regular panelist on the NPR quiz show *Wait Wait . . . Don't Tell Me!*

Josh Swiller is the author of *The Unheard, a Memoir of Deafness and Africa*, and *Bright Shining World*, a young adult novel. He has won numerous awards for his fiction and journalism. He lives with his family in upstate New York.

"I Have a Dream…"

Peroration by Dr. King Sums Up A Day the Capital Will Remember

By James Reston

WASHINGTON, Aug. 28—Abraham Lincoln, who presided in his stone temple today above the children of the slaves he emancipated, may have used just the right words to sum up the general reaction to the Negro's massive march on Washington. "I think," he wrote to Gov. Andrew G. Curtin of Pennsylvania in 1861, "the necessity of being ready increases. Look to it." Washington may not have changed a vote today, but it is a little more conscious tonight of the necessity of being ready for freedom. It may not "look to it" at once, since it is looking to so many things, but it will be a long time before it forgets the melodious and melancholy voice of the Rev. Dr. Martin Luther King Jr. crying out his dreams to the multitude.

It was Dr. King who, near the end of the day, touched the vast audience. Until then the pilgrimage was merely a great spectacle. Only those marchers from the embattled towns in the Old Confederacy had anything like the old crusading zeal. For many the day seemed an adventure, a long outing in the late summer sun— part liberation from home, part Sunday School picnic, part political convention, and part fish-fry.

But Dr. King brought them alive in the afternoon with a peroration that was an anguished echo from all the old American reformers.

Roger Williams calling for religious liberty, Sam Adams calling for political liberty, old man Thoreau denouncing coercion, William Lloyd Garrison demanding emancipation, and Eugene V. Debs crying for economic equality—Dr. King echoed them all.

"I have a dream," he cried again and again. And each time the dream was a promise out of our ancient articles of faith: phrases from the Constitution, lines from the great anthem of the nation, guarantees from the Bill of Rights, all ending with a vision that they might one day all come true.

Find Journey Worthwhile

Dr. King touched all the themes of the day, only better than anybody else. He was full of the symbolism of Lincoln and Gandhi, and the cadences of the Bible. He was both militant and sad, and he sent the crowd away feeling that the long journey had been worthwhile.

This demonstration impressed political Washington because it combined a number of things no politician can ignore. It had the force of numbers. It had the melodies of both the church and the theater. And it was able to invoke the principles of the founding fathers to rebuke the inequalities and hypocrisies of modern American life.

There was a paradox in the day's performance. The Negro leaders demanded equality "now," while insisting that this was only the "beginning" of the struggle. Yet it was clear that the "now," which appeared on almost every placard on Constitution Avenue, was merely an opening demand, while the exhortation to increase the struggle was what was really on the leaders' minds.

The question of the day, of course, was raised by Dr. King's theme: Was this all a dream or will it help the dream come true?

No doubt this vast effort helped the Negro drive against discrimination. It was better covered by television and the press than any event here since President Kennedy's inauguration, and, since indifference is almost as great a problem to the Negro as hostility, this was a plus.

None of the dreadful things Washington feared came about. The racial hooligans were scarce. Even the local Nazi, George Lincoln Rockwell, minded his manners, which is an extraordinary innovation for him. And there were fewer arrests than any normal day for Washington, probably because all the saloons and hootch peddlers were closed.

Politicians Are Impressed

The crowd obviously impressed the politicians. The presence of nearly a quarter of a million petitioners anywhere always makes a Senator think. He seldom ignores that many potential votes, and it did not escape the notice of Congressmen that these Negro organizations, some of which had almost as much trouble getting out a crowd as the Washington Senators several years ago, were now capable of organizing the largest demonstrating throng ever gathered at one spot in the District of Columbia.

It is a question whether this rally raised too many hopes among the Negroes or inspired the Negroes here to work harder for equality when they got back home. Most observers here think the latter is true, even though all the talk of "Freedom NOW" and instant integration is bound to lead to some disappointment.

The meetings between the Negro leaders on the one hand and President Kennedy and the Congressional leaders on the other also went well and probably helped the Negro cause. The Negro leaders were careful not to seem to be putting improper pressure on Congress. They made no specific requests or threats, but they argued their case in small groups and kept the crowd off Capitol Hill.

Whether this will win any new votes for the civil rights and economic legislation will probably depend on the over-all effect of the day's events on the television audience.

The Major Imponderable

This is the major imponderable of the day. The speeches were varied and spotty. Like their white political brethren, the Negroes cannot run a political meeting without letting everybody talk. Also, the platform was a bedlam of moving figures who seemed to be interested in everything except listening to the speaker. This distracted the audience.

Nevertheless, Dr. King and Roy Wilkins, head of the National Association for the Advancement of Colored People, and one or two others got the message across. James Baldwin, the author, summed up the day succinctly. The day was important in itself, he said, and "what we do with this day is even more important."

He was convinced that the country was finally grappling with the Negro problem instead of evading it; that the Negro himself was "for the first time" aware of his value as a human being and was "no longer at the mercy of what the white people imagine the Negro to be."

Merely the Beginning

On the whole, the speeches were not calculated to make Republican politicians very happy with the Negro. This may hurt, for, without substantial Republican support, the Kennedy program on civil rights and jobs is not going through.

Apparently this point impressed President Kennedy, who listened to some of the speeches on television. When the Negro leaders came out of the White House, Dr. King emphasized that bipartisan support was essential for passage of the Kennedy civil rights program.

Aside from this, the advantages of the day for the Negro cause outran the disadvantages.

Above all, they got over Lincoln's point that "the necessity of being ready increases." For they left no doubt that this was not the climax of their campaign for equality but merely the beginning, that they were going to stay in the streets until they could get equality in the schools, restaurants, houses and employment agencies of the nation, and that, as they demonstrated here today, they had found an effective way to demonstrate for changes in the laws without breaking the law themselves.

—*The New York Times* | Aug. 29, 1963

The Saving of the President

It was one of the most dramatic stories in the city's history. Here is what really happened—plus what doctors and nurses remember from that fateful day that President Ronald Reagan was shot outside a hotel near Dupont Circle.

By John Pekkanen

For four tense hours on March 30, 1981, Washington and the rest of the world held its breath awaiting word on the fate of President Ronald Reagan. If history were to repeat itself, this president would die, just like the previous four American presidents struck by an assassin's bullet.

That did not happen because of the skill of a team of doctors and nurses, and a little bit of luck. Just two months in office when he was shot, Reagan went on to establish himself as one the most important presidents of the 20th century.

The assassination attempt became a watershed event in his life and presidency. Reagan believed he had been spared for a reason, a sentiment he expressed in his diary on his first evening back in the

White House. "I know it's going to be a long recovery," he wrote. "Whatever happens now I owe my life to God and will try to serve him every way I can."

This article originally ran in the August 1981 *Washingtonian* and tells how perilously close to death President Reagan came. To accompany this story, the author, John Pekkanen, went back to the key people involved in the saving of the President to get their 2004 perspective on one of the most dramatic events in the history of Washington.

About 2:30 PM on Monday, March 30, President Ronald Reagan walked out of the VIP entrance of the Washington Hilton Hotel after speaking to a labor audience. As a reporter shouted, "Mr. President, Mr. President," a series of shots, sounding like firecrackers, were fired. Secret Service agent Jerry Parr instinctively pushed the President into his waiting limousine, which sped away. As Parr recalled the moment: "I pushed [President Reagan] up to the right rear [of the car]. I ran my hands over his body looking for some kind of wound. He claimed that I had hurt his ribs in landing on top of him, so I told the driver to head to the White House, the safest place. Shortly after that, I would say in a space of 10 or 15 seconds, he started coughing up a little blood. It was bright red, and I knew from my training that this was oxygenated blood—this is blood coming out of the lung. This occurred just as the limousine was in the tunnel [on Connecticut Avenue] beneath Dupont Circle. As soon as I saw the blood, indicating a wound in the lung, I told the driver to head for George Washington. . . . "

They call it "The White Phone," and it sat, all but forgotten, in the emergency room of George Washington University Hospital. It was a Princess phone, hidden away on the corner of a desk at the nurses' station, with a direct link to a communications signal board at the White House.

On that Monday afternoon it rang. Wendy Koenig, an emergency-room nurse, answered. The voice she heard was brusque: "The presidential motorcade is en route to your facility."

That was all the voice said.

Her first thought was that someone had become ill, but not the President—they would have mentioned the President. She moved automatically to the trauma bay at the far end of the emergency room to set up intravenous lines.

Moments later the white phone rang again. Herman Goodyear, the emergency-room secretary, answered. A man's voice said, "We have three gunshot wounds coming in."

The news sped through the emergency room. Something big; multiple trauma. ER personnel moved quickly to make room. A woman who had suffered a cardiac arrest on the street minutes earlier was in the trauma bay with the resuscitation team working on her. She had to be moved.

Kathy Paul, a 28-year-old ER nurse, heard part of a report coming over the radio of the police officer who had accompanied the stricken woman. There had been a shooting at the Hilton. A police officer had been hit.

But not a word about the President.

The section of the ER set up for major trauma now clear, Kathy Paul walked toward the ER main entrance, which faced Pennsylvania Avenue. It had been less than three minutes since the first call on the white phone.

She watched as a black limousine pulled into the ER driveway, stopped, and out of the rear door stepped the President of the United States. She noticed he was dressed in a blue pinstriped suit, but her eyes riveted on his face, which was ashen. He looked frightened.

He walked through the three sets of double doors and said, "I feel like I can't catch my breath." He groaned, his knees buckled, and he began to fall backward. At that point Kathy Paul no longer was awed. The President now was a patient.

She grabbed his arm and, with a paramedic and two Secret Service agents, helped carry him the 40 to 50 feet to the trauma bay at the rear of the ER. They put him on a stretcher in 5A.

The trauma bay gleamed with the latest medical technology. Looming over the President's left side was a rectangular column that held the paraphernalia of trauma resuscitation, including bottled oxygen. Intravenous bottles filled with saline and lactose solutions hung at the ready. Shelves of gauze bandages, syringes, and sterile instrument packs surrounded him.

The President lay flat on the stretcher, bright lights in his eyes, his brows furrowed, his expression worried. There wasn't any obvious sign of injury, and hospital staffers had received no word in those first confusing minutes that the President might have been injured.

"I feel so bad," he said, laboring for air.

They began the trauma protocol.

Kathy Paul leaned over the President and started ripping and cutting off his clothes. All of them. The President kept repeating that he felt bad, that he didn't understand why he was finding it so hard to breathe. She thought he must be having a heart attack: His paleness, his breathing and chest discomfort all fit. She kept ripping. So did Wendy Koenig, who noticed a RR monogram on his shirt just before she tore it off.

Now standing at the bottom end of the President's stretcher was the tall figure of Dr. Daniel Ruge, his personal physician. Ruge had been at the Hilton. After making certain none of the injured on the sidewalk was the President, he had jumped into an official car that followed the presidential limousine to GW. A well-known neuro-surgeon, he now put his hand on the President's foot to monitor his pulse, which was steady and strong. Ruge offered reassuring words to the President.

A crowd of Secret Service agents, DC policemen, and hospital personnel hovered in the ER. Radios squawked. The sounds of sirens still echoed outside. The noise in the ER mounted. At times it was nearly deafening.

Wendy Koenig put a blood-pressure cuff on the President's arm. She pumped it up and waited for the thumping sound of the pulse in her stethoscope.

Not a sound.

"I can't hear anything," she yelled.

"I can't get a systolic pressure."

The President is arresting, she thought, right here in front of me. She had to fight back tears. She remembered a nightmare she'd had a few months earlier, just after Ronald Reagan was elected president. He had been in the ER, ill and under her care. The memory of the nightmare was vivid. And now it was happening.

She pumped up the cuff again. Nothing.

She couldn't tell whether the President's blood pressure was too low or the noise level in the ER too high.

She pumped up the cuff one more time, and she palpated an artery with her fingers. She felt the first throb, somewhere between 50 and 60 systolic, a low pressure, suggesting shock. Normal would be 130.

Two minutes had elapsed since Ronald Reagan had walked in.

Cindy Hines, a medical technician, had automatically begun inserting intravenous (IV) lines into the arm of the man lying in front of her. In the excitement she'd never learned who he was. Not until she had put an IV line in his arm did she take the time to look up and see his face.

In trauma resuscitation there is nothing more precious than time; speed is the inviolable first principle. It is during the "golden hour"—the first 60 minutes—that most trauma patients are saved or lost. Most of those lost die from shock, caused when the body's blood volume becomes so depleted that there is not enough to go around. People in deep shock can be resuscitated. But if too much time is lost before shock is reversed, the major organs can't support the body, and the patient dies.

The President was ashen because his involuntary nervous system had taken over, redirecting his blood flow away from his skin and extremities and into his vital organs. There is little question that in those first few minutes the President was very close to shock if not in shock itself—as one of his physicians later said, the President was "on the brink."

No one knew what was wrong, because there was no obvious sign of injury. Jerry Parr, the Secret Service agent who had landed on the President in the limousine and then directed it to GW, an act which probably saved Ronald Reagan's life, thought he might have cracked one of the President's ribs. But in those first two or three minutes none of the nurses noticed any blood or other sign of injury. It was only when Kathy Paul saw blood on the President's hand and Cindy Hines noticed blood inside his mouth that they knew he wasn't arresting; he was hurt.

Urgent messages had already been dispatched by the paging operators throughout the hospital: "Trauma team to the emergency room." Many doctors also were paged individually.

A meeting of department chairmen and administrators on the top floor of the Burns Building, just across 23rd Street from the main hospital, was interrupted when Michael Barch, administrator of the Medical Center, answered his page. He came back in the room and announced that the meeting was over because the President of the United States was across the street in the emergency room.

Three physicians—surgical residents David Gens, Brad Bennett, and Paul Colombani—meeting for their regular Monday-afternoon discussion group in an on-call room, heard their pagers go off at the same time. Bennett answered. "You're wanted in the emergency room. Stat."

Stat, says a doctor, "means you get there before your clothes."

They came running.

Dr. Sol Edelstein, director of the emergency room, had just driven his wife home from the hospital, where she'd given birth to a son five days earlier. She had extracted a promise from him that he would take a week off. His pager went off minutes after they walked in the door.

Edelstein made the 20-minute drive from his home in Glen Echo Heights to the hospital in seven minutes.

"I can't breathe," the President repeated. The nurses took turns holding his hand and reassured him. He lay with his arms at his sides, his expression worried, but he was conscious and calm.

Three IV lines were now pushing fluids and packed red cells into him, boosting his rapidly depleting blood volume and blood-oxygen level.

Perhaps three minutes had elapsed since the President's arrival.

The first GW physicians to treat the president were Dr. Wesley Price, a senior resident who was not on the trauma team but who hurried down from an upstairs pathology office when he saw the motorcade heading into the hospital, and Dr. William O'Neill, an intern on the trauma team.

O'Neill thought his page was routine until he rounded the final corridor to the ER. From there he noticed a black limousine parked where the ambulances usually were, and he saw the presidential seal. "I hope it's not the President," he thought to himself.

Secret Service men made quick checks and allowed Price and O'Neill to go into the trauma bay. Both were stunned when they saw the President on the stretcher with lines going into his arms.

"Can anybody tell me what happened?" Price asked. No one seemed to know.

O'Neill, who had worked in the emergency room as an undergraduate, had seen a lot of trauma. "You develop an immediate gut feeling as to who is really sick and who isn't," he said later. When he saw the President he felt he was looking at someone potentially in jeopardy.

The President's palpable blood pressure was up to 78 systolic—still abnormally low but an improvement. The fluids were doing their job. The President's pulse was 88 and steady, an encouraging sign.

"Mr. President, where do you hurt?" O'Neill asked.

"My chest hurts, and I'm having trouble breathing."

"Do you know what happened?"

"Not really."

"Are you hurting anywhere else?"

"No, I don't think so."

The President was thinking clearly and able to move all four limbs. To ease his breathing, they propped his head up about 30 degrees.

Wesley Price, the son of a North Carolina preacher, put a stethoscope to the President's chest and listened for breath sounds. Listening to the right lung, he heard crackling noises. The breath sounds on the left side were diminished. Air was not moving in and out freely. As Price continued to listen to the left side he noticed a small, jagged slit, like a buttonhole, just below the President's armpit. There was a black spot around it, and blood was trickling out.

More doctors were arriving.

Dr. Drew Scheele, a general-surgery intern who had been a helicopter pilot in Vietnam, where he'd seen many gunshot wounds, including his own, looked at it with Price. They both realized they were looking at the entry wound of a bullet. Two other new arrivals, Gens and Bennett, also thought it was an entry wound.

Price turned to Jerry Parr, the Secret Service agent. "It looks like he's been shot," Price said.

Dr. Ruge gave Ronald Reagan this news. The President nodded. Ruge added reassuringly: "Everything is okay."

Wendy Koenig asked the President if he'd had a tetanus shot recently. He couldn't remember. She gave him one.

They gently rolled the President from side to side, looking for an exit wound. There was none, so the bullet had to be in him. Then Price and O'Neill thought they noticed distended neck veins, a disturbing sign because it could be caused by cardiac tamponade, the filling of the pericardial sac surrounding the heart. This could mean the bullet had struck the heart. On the other hand, heart sounds were normal. It was too early for certainties.

The physicians treating the President during these first few critical minutes were all very young. Most were around 30 and had been doctors for only the three or four years of their residency training. Bill O'Neill had been a doctor for only eight months.

They wondered what was going on in his mind when they poked at him, listened to him, and tried to speak reassuringly to him. He knew none of them. They realized the President was worried, perhaps frightened, although he was masking it well. They admired his coolness.

The young physicians had moments when, for a flashing second or two, they were awed by what they were doing. And more than once the thought skittered across the mind: My God, this is the President—I'd better not screw up. For some, it caused a temporary reluctance to treat him.

But most of them had completed a three-month rotation at the shock-trauma unit in Baltimore, the premier trauma unit in the country. They also had gained experience with trauma at GW. Moreover, the trauma team—formed at GW just three years earlier— had, under the direction of Dr. Joseph Giordano, drilled and drilled until they knew the treatment protocol instinctively.

Now the protocol was doing what it was designed to do. In times of serious injury, confusion, exhaustion, or all of these, the protocol becomes the thinking process—it tells the team what to do and how to do it. It is based on logic and is designed for speed. Critical to its success is aggressive overtreatment, searching everywhere so that not only the most obvious injuries are treated but also the smaller, more insidious ones that can quietly kill the patient.

Following protocol, David Gens examined the President's abdomen. He found no tightness, no sign of abdominal injury.

The President's left chest was thumped with hands and fingers. Where it should have sounded hollow, there was a dull, flat resonance. His left pleural cavity—the space between his left lung and the chest wall—was filling with blood.

Dr. George Morales, an anesthesiologist, placed an oxygen mask over the President's nose and mouth and kept reassuring him that everything was under control. The President repeated that he was having difficulty breathing. Someone had placed a sheet over the President's lower body after Dr. Gregory Hornig, an intern, had inserted a Foley catheter into his bladder to monitor urinary function.

Twelve minutes had passed since President Reagan's arrival at GW.

Press secretary James Brady, 40, grievously wounded, was wheeled into trauma bay 5B, next to the President, separated only by a curtain. His arrival was followed by that of Secret Service agent Timothy McCarthy, 31, the least seriously wounded victim of the Hilton shooting. He was put in ER 3, just a few feet from the trauma bay. Doctors and nurses split off to attend Brady and McCarthy.

The crowd in the ER kept growing. The noise increased; the air grew hot. Brad Bennett, a member of the trauma team, tried to remove everyone without a specific function. When he wasn't doing that he was squeezing the red-cell blood packs to force the vital, oxygen-carrying cells into the President as fast as possible.

Farther away, Doctors Dennis O'Leary and Sol Edelstein and administrator Mike Barch were attempting to control the crowd. Excitement, tension, and fear gripped many in the ER, but panic was never a factor.

Senior faculty physicians continued to arrive, some still perplexed about why they had been summoned. One asked aloud: "Why the hell was I paged?" A curtain of people in front of him parted slightly and he saw the face of the President. He said no more.

The attending physicians asked Dr. Ruge, who was observing, about the President's health.

Blood type?

O positive.

Any allergies?

Adhesive tape and sulfa drugs.

Any medical conditions?

An old prostatectomy 15 years ago. Nothing else.

The President's blood pressure continued to rise.

A chest tube was readied to remove the blood flooding his left lung. Wesley Price put a shot of Xylocaine into the President's side, between two ribs, to dull the pain of the incision and tube insertion. As he prepared to cut, he heard the voice of Dr. Joseph Giordano, a faculty surgeon and head of the trauma team.

"You'd better let me do this one," Giordano said. Price realized it was appropriate that the senior physician take over.

Giordano cut an opening through the skin and muscle wall. He stuck his finger into the opening to make certain he was into the pleura, put a clamp on the tube, and popped it into the hole. The President winced at the pain. The other end of the tube was connected to a suction device called a Pleur-evac. Wendy Koenig had to fill the Pleur-evac partially with sterile water to begin the suction process. In the excitement, she poured a bottle of water into her shoe. The next time she hit the target.

Blood gushed out of the President's chest tube—1,300 cc's of it, perhaps a fourth of his total supply. No one was alarmed; chest tubes normally pull out a lot of blood when they are first inserted into a wounded chest.

But the blood continued to come, and one man was keeping an especially wary eye on it.

Dr. Benjamin Aaron had been in his office in the Burns Building doing paperwork when he was paged to the ER. He had been up until 2 AM the night before, repairing a complication from an open-heart operation, and earlier that day he'd done a coronary bypass operation.

A 48-year-old chest and heart surgeon, and a Navy surgeon for 22 years before he came to GW in 1979, Aaron was calm and understated, a man not only accustomed to the tight tolerances and demanding pressures of cardiac surgery but one who thrived on them. After he arrived at the ER, he saw that an arterial line had been hooked to the President's left wrist, and doctors were getting readouts of his blood pressure and pulse on a monitor. His blood pressure was now above 100. His pulse was steady. Aaron saw that the EKG monitor reading indicated a strong, normal heartbeat.

Usually, when a chest tube is inserted and the lung reexpands, the injured vessels close off and the bleeding stops. In about 90 percent of cases involving this type of chest wound, surgery is not performed.

But in Ronald Reagan's case the bleeding didn't stop. That was the first thing that disturbed Ben Aaron. The second was the color of the blood. It was not the bright red of freshly oxygenated blood. It had a darker cast to it, suggesting venous blood. Aaron knew that venous blood coming out of the chest meant some part of the pulmonary artery—through which venous blood is pumped from the heart to the lungs—was injured.

He tried to drive from his mind the thought that he was treating the President of the United States, tried to concentrate on the simple thought that he was attending a 70-year-old man with a gunshot wound. He said little. He listened to the President's lungs. He watched the ruby-colored blood flowing out of the President's chest.

In 5B there was little hope for James Brady. The hole through his skull, just above his left eye, leaked cerebral tissue. His eyes were so swollen that they could no longer be examined to see if his pupils were fixed and dilated, and the only hopeful sign was that on arrival they still reacted to light. His left eye had swollen to the size of an egg. He was unconscious, but his body sometimes thrashed.

The bullet had traversed the two hemispheres of his brain, and nearly 90 percent of such wounds are fatal. His brain had begun to swell. When swelling is uncontrolled, the brain "herniates" down—the only direction it can go in the confines of the skull—and compresses the brain stem, which regulates heartbeat and other vital functions of the body. When this happens, the patient dies.

The swelling had already caused an increase in Brady's intracranial pressure—which in turn shot his blood pressure up to 240/160, a very high reading. It was his body's way of compensating, of trying to force blood into the brain to oxygenate the tissues. But he had used up all his reserves.

Everything that could be done in those first few minutes was done. Major credit for this should go to Dr. Judith A. Johnson, an anesthesiology resident who switched to Brady from treating the President, when she realized that there were enough people to attend to him.

She put an endotracheal tube into Brady's windpipe, a delicate procedure when a patient has a serious head wound. To prepare him she had given him Pentothal and a curare-type drug to paralyze him so he would not fight the tube he needed for breathing. His head was elevated 45 degrees to relieve intracranial pressure.

Working with Dr. Jeff Jacobson, a neurosurgery resident, Dr. Johnson gave Brady a large dose of mannitol and steroids to decrease the intracranial pressure.

All this was done within Brady's first eight to ten minutes in the ER.

Dr. Arthur Kobrine, a neurosurgeon on the GW faculty, was paged to the trauma bay, where he saw Dr. Ruge, a friend from their days together at Northwestern Medical School. Ruge once taught at Northwestern, and Kobrine did part of his residency there. Ruge asked Kobrine if he would examine Brady. Kobrine was blunt with Dr. Ruge after the examination.

"Dan," he said, "I don't think he's going to make it, but I think we ought to operate."

Ruge told him to do whatever he thought he had to do.

It was crucial that Kobrine move quickly. Within 20 minutes of Brady's arrival at the hospital, he was wheeled into the CT scan room. There, thanks to a computerized x-ray technique called tomography, doctors would see the extent of his injuries and would know if surgery held out any hope for what seemed to be a doomed patient. Despite the medication he was receiving, Brady's brain was continuing to swell.

In ER 3, Secret Service agent Tim McCarthy was in stable condition. The only outward sign of injury was a small, bloodless hole in his right chest. A peritoneal lavage was performed—a procedure in which sterile fluid is put into the abdominal cavity and washed out to determine if any blood is present. There was. Exploratory surgery would be necessary.

McCarthy asked about the President. Dr. Stephen Pett, a thoracic surgeon, and Doctors Jack Fisher and Norman Odyniec were among those attending him.

It was several days later that McCarthy talked about his ordeal. As he lay on the sidewalk at the Hilton, he said, he could feel no wound, no blood, although he thought he'd been hit twice. Then a paramedic rushed up to him and asked if he'd been hit. I think so, McCarthy said. The paramedic couldn't find a wound, and told McCarthy he didn't think he'd been hit. Well, then, you'd better shoot me, McCarthy thought to himself—I don't want the world to think I just fell down out here.

Perhaps 18 minutes had passed since the President's arrival at the hospital.

Ben Aaron kept watching the ruby-colored blood flow out of the President. Not a flood, but more than a trickle.

The President's blood pressure was now nearly normal. His color was better, but he couldn't breathe without difficulty. If the President kept losing blood, the doctors would not be able to keep giving him fluids indefinitely. When blood is replaced by fluids, the patient's hemoglobin diminishes; even though the blood pressure is normal, the tissues are deprived of oxygen, and the kidney, heart, and lungs lose function. If whole blood is administered for too long, the patient's blood loses its ability to clot. That possibility was approaching.

A portable x-ray machine was wheeled into the trauma bay, and within two minutes a chest film was taken and developed. Dr. David Rockoff, the head of chest radiology, was there to read it.

It showed that with the blood draining out through the chest tube, the lung had reexpanded. Rockoff also noticed an irregularly shaped, hazy area where blood remained in the left chest cavity. Then he saw a small, slender metal fragment shaped almost like a comma in the shadow of the heart. It was the bullet. Ben Aaron looked at the film. According to their viewing angle, the bullet could have hit the heart, the aorta, or the pulmonary artery. But the dark color of the blood coming from the President's chest still suggested that its source was the pulmonary artery, not the aorta, which produces bright-red blood.

Rockoff needed to know the caliber of the bullet. If it was a .22, they were seeing all of it. If it was a larger caliber, another fragment might have hit a rib and been deflected into the abdominal cavity.

He turned to a Secret Service agent standing next to him and asked: "What caliber bullet was it?"

The agent said he didn't know but would find out. What followed was one of the most inexplicable incidents in the President's shooting.

Rockoff listened as the agent turned to a superior and said, "They've got to know the caliber."

The superior said, "Then call the FBI. They've got the gun."

The Secret Service agent went to a phone and called the FBI. This is what was then overheard in the GW emergency room:

"What do you mean you 'can't' tell me?" the Secret Service agent said. "The doctors here have to know."

He turned to his superior and shouted: "They won't tell me."

"You tell them they've got to tell you! It's the President."

His voice rising, the Secret Service agent told the FBI: "We've got to know, and we've got to know now!"

There was a moment's silence before the agent turned to Rockoff and said: "It's a .38."

Rockoff relayed the news to colleagues. "We need a belly film to look for the rest of the bullet," he said.

This occurred 20 to 25 minutes after the President was admitted. The physicians treating the President worked under the assumption that he had been shot with a .38, and they would continue to assume that until, about an hour later, a .22-caliber bullet was removed from Tim McCarthy.

An abdominal x-ray—the "belly film"—of the President was taken immediately. One would have been taken anyway, but if the doctors had had correct information about the caliber of the bullet, it would have been done later. If time had been a more critical factor, the misinformation about the bullet could have been costly.

The abdominal film was negative. The doctors then assumed—because they could find no evidence of a bullet anywhere else—that it had probably hit something and shattered, and only a fragment had entered the President.

Dr. Neofytos (Newt) Tsangaris, acting chairman of surgery, was on the phone. "We're probably going to need three ORs," he said. Only two operating rooms were available now; another would be ready in a few minutes.

Nancy Reagan was ushered through the crowd in the ER and into the trauma bay. She held her husband's hand and leaned over to kiss his forehead. "Honey, I forgot to duck," he said.

After a brief visit, she returned to the small room at the entrance to the ER to join Edwin Meese, James Baker, and Lyn Nofziger, members of the President's staff.

Gens and Bennett tried to insert a large-bore line into the President's jugular vein to push in more fluids. This required the President to lie completely flat. It was very hard for him to breathe. He said he could take lying flat for only a few seconds. They failed to put the line in the first time and abandoned the attempt.

Ben Aaron was still watching the blood flowing out of the President. "When you see blood coming out of the chest that fast, and that persistently, without letup," Aaron would say later, "then you have to make some decisions."

It was now obvious that surgery was the safest course. Was a large blood vessel in the wound ready to burst? Would the blood flow suddenly increase? Those were the questions on Aaron's mind. He didn't want to be wheeling a 70-year-old patient who was in shock into the operating room for chest surgery.

Aaron now told the President that he wanted to go in and find the source of the bleeding and stop it. The President said go ahead. Aaron then spoke with Mrs. Reagan and explained options. She said go ahead.

The President had been in the hospital for about 30 minutes.

The CT scan of James Brady's brain was more discouraging than the original x-rays and clinical findings. Dr. David Davis, chair of radiology at GW and a neuroradiologist, looked at the scans—three-dimensional sectional views of the interior of the brain—and said he did not think Brady would survive. Besides the widespread bone and metal fragmentation, there was continued brain swelling, and the CT scan had picked up a very large clot developing in the right frontal region. That clot was as dangerous as any of the other injuries and was contributing to the swelling and intracranial pressure. The scan also showed that the bullet had traversed the brain's ventricular system—the walls of which make spinal fluid—further decreasing his chances of survival.

There was some talk of not operating at all, but Kobrine and the rest of the physicians in the CT room realized that they had no choice. To save time, Kobrine aborted the CT scans when he had enough information to prepare himself for the operation. He knew that it was crucial to begin quickly. He spoke briefly with Brady's wife, Sarah, but could offer little encouragement.

As Kobrine rushed Brady to OR 4—one of the neurological operating rooms—he figured Brady's chances of survival were less than one in ten. As they neared the OR suite, Kobrine was annoyed to see someone being wheeled in ahead of his critically injured patient.

"Who's that?" Kobrine asked.

"The President," he was told.

The President's stretcher had been wheeled from the ER straight down the hall to the 13-room operating suite. He was accompanied by IV poles carrying blood and fluids and by Secret Service agents, physicians, nurses, and technicians. At his side was Mrs. Reagan, holding his hand.

Sol Edelstein, the ER director, walked in front of the stretcher to stop it from moving too fast. He was afraid the IV lines could be yanked out of the President's arm. Another doctor held the President's foot because the stretcher had no sides. They took a shortcut through the recovery room. The patients there, still groggy from anesthesia, lifted their heads to see what the commotion was about.

David Gens was in his street clothes. He was to assist on a peritoneal lavage or "belly tap" and didn't want to take the time to run to the men's locker area to change into his sterile greens. He went into a small closet near the OR, closed the door, and changed in darkness. Dr. Ruge, wearing a warm wool suit, removed it, wound it up in a ball, and put it on a windowsill when he changed into his greens. Ruge continued to reassure the President that things were going well, that he was in good hands.

There were medical gawkers. One, a GW staff member, remained on the telephone in the posting area just outside the OR and talked and talked, refusing to hang up. Mike Barch, the Medical Center administrator, threatened him with arrest if he didn't leave. He left. Another gawker, a gynecologist, stayed on in the operating room. He just wanted to help, he kept saying. He was shown the door.

A Secret Service agent removed his shoes. He thought it was necessary before entering the OR. "You could tell the Secret Service men," one doctor said. "They all had some part of their OR greens on wrong."

The President was taken to OR 2, the cardiac-surgery room with an amphitheater. Brady went into OR 4 with Kobrine, and McCarthy into OR 5 with Tsangaris and chief surgical resident Colombani. The three patients arrived at the operating suite at virtually the same time.

The ORs are lined with green ceramic tiles that often give off a hollow sound. OR 2 was filled with too many people for that.

Stephen Pett, a thoracic surgeon who was in the operating room to assist Aaron if necessary, was asked by a Secret Service agent to identify anyone he didn't know. Pett glanced around, then focused on one face.

"I don't know that guy," he said, pointing to a tall man.

"That's the President's doctor," he was told.

As the President was lifted off the stretcher and onto the operating table, he looked around and, in a move his doctors interpreted as an attempt to break the tension, said: "Please tell me you're all Republicans."

Dr. Joseph Giordano, a liberal Democrat who was there to do the belly tap, said, "Today we're all Republicans, Mr. President."

Dr. George Morales, an authority on anesthesiology, continued to attend to the President.

"How are you going to put me to sleep? I can hardly breathe now," the President said.

Everything would be fine, Morales assured him.

Assisted by Dr. Manfred Lichtmann, chief of anesthesiology at Walter Reed Army Hospital until he joined the GW faculty, Morales faced the risky problem of putting to sleep a 70-year-old man who was injured seriously and had just eaten, a factor that could provoke vomiting.

Valium was administered, followed by a synthetic narcotic and then Pentothal. As the President was drifting under, Lichtmann performed what is called the Sellick maneuver: With his fingers, he pressed the cricoid cartilage—a ring-shaped cartilage on the upper trachea—against the esophagus, exerting enough pressure to block the esophagus and prevent any backward flow of food and stomach acid if the President vomited. The major risk occurs if food and acid come up and go into the trachea and are drawn into the lung.

The Sellick maneuver was brought off beautifully, and, with remarkably little Pentothal, the President went under. A tube was introduced into his trachea to permit him to breathe during surgery.

Giordano, Gens, and Price began the belly tap. Giordano made a small incision just below the navel and inserted a catheter through it into the abdominal cavity, sealed off from the chest by the diaphragm. They poured in a liter of sterile saline solution and then shifted the President's position to wash the fluid around and out. When the cavity emptied they examined it, and it was clear. The procedure had taken 30 minutes, and they were now 99 percent certain that he had no abdominal injury. To be 100 percent certain, they sent the fluid to the laboratory for analysis.

As Gens was closing the abdominal incision, a thought struck him. He looked up at the faces surrounding the President on the operating table and asked: "Does anyone know what's going on out there?"

There was silence. Then Gens was asked what he meant.

"A lot of people were shot," Gens said. "Is there a conspiracy?"

No one knew. No one had had time to give it much thought.

For the exploratory operation, Dr. Aaron would be assisted by Dr. Kathleen Cheyney, a thoracic fellow at GW and Aaron's regular surgical assistant. Dr. David Adelberg, an intern, would also assist. Lula Gore and Thomas Rhodes would be scrub nurses, and Deborah Medenhail and Priscilla Segal were circulating nurses.

Aaron insisted that the President be treated like anyone else. He feared what doctors call the "VIP syndrome," in which famous people are accorded deferential treatment and usually are much the worse for it.

They turned the President on his right side at about a 45-degree angle and made a six-inch incision along the front and left side of his chest.

Aaron "opened," and Cheyney retracted the incision as Aaron cut. The President's chest muscles were parted and his ribs were spread with a large chrome rib separator. When Aaron got inside the chest he found a 500-cc clot of blood in the left lower lobe. Now the full amount of blood lost by the President was nearly 3,000 cc's, about half of his total supply.

The entry point of the bullet was a jagged slit, but as the bullet had moved into the lung tissue it had made a round hole, about the diameter of a dime.

Aaron saw that the blood flowing out of the wound was still dark. He was convinced that part of the pulmonary artery down in the lower lobe had been struck.

He kept exploring. He opened an area near the heart and looked at it. The pericardium had not been hit. The aorta also was untouched. Aaron now began following the bullet track. The bullet had apparently headed on a downward course until it hit the top of the seventh rib and was deflected toward the upper middle of the chest.

He held the President's lung in his hands, feeling in the soft, spongy material for the hard fragment of bullet he was determined to find and remove. He was as impressed by the texture of the lung as he had been by the muscle tone of the President's chest. Both resembled those of a much younger man.

"It made sense to take the bullet out of the President," Aaron later said. "What I wanted was a nice, clean operation. I didn't want to back out and leave the bullet in there."

But he couldn't find it.

He kept fingering the lung—squeezing, probing—but the bullet wouldn't turn up.

Then the fear hit him. Maybe it had gotten into the pulmonary vein. If that had happened, it could have gone into the heart and now be moving out into the arterial tree. That, Aaron knew, could be very serious.

He asked Ruge: How important is it that I get the bullet out?

What's important is that the President survive, Ruge answered.

Aaron kept looking. Several minutes passed. Tension in the OR mounted.

Lichtmann, often the anesthesiologist when Aaron performed heart surgery, had seen him in tight spots before. He knew the signs—the knit brow, the tight expression—and he often tried to break the tension. He tried it now.

"You enjoying yourself, Ben?"

Aaron glanced up and smiled for a split second.

Lichtmann and Morales kept monitoring the President's vital signs. His arterial pressure was good. But the EKG picked up a minor electrical-conduction abnormality in the President's heart. It was a preexisting condition, they were told.

Aaron called for another x-ray—a side view—to get a better fix on the bullet's location. The film was rushed down to the lab for developing.

In OR 5, everything was moving routinely. Paul Colombani was performing most of the surgery on Tim McCarthy. The bullet had traversed McCarthy's right lung, diaphragm, and right lobe of the liver.

They found the bullet behind the liver, and when Colombani plucked it out he thought it looked strange. It appeared to have a hollow point, shiny on the inside and copper-colored on the outside. It was hardly deformed at all.

He gave the bullet to a Secret Service agent who was holding out a cup. Another agent took extensive notes. The news was rushed to

OR 2 that the weapon used in the shootings was a .22 caliber, not a .38.

McCarthy's vital signs remained stable. They were sure he would survive.

In OR 4 where James Brady lay prepped and ready for brain surgery, the story was quite different: A life was hanging on the edge. Dr. Kobrine looked at the CT scans a final time to consider his options and decided on a coronal opening. This is an ear-to-ear incision over the top of the head. Kobrine thought it would afford the best possible exposure. The operation began less than an hour after Brady was shot.

There was concern about Brady's left eye. The swelling was so pronounced that it was putting pressure on the eye. Dr. Mansour Armaly, an ophthalmologist, made a small incision to drain the clot on the eye.

As he peeled away the scalp, Kobrine could see the bullet hole through the skull. It was less than a centimeter in diameter. (To this day, Kobrine is uncertain whether the bullet—later identified as a "devastator"—exploded on impact. It probably didn't, nor did any of the others.) Kobrine saw that the bullet had gone through the sinuses and realized that this would greatly complicate Brady's recovery if he survived. The injury there created a direct air passageway to the brain that could lead to infections.

A saw was used to cut the skull and expose the brain.

Kobrine initially focused his attention on an opening made by the bullet in the dura, the outermost membrane covering the brain. He widened it to work down deeper into the left frontal lobe, from which he cleaned out the bone and bullet fragments and removed dead tissue.

One of the several doctors shuttling between the operating rooms and the second-floor offices where hospital and White House officials waited popped his head into OR 4. "The networks report that Brady is dead," he said.

"No one has told Mr. Brady or me that," Kobrine replied without looking up.

Neurosurgery is called the queen of surgery because such precision is required. Wearing a microscopic lens and illuminating the small surgical field with a high-intensity light attached to his fore-head, Kobrine moved quickly. Brady's intracranial pressure remained very high.

Kobrine now moved to the right side, where he made a large opening through the dura to suction out a small hematoma near the surface.

Suddenly something entirely unpredictable happened—something that in great part is the reason Brady lives today.

Deep within the right side of Brady's brain, a large blood clot—the same clot that was so worrisome when Kobrine saw it on the CT scan—spontaneously burst. It could have been a catastrophe. Instead it was a godsend.

Its force was so great that it gushed up and through Brady's brain tissue, literally creating a fountain of blood when it broke through the outer surface of the right frontal lobe. If someone could have selected a place for that clot to burst its way out of Brady's brain, it would have been in the right frontal lobe. This is one of the less important areas of the brain, especially for someone who is right-handed. The bursting of the clot opened up a world of possibility unthinkable only moments before. It decompressed the potentially fatal pressure buildup within Brady's brain. His high blood pressure returned to normal.

The opening made by the bursting also provided Kobrine with an access route down into the brain. From this he was able to retract the right hemisphere and control the bleeding from two major damaged vessels with silver clips and electrified forceps. One of the vessels was the anterior cerebral artery, which had been severed by the bullet. He then slipped his finger into the opening and felt the main fragment of the flattened bullet near Brady's right ear. He extracted it with forceps.

There was still much to be done, and Brady remained in critical condition. But something close to a miracle had taken place.

The President's x-ray indicated that Dr. Aaron had been looking too low for the bullet. Now he put a catheter into the bullet track and began to follow the path. Minutes passed. He thought of closing the chest and leaving the bullet inside but decided to stay with it a while longer.

Finally, his fingers felt something hard. Sounds of relief filled the room as Aaron removed the bullet by carefully squeezing it out through the lung tissue.

Now he knew why it had been so hard to find: It was flattened to the size and shape of a dime. It was thin at the edges, thicker in the middle. Rifling marks were still evident on the edges. As before, a Secret Service agent extended a cup for the bullet.

The bleeding from the wound had finally stopped, and Aaron left a drainage site where he removed the bullet, irrigated the wound area, and began to sew over it, having made certain no major section of the pulmonary artery was damaged. Two tubes were left in the President's chest, one at the top for air retrieval, one at the bottom for drainage. Now, more than three hours after the President entered surgery, the doctors began to close his chest.

There was some debate as to where the President should spend the night—the intensive-care unit or the recovery room. Aaron wanted him in the recovery room. It was near the operating suite and, in the case of complications, provided quick access to the OR.

Shortly after 6:30 in the evening, the President, still breathing through the endotracheal tube, was wheeled across the hall into a corner of the recovery room.

Aaron's day wasn't finished. Now he was called to examine another patient—one he'd operated on recently for a heart-valve replacement—who was bleeding. One look at the patient and Aaron realized he had to go back to the OR. He would spend 14 hours in surgery during a 24-hour period.

George Morales returned to his small office in the anesthesia area near the OR suite. He found it filled with communications equipment. On his door a makeshift sign read "Temporary White House."

After receiving a thorough medical briefing from Aaron and other doctors, Dennis O'Leary, dean for clinical affairs, left his hospital office to brief the nation at a press conference. He and Dr. Ruge were the candidates for the spokesman job, but Ruge declined, saying he thought there might appear to be a conflict of interest if he took on the role. He said that someone from the hospital ought to speak for the hospital.

Darkness had fallen when O'Leary crossed 23rd Street on his way to Ross Hall, where he was about to address the nation via TV and radio. As they walked, presidential aide Lyn Nofziger said: "Remember, you don't have to answer a question just because someone asks it."

As the world was hearing that the President had sailed through surgery, the specialists surrounding him in the recovery room were considerably more guarded in their optimism. The President's first postoperative x-ray showed white shadows that indicated pockets of airlessness in the lungs. It also showed considerable plugging of the small sacs and vessels from secretions. Toward the bottom of the film there was a shrunken, whitish area where blood had pooled. The x-ray also showed that the left lower lobe was collapsed. To some of the doctors the findings were worrisome; they could not understand why the lower lobe was collapsed. To others the collapse as well as most of the other complications were predictable and not alarming.

A finding that concerned all the doctors was the level of oxygen in the President's blood, a measure of his lungs' gas-exchange process. The lab analysis showed it wasn't working well. His blood's oxygen level was normal only when the respirator was giving him 80 percent oxygen compared with 20 percent in normal air. They began taking readings every few minutes by drawing blood out of the arterial line in his wrist.

The respirator was set to give the President something called PEEP, an acronym for positive end expiratory pressure. This allows the respirator to trap gas in the lung at the end of each breath to open up and prevent the collapse of lung airways.

The President was not yet conscious. He lay on the stretcher, with the endotracheal tube down his throat. He was hooked up to an EKG monitor, blood pressure and pulse monitors, and IV lines. His head was tilted up at 30 degrees, and he was surrounded by a small army of medical personnel, Secret Service agents, and some of his aides, Baker and Meese most prominently. The aides asked when the President would be able to make decisions but didn't receive a precise answer.

The President began to regain consciousness at about 7:30 PM, and he indicated that he couldn't catch his breath. It is a sensation many people on respirators experience, and it can be frightening. He was assured the respirator was doing his breathing for him.

Between 7:30 and 8 the President's wife, Nancy, and their son Ron visited briefly. They held the President's hand. Mrs. Reagan kissed him, and Ron leaned over and whispered into his ear. Although he was aware of their visit, the President remained groggy. Mrs. Reagan expressed the President's concern—and her own—that he felt he could not breathe. It was an advocate's role she was to play throughout his stay in the hospital. But they understood her concern and patiently tried to keep her abreast of developments.

Mrs. Reagan was now reassured that the President was breathing as he should with the respirator and, at the doctors' urging, she prepared to leave. Standing alone in the open doorway of the recovery room, she looked back intensely at her husband's bed for what seemed like minutes.

At about 8 PM the president experienced pain and was given morphine. He would be given it periodically for the next several hours. For security reasons, most of the President's drugs and meals were brought from the White House. Secret Service agents randomly selected other drugs from the hospital pharmacy.

Dr. Ruge remained in the recovery room that night and would stay at the hospital around the clock until the President was discharged. His role was important not so much for what he did but for what he didn't do. At no time did Ruge intrude, impose his judgment, or demand that outside consultants be brought in. He was in the spot to do that, and it might have afforded him some protection from second-guessing if he had. But he had confidence in the GW doctors, and they in turn trusted him. Nor did Ruge consider moving the President to Bethesda Naval Hospital, which was suggested by the Secret Service.

Ruge's attitude helped avoid the VIP syndrome. That evening two chief surgical residents, David Gens and Paul Colombani, were assigned to take continuing care of the President. Although some physicians at GW felt this was a mistake, that a large team of senior specialists should have been assigned, the more standard approach was taken. "Medicine by conference would have been the worst thing we could have done," one of his doctors said later. The President was, in the words of another of his doctors, "treated like any other 70-year-old man with a gunshot wound."

Different doctors focused on different things during those first few hours in the recovery room. Dr. Samuel Spagnolo, pulmonary-medicine specialist, fixed on the rhythmic beeping and the steady line blipping across the screen of the EKG monitor. In all the hours Spagnolo watched, the President's heart didn't miss a single beat.

Sol Edelstein marveled at the powerful muscles in the President's chest, developed from outdoor work. Ruge said he'd seen the President toss around ranch posts as though they were bamboo sticks.

They now took another blood-gas reading, and the results were no more encouraging than the earlier ones. More x-rays were taken, and they showed the lower lobe still collapsed. There was concern that the President might have to stay on the respirator for up to three more days unless there was quick improvement. To keep him on 80 percent oxygen would invite other problems for his lungs.

The President was handed the back of a hospital progress sheet attached to a clipboard to write on. And write he did. Early notes continued to express his worry over his breathing, but their tone lightened at times.

"Am I alive?" he asked in one note after waking from a nap. Another said he'd like to shoot the whole scene over, beginning at the hotel.

Because his lungs were so congested, there was an attempt to perform a bronchoscopy. This involves slipping a fiber-optic tube down into the bronchi and clearing out clotted blood or other debris. The attempt failed because a bend in the endotracheal tube blocked the bronchoscope's passage.

Jack Zimmerman, director of the intensive-care unit and considered one of the best clinicians at the hospital, had come to the recovery room to assist. When the bronchoscopy failed, he had nurses Denise Sullivan and Kathy Edmonston take a small volume of saline solution and insert it into the endotracheal tube. It caused the President to cough, freeing mucous plugs and thinning out secretions, which were then suctioned out. In the midst of this the President wrote the note that echoed W.C. Fields: "All in all, I'd rather be in Philadelphia."

Most doctors and nurses took the note writing to be a reflection of the President's exuberance at being alive and as his way to break the tension.

The notes kept coming. One to Denise Sullivan, the head recovery-room nurse, read: "Does Nancy know about us?" The Secret Service took that note and all the others the President wrote.

Then came a different kind of note: "Was anyone else hurt?"

Sullivan, a quick woman with 15 years of nursing experience, froze for half a second and thought quickly. Two others were hurt, she told him, but not seriously. She had not heard of the fourth victim, Officer Thomas Delahanty, who had been successfully operated on at the Washington Hospital Center for a wound to his upper spine.

Then another note: "Did they get the guy?" Yes, Denny Sullivan told him, they did.

Ruge then conferred with the medical staff. There was agreement that if the President asked again, he was not to be told of the seriousness of the injuries to the others, particularly Jim Brady. Considering the President's condition, an emotional jolt was too much of a risk.

A new blood-gas reading was taken, and it showed improvement. The news was greeted with relief.

Tim McCarthy had been taken directly from the OR to the intensive-care unit for postoperative observation. He was doing well; his vital signs were strong and stable.

Toward 8:30 PM the six-hour operation on James Brady was ending. Dr. Kobrine had no certainty that Brady would ever be able to function again, but he was more encouraged now than he had been before surgery. Brady was wheeled into the recovery room at about 9, and Kobrine went to look for Sarah Brady.

Optimism took hold as the president's blood-gas level continued to improve. The oxygen from the ventilator was slowly reduced as his blood oxygen slowly increased—which meant his lungs were resuming function.

He remained alert and continued to write notes. "I don't think I've ever seen a person that age with that kind of injury do that well," Zimmerman said of the President's recovery-room performance.

As the hour neared midnight, it was becoming clear that if improvement continued, the President could be allowed to breathe without assistance before daybreak.

He apparently became unnerved momentarily when he overheard Ben Aaron describing to other doctors the condition of the heart patient he'd treated after he'd operated on the President.

"Is that happening to me?" the President wrote.

Marisa Mize, a recovery-room nurse who had come on at 11 PM for the night shift, reassured him that it wasn't. An attractive woman of 26, she sat next to the President for long periods of her shift—holding his hand, talking to him. At one point she rose to leave. The President seized her hand. His look told her not to go. She sat back down next to him.

At times she kidded him. "Don't worry," she said to him once, "your wife isn't holding dinner for you."

"I'm not that hungry, anyway," he wrote.

At about midnight James Brady slowly to come out of anesthesia. Small tremors rippled over his body—a good sign. Often in cases of serious brain damage the patients do not have these postanesthesia tremors because the neurologic damage is so great. Brady started to move one of his toes. And then a nurse insisted that he had squeezed her hand.

Kobrine had realized during surgery that Brady's left side was not going to be as good as his right. The right hemisphere of his brain had taken most of the damage, and it controls the left side of the body. The major vessel damage was to vessels that led to areas of the brain involved in motor function. It became clear watching him in the recovery room that the motor functions of Brady's left side were substantially damaged.

But Kobrine found another hopeful sign. The swelling around Brady's eyes had now abated enough for Kobrine to put a light to them, and he found that they were not fixed and dilated.

Postoperative CT scans showed marked improvement over those taken just before Brady was wheeled into surgery.

Maybe he's going to do better than we all anticipated, Kobrine thought.

At 1:30 in the morning the President thought it was 6:30 in the evening, but other than that, he was experiencing little disorientation. Doctors explained to him what had gone on in the OR. He was now given morphine for pain, but his blood gases came closer to normal.

Slowly the attending physicians began to wean him from the respirator, and, as they did, he began to "buck"—to get out of sync with it. He started coughing and became agitated.

At 2:30 in the morning, the President had another scare. As doctors began removing the endotracheal tube, they kept saying, "This is it," meaning that the time had come to take him off the respirator.

Marisa Mize saw the fright in his eyes. "What do they mean, 'This is it?'" the President scribbled.

She explained, and he calmed down.

By 2:45 AM the President was off the respirator for the first time in nearly 12 hours. He had an oxygen mask on but was able to speak. His voice was hoarse.

He expressed concern for the others who were wounded and asked about the motives of the assailant.

No one in the recovery room dared to say anything about the other victims.

The President continued to talk with his doctors, nurses, and aides. They soon realized he had a partial hearing loss in his right ear that predated the shooting. By 4:30 the recovery room had pretty well thinned out, and several lights were turned off so the President could sleep. Joanne Bell, a recovery-room nurse, put a gauze pad over his eyes to block the light and moved away to let him sleep. Within seconds he had the pad off and was talking again. She walked back to the President's bed, took the pad in her hand, and said: "Mr. President, in the most polite way I can tell you, when I put this over your eyes, that means I want you to shut up."

He looked up at her, winked, and took a 45-minute nap.

Ben Aaron went to sleep on a stretcher. Gens and Colombani found beds in the kidney-dialysis unit, but it was so hot that Gens woke up at 3 AM and returned to the recovery room, where, with Zimmerman, Spagnolo, Edelstein, and Price, he stayed until early morning.

At 6:15 Tuesday morning the President was wheeled from the recovery room to the intensive-care unit (ICU) on the fourth floor. His room's curtains had been drawn. The room was crowded with people and medical equipment.

The ICU nurses now began giving him respiratory therapy, which consisted of having him cough and breathe deeply and of pounding him on the back.

Nurse Carolyn Ramos helped the President brush his teeth, and then she brushed his hair. "Now you can tell everyone I don't dye my hair," he said. Indeed he doesn't, a fact that his nurses and doctors can confirm and one that, to their surprise, several members of the President's staff took pains to point out.

What also surprised those who took care of the President was his ability to put them at ease—to kid with them, talk with them, to give them the impression that he was a totally accessible and secure man. Republicans and Democrats alike came to admire him.

In the ICU, where the President was to remain that day, Carolyn Ramos felt enough at ease to joke with him. Sometimes, she told him, patients who have undergone surgery are asked questions to determine how oriented they are. Typically, she said, they are asked the year, their whereabouts, and the name of the incumbent president. "In your case," she said, "we'll skip the last question."

The President laughed.

Then she told him that a recent patient, when asked who the President was, said: "That actor fellow . . . Jimmy Stewart."

He laughed again.

The President's aides visited early that morning, a practice they would continue throughout his stay at GW. The President said to them that he'd known that missing a staff meeting would be too much to hope for.

The same morning the President signed into law a bill eliminating a scheduled increase in dairy price supports. He'd been given a total of 30 milligrams of morphine for pain over the last several hours, and some of the nurses wondered how a man who'd taken that much morphine could understand what he was signing. They kidded among themselves that they should put the student-loan bill in front of him to sign.

The President showed a persistent curiosity about who had shot him. And although he seemed satisfied when told that the others were not hurt badly, he continued to ask about them.

Later that morning Dr. Ruge finally told the President about the seriousness of the injuries to James Brady and the others. He appeared shaken by the news and said he felt guilty because he realized he had been the target. He didn't need a supporting cast, he said. That morning Ruge talked to members of the Cabinet and spoke very optimistically of the President's condition.

The President's room in intensive care became hot because of the large number of people now gathered there. It was unseasonably warm and the hospital's air conditioning was not yet turned on. Nancy and Ron Reagan visited in the morning; daughter Maureen came in the afternoon. Mrs. Reagan wanted him moved as soon as possible. But because the suite on Three South that he was to occupy had yet to be prepared and made secure, the President had to wait all day in this little room in intensive care.

That afternoon x-rays of his lung showed that his left lower lobe, which had collapsed after surgery, had fully expanded. But he was in pain and was given codeine.

The next day, Wednesday, it was decided to cut back the number of medical people with access to the President, in part because the President and Mrs. Reagan were being made uncomfortable by people in such number in such a space.

Ben Aaron, pulmonary specialist Sam Spagnolo, and Gens and Colombani, the chief surgical residents, were to be the only physicians with direct access. It would be Gens and Colombani, both in their thirties, who would write the President's chart, give him his IVs, draw his blood, change the dressings on his wound, and otherwise look after him on a day-to-day basis. Aaron was in overall charge. Ruge kept Reagan informed. They would all meet early each morning to examine the President and then, after the chest x-ray was taken, would confer with Rockoff, head of chest radiology. Later that first week, the list of GW doctors with direct access would be narrowed further, with Spagnolo acting as a consultant.

By 9 PM Tuesday, the President's second night at GW, the Three South hallway was secured and turned into a miniature presidential compound, with a sitting room for Mrs. Reagan, a room for Ruge, two rooms for Secret Service agents, and a conference room. The President's room had two easy chairs and a sofa, and a Secret Service agent was there at all times. The windows were bulletproof.

Although chest-surgery patients are normally kept on the sixth floor, the Secret Service did not want the President on the top floor, for security reasons. In every move the President made at the hospital, the Secret Service took all security precautions, checking halls, doors, anything that could present a problem. The agents moved quietly through the hospital, their identity made clear by the small button in the lapel and the jacket bulge. The hospital staff realized that some carried Uzi submachine guns in their briefcases. A SWAT team remained on the hospital roof. All hospital entrances except the one on 23rd Street were sealed.

The Secret Service agents, the doctors and nurses said, were unfailingly courteous and professional. They came to be admired by the GW staff.

With the President's arrival imminent, Sylvia LeBlanc, a young nurse on duty at Three South, felt her hands growing cold. She knew that she'd have to pound the President's back as part of his respiratory therapy. She decided to wash with warm water just before the therapy because she wouldn't want to hit a president with cold hands.

That first night in Three South was uneventful, but in the early-morning hours of Wednesday Colombani realized that the President had not urinated since the Foley catheter was removed Tuesday afternoon. Colombani had no choice: He woke up the President and told him he'd have to get out of bed and walk around. Colombani hoped the movement would stimulate urinary output. It didn't. Now Colombani was faced with the unpleasant task of telling the President of the United States that the Foley catheter would have to be reinserted.

The President had dealt cheerfully with most of his medical problems, but he did not cheerfully accept the news Colombani now had to give him. Gens and Colombani took alternate nights on the presidential watch, and it became a running joke between them that the bad things always happened on Colombani's shift.

In general, the President's recovery continued to go well. However, while reexamining the President's abdominal x-rays, Rockoff saw an abnormality that disturbed him. It was not in the chest but in the back. What he detected was a small, gray shadow on a vertebra in the President's lower spine—a lesion of some kind, about the size of a pencil eraser. He was unsure of what it was, and there was some fear it might be malignant. This information was shared with very few doctors. They did not tell the President. They wanted to study it further.

The President continued to cough up blood, but it was dark blood, a natural consequence of his injury. Dave Gens told the President, who was concerned about it: "It's good—you're coughing up old blood."

"Don't you know what they said about me during the campaign?" the President answered. "I'm full of old blood."

The one-liners kept coming. And the President did a good Jimmy Stewart impersonation.

Mrs. Reagan expressed concern because the President was still occasionally disoriented about time. Gens explained to her that many patients sealed away inside a room with the curtains drawn and without clocks lose track of time.

Assistant Secretary of State William Clark, longtime friend of the President's, was there complaining that he'd just had a terrible day on Capitol Hill. He said he felt useless and wanted to do something to feel useful, so he'd buy the President a clock.

He did. A big Mickey Mouse clock hung in the President's room for the remainder of his stay.

That first Wednesday, the President's blood-oxygen level dropped dramatically. He was put back on oxygen, now given to him through nose prongs instead of a mask. IVs still came into his arm. A picture of the President and Mrs. Reagan, taken that first week, showed the

President smiling as he stood in his robe. Cropped out of the picture was a nurse, standing to his immediate left, holding the Pleur-evac connected to the chest tube, which came out from under his robe. Mrs. Reagan was very particular about that photo: She did not want her husband to be pictured as an invalid.

Forty-eight hours after surgery, the President was taken off precautionary antibiotics. Standard procedure. He had an emotional visit from Sarah Brady. He expressed sorrow, and she told him that her husband was doing better, that she was hopeful. Every night when Dr. Ruge came by, the President would ask how Jim Brady was doing.

When Dave Gens arrived back in the on-call room across the street from the hospital late that Wednesday night, his first night on the President's watch, he sat on the bed for a few moments and realized that with all the security arrangements, it would take him three or four minutes to get back to the President's bedside if there were an emergency. Too much time would be lost.

He promptly got up, walked back to the hospital, and went to sleep on the sofa in Mrs. Reagan's sitting room, adjacent to the President's room. He did this every night he was on duty. He made certain, however, that he was always up very early. He didn't want to be caught sleeping in the First Lady's room.

Thursday morning, April 2, the abdominal stitches from the President's peritoneal lavage were removed, and it was learned that a "devastator" bullet had been used by the assailant. Hurried calls were made to determine whether lead azide, a component of that type of bullet, was dangerous. An authority in Colorado assured the GW doctors that it was not.

The President had been awakened twice each previous night, for respiratory therapy, and it was now decided to let him sleep through. His spirits were high. He still kidded with the nurses and doctors, watched TV, and read everything he could about his shooting. He seemed to prefer entertainment on TV, one night passing up a documentary on El Salvador to see *The Birds*, an Alfred Hitchcock movie. He continued to confer with his aides—Meese and Baker, among others—daily.

On Thursday night the President's recovery came to a halt; a fever was detected. His temperature ranged between 102 and 103 and was soon accompanied by other problems. Tylenol helped somewhat, but the moment its effects wore off, the fever would peak again. His color worsened, and he became more tired. His white count went up. Colombani, on duty that night, called Ben Aaron at home. Aaron said to continue with the Tylenol. The President's one remaining chest tube was examined as a possible infection source. It was "clean." The few people who knew about the fever were disturbed by it. It was a setback.

The President's fever continued, and on Friday night he began to experience chills. He asked about the source of the new problem, but no one knew what was causing it. The daily x-rays continued to indicate that there was some fluid in the lungs, which could mean pneumonia. Concern about his condition grew. Aaron decided to do a bronchoscopy to try to clear up the bronchial tubes. To prepare a patient for a bronchoscopy, a spray solution of Xylocaine is used to deaden sensation in the throat, and often Valium is administered to relax the patient. Edward Yob, a White House physician, approached Dave Gens and asked whether Valium was going to be used. Gens said it probably was.

Yob asked if they could hold off giving the President major sedatives. Gens asked why. Yob said he didn't know but something very important was going on in the world, and unless it was absolutely necessary to sedate him, the President was to be kept fully alert. Gens never learned the nature of the crisis.

Valium was not necessary. Aaron suctioned out some old, clotted blood with the bronchoscope and, through the eyepiece, viewed the bronchi. He found no pus or other sign of infection.

There was no change in the President's fever that night. His appearance and spirits continued to sag. One doctor remarked to another, "The President looks terrible." President Reagan's fever was being described to the public as "moderate." There was no public hint that his doctors thought it possible that he had a lung infection.

On Saturday, five days after the shooting, another complication developed. The President had been coughing up blood all week, but the color was dark—it was obviously old, clotted blood and thus not alarming. However, the color of the blood he coughed up Saturday morning was bright red—fresh blood. Taken in combination with the fever and chills, it was "an ominous sequence of events," Aaron said later. The President had been put back on his original antibiotics, but to no avail. The fever persisted. So did the red blood coming up.

Aaron told Dennis O'Leary and Ruge Saturday that he thought the President was very vulnerable, that the new blood coming up could be a prelude to a major lung bleed. At one point, Aaron considered the possibility of going back in and surgically removing the left lobe, the source of the President's problem.

"It was a terribly depressing time," one doctor recalls of that period. "The President was a lot sicker than most people realize."

Aaron was more worried about the new bleeding than the fever. But at about the time his worry was deepening, the bleeding stopped. He suspected that a small clot had let go, causing the bleed; at any rate, he was relieved of the risky task of operating a second time.

Yet the fever persisted. What was causing it? No one knew; opinions of internists and surgeons divided sharply. The head surgeon, Aaron, held that the fever was a result of an inflammatory process, a natural consequence of the injury. Gens and Colombani agreed.

Internists such as Spagnolo and Rockoff had a darker worry— that the President had developed an abscess within the lung. If this proved to be the case, surgery might be required to remove it.

These two factions continued to disagree—not angrily but firmly. The surgeons argued that they were seeing the President daily and that he did not appear to be seriously ill. Rockoff at one point countered by saying, "I'm here to keep you from getting too optimistic."

That same Saturday there was good news. A new series of small x-ray pictures called tomographs gave a detailed picture of the suspicious shadow on the President's vertebra. Rockoff now determined that the suspicious lesion was not invading the bone, as cancer would. The diagnosis was that it was sclerotic in origin—benign.

Rockoff, who had downplayed the possible significance of the shadow on the vertebra in discussions with the President, now told him that everything was fine. The President looked wearily at Rockoff and said of this latest series of x-rays: "Could we make picture post-cards out of them so I can send them to my friends?"

The fever continued. A pivotal meeting was held early Sunday morning in Rockoff's radiology office. Besides Rockoff, physicians on hand were Gens, Colombani, Ruge, O'Leary, Aaron, and Carmelita Tuazon, director of infectious diseases at GW. When they reviewed the week's x-rays of the President's lung, they noted that those taken on the large, stationary machine were of a much higher quality than previous x-rays and revealed the lung densities clearly. Whether these densities had been there earlier or were new was not the major question. The major question was what could be done to get rid of the fever.

Tuazon, who had not been called in to consult until Sunday—a day or two too late, some doctors complained—had studied the sputum slides and the blood and urine cultures and suspected that the President had a bacterial infection.

After discussing a number of treatment possibilities, the consulting physicians decided to take the President off his present antibiotic and put him on two new ones, penicillin and aminoglyco-side, to deal with the suspected bacterial infection.

They waited Sunday and Monday for the fever to break; it didn't. On Tuesday, eight days after the shooting, there was a little opti-mism because the President's peak temperature was lower than it had been for several previous days. It dropped further on Wednesday. Gens and Colombani now plotted a temperature curve and boldly predicted that his fever would be gone by Friday. They were off by a day; it ended Thursday. The President looked better, felt better, was better. The crisis had passed.

On Thursday of the President's second week at GW, he was doing so well that some thought was given to taking him off penicillin. But Tuazon, wanting to take no chances with a possible infection, dug in her heels and insisted that he remain on penicillin for another ten days. He did.

The President's strength continued to return. Ben Aaron noticed the change: "He slowly emerged from being the perfect patient to a restless man, anxious to get back to work."

In high spirits, the President made a practice of walking "laps" in the hallway and telling Maria Blaz, one of his nurses, how many he had done each time he approached the nurses' station. Once, after he had done three, he turned to her and called: "That's eight." She glanced up to catch him smiling.

Blood, urine, and sputum cultures continued to be negative. The patient was almost healthy enough to be discharged.

James Brady's condition was improving. He was responding to questions, remembering details about his life, and showing a sense of humor. Mobility on his right side had improved. His left side showed little motor movement. On Saturday morning, April 11, all the physicians involved in the President's treatment met for a last time, in Rockoff's radiology office. The President's x-rays were very encouraging; his lungs sounded and looked better. He would remain on intravenous penicillin one more day and then be switched to oral. There seemed no further need to keep him at the hospital. They decided to discharge him that morning.

Gens and Colombani, the doctors who had the most contact with the President while he was at GW, went to his room to say goodbye. The President shook their hands and thanked them. Gens, who had spoken often with Mrs. Reagan during the President's 12-day stay, joined Colonibani in seeking her out. They found her in the corridor talking with Sarah Brady. She thanked them, hugged them, and kissed them on the cheek.

Doctors and nurses were asked to line up in the hallways so that they could wave to the President as he left. As he was heading out, at about 10:30 that morning, he kept stopping and reaching out to touch or shake hands with the people who had cared for him. Many were touched by his warmth.

At the 23rd Street entrance, the President, wearing a cardigan sweater over his bulletproof vest, said his goodbye:

"From the time we came here, in confusion, until now, you have made us all welcome. God bless you all."

Several days after the President's release, Doctors Aaron, Gens, and Colombani went to the White House to make a house call.

They were ushered upstairs to the President's working office on the second floor.

Ronald Reagan greeted them by holding out his arms in the fashion of a man accustomed to having needles inserted, smiled, and said, "Here, is this what you guys want?"

They laughed, examined him, and found him well.

—*Washingtonian* | August 1981

Prisoners of Overachievement

The residents of Washington have a work ethic like no other town. They looooove their work. Just ask them.

By Walt Harrington

Workworkwork. In Washington, we workworkwork. It is the way we like to see ourselves, sell ourselves. Obsessive-compulsives. And proud of it. Hand washers, redirected. Toward ambition—pure ambition, ambition as evident and invisible as air.

Imagine Monday mornings at the water cooler:

"I worked Saturday morning!"

"I worked Saturday morning *and* Saturday afternoon!"

"Oh, yeah, I worked the whole weekend! I abandoned my family and skipped meals and prayers and showers. Oh, yes, I will die young, yet I will know that my amendment to the rider to the House bill on bilateral wastewater disposal procedures will live forever." As a monument to what we in Washington seek: to matter.

Like Dr. Frankenstein.

In Washington, we are doers, people who make a difference. *I do, therefore I am.* We are Washington—the most important city on the most important planet in the most important solar system in the universe. We are Rome. We are one big deal.

Just ask us.

Snapshot No. 1 from Washington's workaday world . . .

The woman had just moved to Washington and was working as a librarian in Fairfax County when a brusque, self-important man came to the desk to return a stack of books. The woman checked and discovered the man owed a small fortune in fines. She told him this. The man was outraged. From his coat pocket he pulled a chain heavy with official government ID cards. With a resentful flurry, he tossed the chain and cards onto the desk.

He announced, "This is who I am!"

Washington lives like a cocoon within America.

It has the highest average household income of any major metropolitan area in the nation, more than $50,000 after taxes. It has the highest proportion of professional workers—40 percent of its working men, 35 percent of its working women. It has the lowest proportion of blue-collar workers, only 16 percent. Its people, black and white, have the highest percentage of college degrees. Most of its women work, about 70 percent, and at least two-thirds of its mothers work. People in Washington more often drive new convertibles, drink foreign brandy and visit the Caribbean than do people in cities all across America. Macy's, Nordstrom and Bloomingdale's have discovered this.

Washington is the good life.

Prosperity's font: workworkwork.

Recall the maxim: "By the work one knows the workman." It is the truth of Washington. Work is the talk, the glue and the currency of the town. The federal government generates a $12-billion-a-year local payroll and another $11 billion a year in purchases from local businesses. This has demanded highly educated, experienced and ambitious professionals, who, in turn, have created a thriving economy of workers to sell these affluent people fine food and clothing, repair their cars, fix their kids' teeth, draw up their wills.

Washington is said to be at the cutting edge of America's economy of the future, the place America is headed in the next century.

Washington: America's primo white-collar ghetto.

Sure, Washington has hamburger slingers, house painters, 7-Eleven clerks, secretaries, government 9-to-5ers, poor people. But they don't create Washington's personality—workworkwork creates its personality. In the white-collar ghetto, work is glorified because it is the vehicle of the city's core value: achievement. In Washington, achievement is communion. It is the work ethic gone berserk.

A Washington Post poll taken for this issue of the Magazine found that 75 percent of people in the metro area believe their work is an important part of "who I am," 62 percent work more than 40 hours a week, and 58 percent believe they work harder than most people. These workworkwork attitudes are heavily concentrated in Washington's huge bubble of professional workers.

And that bubble is growing. The heart of Washington's workworkwork world has always been its lobbyists, downtown lawyers, Capitol Hill aides, journalists, GS-16s, Pentagon officers and political appointees. But Washington's professional work force more and more includes consultants, Beltway Bandits, office managers, stockbrokers, real estate lawyers and others who prosper at the fringes of the government-driven prosperity. The cycle creates itself; by the year 2000, an even greater share of Washington's workers will be professionals.

But there is a price. "People in Washington have no concept of what reality is," says Washington attorney G. Jerry Shaw, who grew up in a Montana town of 1,000 people. "We make more money here. We have different expectations. It's a tremendous town, but a town you have to get out of to remember how the rest of the world lives. I love Baltimore, Philadelphia, New York for their ethnicity. You come to understand that people bring a heritage to their lives. Here, it is acceptable and encouraged for children to leave their roots and go achieve, make their way by accomplishment."

Everyone—children, truck drivers, secretaries, even the army of professionals themselves—is affected by the dominance of Washington's achievement elite. Its members shape everything from the brands of vodka and blue jeans available to the popularity of Volvos and natural spring water. Their fat incomes push up home prices. Their enthronement of achievement shapes the area's ruthlessly competitive schools.

But more than anything, Washington's achievement elite establishes the standard for everyone, and that standard is high, perhaps dangerously high. It reminds people who aren't affluent and successful that they aren't affluent and successful, and it even takes a toll on its own. "You can only be important relatively, not absolutely," says sociologist Mady Wechsler Segal, and it's possible to be successful yet feel like a failure compared with your grand expectations. There are a lot of people like that in Washington.

"We call them the 'worried well,'" says Segal.

Over the years, professionals put a lot of themselves into their work. They compete through college, graduate school, law school and apprenticeships in backwater cities. Work becomes their religion. Drop all these people into Washington, and this occurs: The realities of the ultimate political town and the obsessions of its elite feed furiously on each other, creating an achievement culture that enshrines the values of the work place as the values of life.

This is the Washington they and their work have created:

Washington is ambition. Have you met a person lately who's going to law school at night? A bureaucrat also writing a novel? The daughter of GS-15 parents who is panicked about her embarrassing 1300 on her SATs? "People are here for results, to make a mark," says Terrence Russell, a sociologist who studies work for the American Chemical Society in Washington. "Nobody came here because 'Gee, it's such a wonderful place to live.'"

Says Jonathan Robbin, the founder of Claritas Corp., a marketing information firm in Alexandria, "What's the old line? 'Washington consists of two kinds of people—lawyers and the wives they left behind.'"

Washington is the mastery of details—budgets, laws, investigations, protocols, direct mail. And it is people who can master these details. It's a favorite source for "Jeopardy" contestants. It's a town with nearly 24 times the national average of people who fall into the U.S.

census work category that includes cipher experts and cryptographers. If you don't have a graduate degree, get one—and not through the mail. A want ad for a management job in Washington, says Paul Maraschiello of Associated Resume Writers, may generate 200 qualified applicants, compared with, say, 20 in other cities.

"You don't find kids with 2.0 averages applying," says John McDermott, who runs the House of Representatives employment office. "They're all Phi Beta Kappas of some kind. They are all of a type."

Washington is conformity to conformity. It's wiry little guys with cuffed pants, collar buttons and tassels on their shoes. It's women with skirts and blouses with floppy bows from Alcott & Andrews. New Yorkers may conform to non-conformity with chic clothing, but conformity in Washington is, well, more classic. Sociologist Theodore Caplow once wrote that professional work demands "standards of decorum, including dignified carriage, inconspicuous table manners, a degree of aloofness, and avoidance of violent language and public daytime intoxication." That about covers it in Washington.

Says a man who has lived in Washington for a decade, "Everyone in Washington is in a headlong rush to achieve the status quo."

Washington is frenzy. It's working husbands and working wives racing to day care before the $1-per-minute late charge kicks in after 6 p.m. It's lawyers billing in computerized six-minute time zones. It's hustling to the HOV car pool. "A lot of people in this town are stimulation junkies," says Georgetown psychotherapist Stephen Shere, who has practiced here for 16 years. "People develop an appetite for it."

If you aren't frenzied, you still had better act frenzied because in Washington, frenzy is often mistaken for dedication to the job. A former Washington attorney who now practices in California says of her adopted state, "Here it's 'cool' to have friends outside of work. People work the same 70-hour week, but it's not 'cool.' So they talk about the weekend trip to Tahoe."

Says Judy Ziewacz, of the National Milk Producers Federation, "It's very 'Washington' to use one-upmanship about who works the longest hours."

Washington is competition. "Politics," wrote Ward Just in *The Congressman Who Loved Flaubert,* "was nothing more or less than an understanding of ambition and the moral and social conditions that produced it." And politics—like the city, the work, the ambitious people it has sired—is fiercely competitive. Says one newcomer to town, "I've never seen a place where people take such glee in other people's failures."

In Washington, competition must always supersede friendship.

But more than anything, Washington is the joy of meaningful work. In an era when so many people seem to feel their jobs are bureaucratized and pointless, it's ironic that workers in the world capital of bureaucracy still feel their jobs matter—feel their work makes a difference to the country and to its people. Maybe this is the real engine of the workworkwork ethos of Washington—and also the reason people in Washington are so often accused of myopia. "People back home ask me why I work so hard for so little money," says Gretchen Hasper Govan, a scheduling aide for New York Congressman Jack Kemp who often worked seven days a week during Kemp's failed presidential bid. "I tell them it's more than a job. It's a grand goal. So many people in Washington say, 'My life is my work.' You can get caught up in that."

Yet to feel, as the craftsman, that your work matters, that it reflects something within you, that it is occupation and avocation, is no small accomplishment today. It is the genuine beauty of work in Washington, where exhilaration is almost as highly prized as achievement itself. "You sacrifice a great deal in time, energy and family," says Judith Aitken, who before moving to Colorado ran the office of then-Kansas Congresswoman Martha Keys. "But you get a lot. You can make a difference. You are where the action is." What was Aitken's proudest accomplishment? She takes a long time to answer and then mentions a piece of legislation Keys got passed into law.

"It's pretty hard to pinpoint anything personally that I did," Aitken says. She ran the office efficiently—that was achievement enough, especially since Aitken can recall only one day in her eight years on Capitol Hill that she was caught up with her workload.

"One day in eight years!" she says, laughing. "I've always remembered that. Washington is so different. I never lost the thrill."

Snapshot No. 2 from Washington's workaday world . . .

The man got to the party and realized it wasn't really a party at all. The sprawling house in suburban Reston was filled with well-dressed people wearing those familiar lean and hungry looks. It was a "networking" party, and the people there weren't so much potential friends as potential commodities, each hoping to rise in some unknown way through the rub of others. Sure enough, when the people around the man discovered he was a reporter for an influential newspaper, they fawned over him. This irritated the man. He went upstairs, where someone again chanted the Washington mantra, "What do you do?"

"I'm a garbage man," he said.

"Oh, you own a garbage company."

"No, I pick up garbage."

A labored silence followed. "Yeah, and you know what bugs me—people who put wet grass clippings in plastic garbage bags. You know how heavy that is? Why don't people think?" The man rambled on and on, knowing that his squirming audience was trapped as long as he talked. When he finally stopped, nobody said a word. Heads turned and soon he was alone.

Q: "WHAT DO YOU DO?"

A: "The hundred-yard dash in 11.5."

Or: "The dishes every night."

Or: "As little as possible."

These answers won't fly in Can-Do Town, U.S.A.

"You just can't avoid the importance of 'role' here," says Charles Peters, who has worked for 20 years as the editor of The Washington Monthly magazine. "It is more powerful than any place I've ever been. You can go to parties, just blink and see blank faces with labels." Congressman, reporter, White House official, lobbyist, Cabinet member. "Every party has to have 'the mix.'" Most people never make it to these clubby bashes, but the attitude that a person is his work still hangs in the ether in Washington.

It's a town of job snobs.

Zy Weinberg learned this when he came to Washington to work as a public-interest lobbyist. "Name-dropping was common," he recalls. "'My husband works in such-and-such an agency.' That is not common elsewhere." Weinberg hated Washington and soon left. Scherrie Goettsch, who lived in Washington for five years while her husband taught college, remembers that people at parties actually walked away when she said she was a housewife.

"It was the kind of town that unless you were a professional out in the real world, you really didn't matter," Goettsch says. "Staying home was not acceptable—or certainly not as important."

This obsession with people's jobs is said to be tied to the simple clarity of Washington's key work pyramid—the federal GS ratings, which rank people neatly. But people also are judged on their nearness to the flame of political power. Political people want to know your job, says Washington novelist and former syndicated columnist Les Whitten, so they can decide if they want to take the time to talk to you. "If you're a teacher at Walt Whitman High School," he says, "nobody wants to talk to you."

The reason: You can't help them make a difference.

Housewives and schoolteachers are diminished by this credo, but so is everyone eventually, even Whitten. During the years he wrote a newspaper column with Jack Anderson, for instance, Whitten often ate with a man who was a top CIA secret operative. The men both enjoyed fine food and poetry, and Whitten came to think of the man as his friend. Big mistake. After Whitten left the Anderson column, he invited his friend to dinner. The spook was busy. From that day on, the men never shared a meal together again.

"I love to see the mighty fall," Whitten says, "but I didn't enjoy it when it happened to me. I thought he was my friend. That's Washington."

To be more charitable, there are reasons for Washington's job fixation that have nothing to do with power and influence. For one, all these ambitious, hard-working, educated people working in one town is akin to a piranha feeding frenzy. These people are used to being at the top of the normal curve, but here they're competing only against the top of the curve. So they push harder.

The result is critical mass. "I meet a lot of people," says Washington psychotherapist Amy F. Scott, "who believe, 'I am what I do, and if I no longer work at my job, I have no value.'"

This abiding fearfulness is not lost on their kids. "There is a high expectation for achievement," says Dr. Lawrence A. Brain, the director of child and adolescent psychiatric services at the Psychiatric Institute of Washington. "They see that their parents have benefited from achievement and feel the need to do as well or better. They have to achieve, but they are afraid they can't." It is achievement devoid of joy. The problem is magnified by the rising number of families with both parents working at demanding professional jobs.

"Surrounded by affluence," Brain says, "there is a deprivation of social support." Ironically, children of the achievement culture can also come to confuse the goal of achievement with its rewards—nice cars, houses and vacations. When Brain asks teens to list their three wishes, for instance, they inevitably say a big house, millions of dollars and a Porsche.

Not a word about family or friends—or making a difference.

Snapshot No. 3 . . .

The crowd at the Capitol Hill reception was knotted in the corner of the room when the woman arrived. She walked over and discovered an unusual guest, high-fashion model Christie Brinkley. When Brinkley left, the woman noticed that the knot quickly scurried over and re-assembled itself around then-White House Chief of Staff Donald Regan. The woman laughed to herself. Only in Washington could Donald Regan attract a klatch of groupies.

Work will set you free, bring you happiness.

It is the great Washington myth.

Richard F. Hamilton and James D. Wright, whose recent book *The State of the Masses* is a review of several thousand surveys dealing with work or life satisfaction over the last 40 years, argue that what makes people satisfied or dissatisfied with their lives usually isn't their work. The social scientists discovered that people's happiness with their family lives and their marriages was a far more potent indicator of life satisfaction than any of the classic sociological variables—job, income, education, race, sex or age.

This is a zinger. Because if workworkwork isn't all it's cracked up to be, people in Washington are in deep trouble. Work and family are on a collision course across America, as more and more husbands and wives work while raising children. As ever, Washington leads the way. You can't help wondering: In order to earn the money, status and satisfaction good jobs can bring, do people in Washington also lead the country in paying a price within their families and marriages, which are the real sources of personal happiness?

Most people seem to understand this intuitively. Seventy-two percent of respondents in The Post poll on work, for instance, ranked "family" as the most important thing in their lives, while less than 2 percent ranked "work" as the most important thing in their lives. But knowing this isn't as easy as living it, because the dirty little secret about Washington's workworkwork ethos is that it is not entirely voluntary.

"I've been amazed," says a professional who moved to Washington from the Midwest a few years ago. "I work 55 hours a week. I feel guilty for not working weekends. I don't think this is healthy. I know a woman with a baby who is quitting because she can't do 60 hours a week. She thinks it's okay for them to ask for 60 hours a week! I know another woman with a baby who looks worse and worse. She fears she's falling behind. I know of a young man with a young child who is under similar pressure. A lot of people here feel this great pressure."

A lawyer who moved to town from another big metro area about a year ago puts it bluntly: "They're compulsive here. I find people incredibly bright and politically aware, a lot of talented, sharp people. But they don't often do arts and crafts or ski or read. They have so much intelligence, but most of it is focused on work. It's not just hours, but it's a whole mentality. It's a very tangible thing. You feel the tension when you walk down the halls. It's a constant fight to remember that there is another world out there."

But perhaps that insight should be turned around: It is people in Washington who must remember that it's another world *in here*—in Washington, inside the achievement culture. Washington is the boy in the bubble. It is people in Washington who are at risk, living at the fringe of what most Americans believe is important in life. It is people in Washington who are out of sync, who are the guinea pigs in a national experiment altering the balance between living and working.

"Work in Washington is a tremendous part of a person's life, and it takes a lot more time than it does at home," says G. Jerry Shaw, the Washington attorney from Montana. "At home, work was a means to an end—leisure time, family time. In Washington, work is not the means, but the end in itself."

That is the heart of workworkwork, the heart of Washington.

And that is a scary thought.

—*The Washington Post* | Nov. 12, 1988

L'Enfant Terrible

Brilliant and Unbearable, Pierre L'Enfant
Made Washington Much of What it is Today

By Howard Means

A pocket biography of Pierre Charles L'Enfant would include the following:

He was born in Paris on August 2, 1754, and studied there, under his father, at the Royal Academy of Painting and Sculpture. Inspired by the American struggle for independence, he joined the French colonial troops with the rank of lieutenant and in early 1777 sailed for the New World.

At Valley Forge, during the awful winter of 1777-1778, he came to the attention of George Washington, who was to become his patron. Two years later, in May 1780, L'Enfant was among those captured in Charleston, South Carolina, when Fort Moultrie fell to an 8,000-man British force commanded by Henry Clinton.

The war, which had begun in 1776, came to an unofficial close on October 19, 1781, when General Cornwallis surrendered at Yorktown, Virginia. The following January the British prisoner L'Enfant, by then a captain, was exchanged for a Hessian mercenary of equal rank. L'Enfant would spend the next year and a half in Philadelphia.

In December 1783, three months after the Treaty of Paris brought a formal end to the War for Independence, L'Enfant returned briefly to France to settle personal affairs. There, at George Washington's request, he had the medals struck that he had designed for the Society of the Cincinnati, the organization of Revolutionary War officers. It was to be his last trip to his homeland.

Returning to America in the spring of 1784, L'Enfant soon established himself as perhaps New York's most successful architect.

Under the Articles of Confederation, the United States had been, since 1781, a loose collection of nation-states. Officially adopted in 1789, the Constitution heightened the need for a national capital to serve as the seat of the newly powerful federal government. The political compromise worked out in the Residence Act of 1790 placed that capital along the Potomac River, and on January 29, 1791, George Washington appointed L'Enfant its planner. It was a position L'Enfant had ardently sought.

L'Enfant arrived in Georgetown on March 9, 1791, and in less than thirteen months plotted what was to become the fundamental geography of the national capital—the plan of its streets, the location of its principal public buildings, the underlying logic that would govern the city's expansion.

On March 27, 1792, in a letter drafted by Alexander Hamilton and sent over Thomas Jefferson's signature, L'Enfant was relieved of his duties. He died here, virtually penniless and largely forgotten, in 1825 and was buried on an estate in Prince George's County. Nearly a century later, his reputation would be resurrected and L'Enfant placed among the pantheon of the city's founders.

Those are the raw facts. What they don't tell you is the troubling texture of the man.

Nor do they hint at the sometimes bitter debate over the true extent of L'Enfant's contribution to the design of the District of Columbia. Did he plan the city, or partially plan it, or crib its design from a variety of ancient and contemporary sources, or merely claim credit for the plan? The jury is still out on that verdict.

Nor do the facts convey the difficulty of the job L'Enfant faced. The new capital he planned—from Rock Creek to the Anacostia, from Florida Avenue south to the Potomac—was raw land. Speculators dogged him nearly every step of the way.

So did the need for urgency. The political compromise that had created the federal district was fragile as a meringue. George

Washington needed a real city, not a drawing-board one, to make the deal stick.

Nor do the facts convey the despair and bitterness that marked L'Enfant's later years. It was not an easy job George Washington handed Pierre L'Enfant. Trying to fulfill it would break him.

He had a tendency, the late French ambassador J.J. Jusserand wrote, to see things *en grand*. The phrase is especially becoming in French. Pierre L'Enfant was a big-picture man, a visionary.

"With the mind of an artist and in some sense of a prophet, perceiving future time as clearly as if it were the present, a man foresaw a century ago . . . what we now see with our eyes," wrote Jusserand, one of those most responsible for reviving L'Enfant's reputation.

He had other character traits as well, not nearly so becoming.

He was a wheedler, a whiner, a sycophant. He was a main chancer, a chronic malcontent. It wasn't only buildings and cities that he saw *en grand*; he saw himself *en grand*, too. He was impossible. He was also, quite probably, a genius.

One has to allow for L'Enfant's sometimes comic difficulty with the language he was forced to communicate in and for the more florid prose style of the time. Nonetheless, something close to his true voice drifts down to us in his letters.

"Sir," he wrote George Washington in early 1782: "A strong desire of convincing your excellency of the sentiments which have ever actuated me since I have had the honour to serve the United States induces me to address this to you and I flater myself you will perceive that my sole ambition has Been to merite your opinion and to owe to you the favor of Congress.

"I have never therefore embraced those opportunities which the success of other stronger [men] offered of soliciting Congress—but on the contrary have submitted in silence to the advancement of persons who were inferior to me in Rank—a very late instance may Be cited in the promotion of a much younger Capt. of Engineer than my-self, I mean *Monsieur Rochefontaine* . . . "

"It is not my intention to intimate anything to the disadvantage of those gentlemen who have been so happy as to obtaine the favor of Congress," he added later in the lengthy letter.

"Right," one wants to shout over the years in reply, "not your intention at all."

Before the decade ended, L'Enfant was writing George Washington again, this time for far larger stakes:

"Sir: The late determination of Congress to lay the foundation of a city which is to become the capital of this vast empire offers so great an occasion of acquiring reputation to whoever may be appointed to conduct the execution of the business that your Excellency will not be surprised that my ambition and the desire I have of becoming a useful citizen should lead me to wish a share in the undertaking."

L'Enfant had other powerful patrons—Alexander Hamilton was one—but only George Washington, the president, the Father of his Country, could have delivered L'Enfant the crown jewel of planning the country's capital. Yet it was a patronage stained almost from the moment L'Enfant set to work.

In Washington's letters, we can see him evolving an attitude toward the planner he had hired, an emerging awareness of those character traits that were to grind L'Enfant's ambition to dust.

"Since my first knowledge of this gentleman's abilities in the line of his profession, I have received him not only as a scientific man, but one who has added considerable taste to professional knowledge," Washington wrote in November 1791 to David Stuart, one of the three commissioners appointed to oversee construction of a national capital.

For planning the capital, "for prosecuting public works and carrying them into effect, he was better qualified than any one who had come within my knowledge in this country."

There's a hedging tone to that, an attempt to clean up, the historical record, a backing away, and there needs to be. L'Enfant had been appointed nearly a year earlier and had been on the job nine months. Things weren't going well.

Three weeks later, Washington wrote to a powerful local landholder of L'Enfant's "zeal in the public cause, [which has] carried him too fast!"

Two weeks after that, he wrote to the District commissioners: L'Enfant's "aim is obvious—It is to have as much scope as possible for the display of his talents—perhaps for his ambition."

"Ambition." The word keeps popping up with L'Enfant. His ambition was *en grand.*

He was haughty, proud, vain, mule-headed when he thought his talent had been crossed. He suffered no fools; he seems to have been incapable of compromise; his demands were non-negotiable.

L'Enfant answered only to George Washington—certainly not to the commissioners—and as much as anything, that is what doomed his role in the creation of the capital.

In the end—in late March 1792, when every appeal to L'Enfant had failed; after L'Enfant had told Washington's private secretary, Tobias Lear, that he had "already heard enough" of chains of command—the president pulled the plug.

"From your letter received yesterday in answer to my last, and your declaration in conversation with Mr. Lear, it is understood you absolutely decline acting under the authority of the present Commissioners," Jefferson and Hamilton wrote L'Enfant, with Washington's concurrence.

"If this understanding of your meaning be right, I am instructed by the President to inform you that notwithstanding the desire he has entertained to preserve your agency in the business, the condition upon which it is to be done is inadmissible & your services must be at an end."

L'Enfant's response was immediate and in character: He went straight to the top.

"Permit me also to assure in the most faithful manner," he wrote Washington, "that the same Reasons which have driven me from the establishment, will prevent any man of capacity, impressed with the same disinterested views, by which in every stage of it, I have been actuated, and who may be sufficiently well convicted of the importance of the undertaking, from engaging in a work that must defeat his sanguin hopes and baffle every exertion."

Defeat his sanguine hopes it did.

L'Enfant started many great projects—the federal city; Hamilton's manufacturing utopia at Paterson, New Jersey; Philadelphia's largest house for the nation's richest man, Robert Morris—but he finished very few.

He was star-crossed, by circumstance as well as by inner flaws— Morris's fortune collapsed as L'Enfant was working; the subscriptions to fund Hamilton's Paterson trickled in slowly.

For all the ambition he exhibited at obtaining major public commissions, he may have been a secret slugabed.

"I am only at present to regret that an heavy rain and thick mist which has been incessant Ever since my arrival here dose put an insuperable obstacle to my wish of proceeding immediatly to the survey," he wrote Jefferson in March 1791, shortly after arriving in Washington. "Should the weather continue bad as there is Every apparence it will I shall be much at a loss how to make a plan of the ground you have pointed out to me and have it ready for the President at the time when he is Expected at this place."

All true, perhaps, but the situation was urgent. America was still clumsily forming, and other powerful cities had hardly reconciled themselves to the inevitability of a national capital on the shores of the Potomac. What's more, Washington's surveyor, Andrew Ellicott, had performed admirably under the same conditions.

"Ellicott did accomplish his mission with remarkable promptness and efficiency, despite inclement weather, an attack of influenza, and a lack of competent assistants," Julian Boyd writes in his introduction to the twentieth volume of Thomas Jefferson's papers. "But mists and rains which had not impeded him in his more formidable task presented to L'Enfant 'an insuperable obstacle.'"

Contempt drips from the sentence.

The standard physical description of Pierre L'Enfant comes from the philanthropist and art collector W.W. Corcoran, whose father the Frenchman often visited.

L'Enfant was "a tall, erect man," Corcoran recalled, "fully six feet in height, finely proportioned, nose prominent, of military bearing, courtly air and polite manners, his figure usually enveloped in a long overcoat and surmounted by a bell-crowned hat—a man who would attract attention in any assembly."

But the portrait shows fracture lines in his later life, after the full measure of his bitterness and despair had settled in.

L'Enfant became an "unsuccessful petitioner before Congress for redress of his real and fancied wrongs, and he was to be seen almost every day slowly pacing the rotunda of the Capitol," the journalist Benjamin Perley Poore wrote in the 1880s, drawing on earlier accounts and his own 60 years in the capital.

"He was a tall, thin man, who wore, toward the close of his life, a blue military surtout coat, buttoned quite to the throat, with a tall, black stock, but no visible signs of linen.

"His hair was plastered with pomatum close to the head, and he wore a napless high beaver bell-crowned hat. Under his arm he generally carried a roll of papers relating to his claim upon the Government, and in his right hand he swung a formidable hickory cane with a large silver head."

Poore's description limns a distinctly modern—and sad—type of Washingtonian. One sees them throughout the downtown: clothes shabby; pockets stuffed with papers documenting claims for a veteran's pension or against the IRS or the FBI. L'Enfant was not the first person driven daft by government.

No description of L'Enfant is more poignant than the firsthand one offered by the engineer Benjamin Latrobe in his journal entry for August 12, 1806:

"Daily thro' the city stalks the picture of famine L'enfant and his dog. The plan of the city is probably his, though others claim it. It is not worth disputing about. This singular Man, of whom it is not known whether he was ever educated to the profession, and who indubitably has neither good taste nor the slightest practical knowledge, had the courage to undertake any public work whatever that was offered to him. He has not succeeded in any, but was always honest, and is now miserably poor. He is too proud to receive any assistance, and it is very doubtful in what manner he subsists."

At the height of his powers as the imperious planner of the federal city, L'Enfant had torn down the partially finished house of Daniel Carroll of Duddington because it intruded on one of his envisioned radials, New Jersey Avenue.

The act was born of hubris, and in the best tradition of classical tragedy, from that moment forward L'Enfant's life would unravel, his losses mount. The Carroll family was powerful; Daniel Carroll was no man to forgive a wrong, least of all from the self-important Frenchman.

Yet at the depth of his despair, L'Enfant was delivered unto the hands of his enemy's descendant. He was taken in first by a wealthy bachelor friend, Thomas Attwood Digges, and later by Digges's nephew, William Dudley Digges, Daniel Carroll's son-in-law. L'Enfant died at the Digges estate—"Green Hill," near Bladensburg—in 1825 and was buried on the grounds. It was not to be the final irony.

Today, Pierre L'Enfant's name survives in the Plaza along Independence Avenue, in the names of dental offices and florists, and in gift and jewelry shops. "L'Enfant" is part of the common parlance of the city's place names.

One hundred years ago it is doubtful that one in a thousand Washingtonians would have known his name. He simply disappeared from local history, as if someone had tied a rock around his memory and thrown it into the River of Forgetfulness.

Yet in 1909, a handful of dust and a few bones, he was to become only the eighth person—the first not native-born—to have his remains lie in state beneath the Rotunda of the Capitol. (The previous seven: Senators Thaddeus Steven and Charles Sumner, Supreme Court Justice Salmon Chase, the Civil War general John A. Logan, and the murdered presidents, Abraham Lincoln, James Garfield, and William McKinley.)

He was a man of extremes, a man of vision and little insight.

With him in charge, it is hard to believe that the city he longed to have his name associated with would have remained the capital. George Washington wanted a new national capital far more than many members of Congress, who found Philadelphia a congenial home, and L'Enfant, the president's agent-in-place in the new capital, was muddying the waters every inch of the way.

But without his contribution, the capital city that finally rose would not have been the same. L'Enfant seems to have had so much of the romantic in him—the Old World's idealistic enchantment with the New one—that he could not help seeing the nation thus as well.

"No nation, perhaps, had ever before the opportunity offered them of deliberately deciding on the spot where their capital should be fixed," he wrote Washington in that 1789 letter seeking the chance to plan the seat of government.

" . . . And, although the means now within the power of the country are not such as to pursue the design to any great extent, it will be obvious that the plan should be drawn on such a scale as to leave room for that aggrandizement and embellishment which the increase of the wealth of the nation will permit it to pursue at any period, however remote."

Modern Washington is that "remote" period of aggrandizement and embellishment, the other end of L'Enfant's vision of both the capital and the nation it was to serve—L'Enfant's dream, as it were, delivered.

To track Pierre Charles L'Enfant's life is to pick a delicate path through a minefield of egos.

His father had been a "painter in ordinary" to Louis XV. The senior Pierre Lenfant—the apostrophe came later—did landscapes and battle scenes commemorating the King's victories. Under his tutelage, young Pierre either studied engineering and architecture, as his supporters claim, or at least became adept at drawing and gained some sense of the design of fortifications.

L'Enfant's name appears sporadically in the history of the American Revolution, always an officer and a gentleman, often attached to more famous names. His bravery seems beyond question.

He served as an aide to Baron von Steuben at Valley Forge. The illustrations for The Army's first "Blue Book"—its manual of regulations—are his. That winter, as the ragged troops neared starvation, he did a pencil portrait of General Washington, at Lafayette's request, and a miniature oil portrait of the wife of General Nathanael Green. His Parisian manners apparently enchanted the general's lady.

By October 1779, he had made his way to Georgia, a part of the American and French forces under Count Pulaski that attempted to retake Savannah from the British. Pulaski was killed. Badly wounded, L'Enfant managed to escape to Charleston, South Carolina, where seven months later he would be taken prisoner by the British.

"[I was] in my bed till January 1780," he wrote Washington. "My weak state of health did not permit me to work at the fortifications of Charleston." Still, supporting himself with a crutch, he fought when the British arrived.

"Your zeal and active services are such as to reflect the highest honor on yourself and are extremely pleasing to me," George Washington had responded to L'Enfant's plea for promotion.

The new commission came in 1783 when L'Enfant was made a major of engineers. Three years later, established as an architect and designer in New York City, he began to make his fortune.

L'Enfant "was the lion-architect of this city," Columbia University research librarian William Hindley wrote of the Frenchman's role in New York. "His voice [was] listened to and work poured in upon him from every direction."

He had a hand in designing Gracie Mansion, the seat of New York's mayors. He executed mansions for Alexander Hamilton and furniture-maker Duncan Phyfe.

The record is spotty on whether he designed the mansion for John Jacob Astor, but beyond doubt the two became intimates. He was networking, building up his list of contacts, and eminent ones they were: Astor, Phyfe, Hamilton, Washington; trade, industry, banking, and government.

He had a hand, too, in improvements to St. Paul's Chapel, and at Hamilton's behest, he designed a dome under which Washington and members of Congress sat at the grand New York banquet of July 23, 1788—a public festival meant to swing the state's vote to ratifying the Constitution.

The dome, a newspaper account notes, was "surmounted by a figure of Fame, with a trumpet proclaiming a new era, and holding a scroll emblematic of the three great epochs of the war: Independence—Alliance with France—Peace."

He saw things *en grand*.

The dome was much admired. So was his work in remodeling New York's old City Hall. In early March 1789 Congress met in the building—by then renamed Federal Hall—for the first time under the new Constitution. It was the site as well of George Washington's inauguration as the nation's first president on March 30, 1789. When Martha Washington visited the hall in June of that year, she had more than enough reason to admire L'Enfant's chimneys of American marble and the eagle with thirteen arrows in its talons that he had designed as the main ornament of the facade's pediment.

Federal Hall was to be another of L'Enfant's projects that would fail to outlive him. In 1812, it was sold at auction for $425 and torn down. For his services on the hall, L'Enfant was granted ten acres of land, which he rejected in pursuit of cash compensation. Twenty-one years later, the Frenchman was still petitioning New York for his pay. The ten acres he rejected today lie just east of Central Park near 68th Street.

Three months after Mrs. Washington's visit to Federal Hall, at the height of L'Enfant's New York career, he wrote the president of his "ambition and the desire" to help "lay the foundation of a city that is to become the capital of this vast empire"—and threw himself headlong into the forces of history that were to strip him of his wealth, his reputation, and some part of his sanity.

"I am fully sensible of the extent of the undertaking," he assured Washington. But he couldn't have been.

The effort to establish Washington as the national capital was "haunted by a demon of discord," James Thomas Flexner writes in the final volume of his biography of George Washington.

"The brilliant L'Enfant had forced his own dismissal; the commissioners had fallen out with the local landowners; and, as inefficiency reigned, auctions aimed at selling lots found few bidders.

"Word circulated that the city would never rise. Pennsylvania, eager to change Philadelphia from the temporary to the permanent capital, announced plans to create at state expense such handsome public buildings as the infant city of Washington seemed unable to achieve."

Flexner's graceful summary only hints at the daunting complexity of problems that L'Enfant faced.

The Residence Act had struck a middle ground between northern and southern interests, but it had been vague on the exact site of a capital. It was to be established somewhere on the Potomac between the river's "Eastern Branch" (now the Anacostia River) and the mouth of the Conococheague Creek, at Williamsport, Maryland, near Hagerstown. But there was never any real doubt what location would be chosen. Navigation on the river stops at Little Falls, and Georgetown and Alexandria were already established ports. Between Georgetown and Alexandria stretched not much more than an improved wilderness dotted by farms and two hamlets—Carrollsburg and Hamburg, where the bulk of public buildings eventually would be built.

Jenkins' Hill, which L'Enfant would write "stands as a pedestal waiting for a monument" (the monument placed there was the Capitol), was densely wooded.

To the west, along what would become the Mall, Tiber Creek meandered toward the Potomac amidst sometimes impassable bogs and thickets.

Northwest, he again found high ground for his "Presidential Palace"—a spot that would add "to the sumptuousness of a palace the convenience of a house and the agreeableness of a country seat." And country it was. What L'Enfant saw *en grand*, he envisioned out of nature's raw materials.

Added to the difficulty of the terrain was the need for deception. The area may have been sparsely settled and only moderately suited to agriculture, but with the announcement that a capital was to arise within it somewhere east of Rock Creek, real estate became what it ever would be—Washington's number-one non-political obsession.

A Scotsman named David Burnes—"an unambitious farmer and a heavy drinker," Douglas Southall Freeman writes—owned 225 acres along the Potomac in and near Hamburg. To bring him to reasonable terms, Washington had L'Enfant begin his planning in the opposite direction, toward the Anacostia.

Feint left, run right—it begins to sound like the Redskins' "counter-trey" play.

Added to the difficulty of often virgin terrain and the need for deception, always, was urgency. Philadelphia, powerful both politically and economically, was plotting. And it was the acting seat of the nation's government. If a capital on the Potomac wasn't ready to receive Congress by the end of the century, Philadelphia was likely to become the permanent capital.

L'Enfant had peppered George Washington with plans, designs, and general maps—in late March, June, and August of 1791, and again, with a fourth revision, in January 1792—but the president needed more than magnificent visions; he needed roads and structures.

"The advance of the season begins to require that the plans for the buildings and other publick works at the Federal city, should be in readiness, & the persons engaged to carry them into execution," Jefferson wrote L'Enfant from Philadelphia in late February 1792.

Get cracking, get a move on, get off that haughty French *derrière*.

"To change a wilderness into a city," L'Enfant wrote back, "to erect and beautify buildings etc. to that degree of perfection necessary to receive the seat of Government of a vast empire the short period of time that remains to effect these objects is an undertaking vast as it is novel—and reflection that all this is to be done under the many disadvantages of opposing interests . . . "

Yes, yes, but perfection wasn't what anyone wanted to hear. L'Enfant was playing the philosopher; the Secretary of State and the president needed a construction superintendent.

The problems were complicated by the distance between them. George Washington was trying to oversee the city that would bear his name by long distance, from Philadelphia. Jefferson, Washington's go-between with L'Enfant, was busy with affairs of state. Lines of communication were frayed, and the planner was not a good listener.

There was the problem, too, of financing the new capital. Plans could be had cheap. Building the roads and structures, the president wanted required cash.

L'Enfant wanted the government to float a loan to fund construction of the capital—$1 million. His budget for 1792 included nineteen boatmen at $8 a month; seventeen "Overseers of the Labourers" at $20 a month; $1,000 for "bellows, anvils, vices & tools for Smiths and Iron, steel grindstones, nails, spikes etc."; $10,000 for "boards, scantlings etc." In all, the tab came to about $300,000.

The government—Washington, Jefferson—wanted nothing of such debt. Building the city would be funded by exploiting its natural resource: land.

In the complicated and ingenious deal George Washington had struck with local landowners, more than 10,000 building lots had remained in government hands. Funding would be raised by the sale of those lots, and the fuel that would drive the fire of funding was speculation.

But L'Enfant abhorred speculation. The premature sale of the land would constrict his ability to alter his plans as new problems presented themselves. L'Enfant was armed only with persistence and complete confidence in himself—and the map that showed the exact location of the lots the government proposed to sell.

Historians differ on why there were no maps of the city-to-be available for display at the public land sale of October 17, 1791: L'Enfant either had difficulty having the plans printed in Philadelphia, or he abetted the difficulty, or he actively created the problem. What is beyond question is that L'Enfant adamantly kept his own copy of the plan to himself as the sale proceeded.

Predictably, the sale was a flop. How, Washington fulminated in a letter to Commissioner David Stuart, could would-be purchasers be "induced to buy, to borrow an old adage, *a pig in a poke?*"

It was a battle L'Enfant had no hope of winning, no more than he had any hope of coming out ahead in his continuing battle with the commissioners over whether he was to answer to them or only to George Washington, no more than he had any hope of prevailing when he pulled down the house of Daniel Carroll. L'Enfant was a man seemingly enamored of trouble.

He plotted the greatest opportunity of his life so that the drama could have only one end. If he had consolation in his later years, it must have been that so many of the speculators he loathed came out no better than he did.

Benjamin Stoddert, the first Secretary of the Navy, invested heavily in Washington land, and spent his last years dodging creditors. So did Thomas Law and William Mayne Duncanson, who had become rich in India only to lose their fortunes in Washington real estate.

By 1792, Samuel Blodget was one of the city's biggest promoters. He sponsored two lotteries. The prizes were to be expensive buildings constructed for the winners; the profits were to fund a national university here. Both lotteries failed, and Blodget was imprisoned for debt.

Of all the speculators, none failed more spectacularly than James Greenleaf, who had amassed a fortune while serving as the American consul in Amsterdam. For $480,000 he and his syndicate partners—John Nicholson and Robert Morris, whose mansion had caused L'Enfant such grief in Philadelphia—purchased 3,000 lots in Washington under a leveraged deal that let them take title to the land before they had completed the purchase. Soon, the syndicate owned more than a third of the land for sale here. A monopoly, it charged exorbitant prices, and land sales ground to a halt. In 1797, beset by this and other failures, the syndicate sank into bankruptcy. Greenleaf, too, would do time.

In all, it was a real estate failure of such epic dimensions that the new capital would not crawl out from under it for half a century. Officially, the government established itself here in 1800. Six years later, as Benjamin Henry Latrobe recorded in his journals, the city was in tatters. The passage deserves quoting in its entirely.

"The families of Workmen, whom the unhealthiness of the city and idleness (arising from the capricious manner in which the appropriations for the erection of the public buildings have been granted, giving to them for a short time high wages, and again perhaps for a whole season not affording them a weeks work) have ruined in circumstance and health, are to be found in extreme indigence scattered in wretched huts over the Waste which *the law* calls the American metropolis, or inhabiting the half finished houses, now tumbling to ruins which the madness of speculation has erected.

"Besides these wretched remnants of industrious and happy families, enticed hither by their own golden dreams, or the golden promises of swindling, or deceived speculators, there are higher orders of being, quite as wretched and almost as poor, tho' as yet not quite so ragged. These are Master Tradesmen, chiefly building artisans, who have purchased lots, and perhaps built houses, in which they invested their all. Many of them brought hither, and have sunk, the earnings of a laborious life, which in any other spot would have given to them ease, and to their children education. Distress and want of employ have made many of them sots; few have saved their characters; most of them hate, envy, and calumniate each other, for they are all fighting for the scanty means of support which the city affords.

"Above these again are others who brought large fortunes to this great vortex that swallowed every thing irrecoverably that was thrown into it. Law, Duncanson, Stoddert, and many others from affluent circumstances, are involved by their sanguine hopes in embarrassments from which nothing but the grave will set them free. Of the adventurers and swindlers whom the establishment of the city brought hither few remain. S. Blodget is confined in the bounds of the prison, and collects $5 subscriptions for the establishment of the University. Greenleaf pays an annual visit to the courts of justice, for the purpose of *testing titles* to lots, and also as agent for his creditors who hold Assignments on his city property. The rest have disappeared or are dead."

If L'Enfant took a perverse pleasure in the bleak prospects of the capital—and given his nature, he probably did—the pleasure must have been qualified. For the experience of trying to launch this capital broke L'Enfant, would have snapped him like a dead twig if he hadn't had such an absolute faith in himself. His pride seems to have been indomitable. It is impossible not to admire his persistence, his stamina in the light of all that befell him.

His supporters are quick to note that L'Enfant waited until after George Washington's death in 1799 to begin demanding his due of Congress. Perhaps it was just that—respect for his patron, "his Excellency"—that kept L'Enfant quiet so long. But Washington had already spoken on the matter, shortly after L'Enfant's dismissal and unfavorably so far as the planner was concerned.

"The plan of the City having met universal applause (as far as my information goes) and Major L'Enfant having become a very discontented man—it was thought that less than 2,500 or 3,000 dollars would not be proper to offer him for his services," Washington wrote the commissioners.

"Instead of this, suppose 500 guineas, and a lot in the good part of the city were to be substituted? I think it would be more pleasing and less expensive."

The offer was conveyed March 14, 1792. Less expensive, it might have been—Washington was ever the practical man. More pleasing, it wasn't.

"Without enquiring of the principle upon which you rest this offer," L'Enfant responded to the commissioners four days later, "I shall only here testify my surprise thereupon, as also my intention to decline accepting it."

Even as testy as he was, with L'Enfant the quality of mercy does indeed seem to have been strained: $2,500 in cash and land was piddling recompense. It also as the best offer he was to get.

He sent three "memorials"—petitions or redress—in 1800, to the city commissioners, to Congress, and the president. Collectively, the memorials address the old grievances of 1791 and 1792—he'd been cut off from access to the president, profits from the map he had drawn of the city had been denied him, errors had been inserted on the map and

Andrew Ellicott's name had been substituted for his own—but the first paragraph of the first one gets to the real and true point.

"A concurrence of disastrous events rendering my position so difficult as to be no longer possible to withstand unless speedy relief be obtained by collecting what yet remains my due . . . "

What was the true value of his services in planning the federal city? Eight thousand dollars, he calculated, for one year of his labor; $37,500 for the profit he should have received from the sale of his map; and an additional $50,000 for "prequisites of right in particular negotiations and enterprise."

In sum, $95,500. What were the "prequisites of right"? No one has ever quite figured that out.

Simultaneously, L'Enfant pressed forward with his incessant defense of his plan, his "sisteme" of streets and isolated settlements built around the intersection of radial avenues that would grow together to create a pleasing whole.

In an exhaustive appendix to his first memorial, he wrote of "Idle talkers and busy brain people as I at best take to be those fault finders who can pretend Ignorance of the conditions upon which that sisteme was framed and presume to Juge of thing the Intention of which the[y] understand not."

Already the sound of frenzy has worked its way into his prose. The memorial itself runs twenty tightly handwritten pages; the appendix another nineteen. Its subtext, always, is obsession.

On April 27, 1810, Congress voted to appropriate him $666.66 for his role in laying out the city, with interest dating back to March 1, 1792—$1,394.20 in all—and by then the creditors were lined up at his door. In the meantime, he became the tragicomic figure, the haunter of the Capitol and the city streets.

Until the Digges family took him in, he lived very nearly hand to mouth. Whatever financial help might have flowed his way from his family in France had been cut off by the revolution there. Occasionally, the odd check would trickle in from an admirer or a fellow countryman.

"I am sending you my dear Major a note for $50 that I promised Soderstrom to have mailed you," said a letter of July 1803. "He has informed me that you are still in the same situation." The letter is signed, "Your friend, V. duPont."

Others tried to help L'Enfant, mostly in vain. Not only did he court failure; he resisted kindness.

In 1812 Secretary of War William Eustis appointed L'Enfant to the faculty of the United States Military Academy at West Point as a professor of the art of engineering.

L'Enfant replied that he had neither "the rigidity of manner, the tongue, nor the patience, nor indeed any inclination peculiar to instructors." It may have been one of his sharpest self-insights. He prated on about the lack of compensation for his work in planning Washington. He had become a Johnny-One-Note.

James Monroe, then the Secretary of State, tried to reason with him. The West Point position will "provide you an honorable station and situation," he wrote L'Enfant. "Your creditors have no hope in your present situation."

Again the answer was no. The appointment, L'Enfant wrote Eustis, was "unaccepted but not rejected"—a distinction from a man prone to hang himself with such fine demarcations.

Monroe did get him a final job.

In August 1814 Fort Washington (then Fort Warburton) had been blown up and abandoned by its commanding officer as the British advanced on the city. Serving as the Acting Secretary of War as well as Secretary of State, Monroe asked L'Enfant to restore it. The final result, a star-shaped fortress drawn from the Middle Ages, would be built in 1822, but by then L'Enfant was long gone from the project.

Old habits, perhaps lingering suspicions on the part of some in government, betrayed him. It was said he was slow to send Monroe a report of the needed changes, that he was too extravagant in his proposals, too en grand. A permanent war secretary came on and replaced the Frenchman. For the nearly sixteen months he worked on the fortifications, L'Enfant was paid $1,866. Again creditors were waiting. It was his last chance at public acclaim, at public redemption.

"A retrospect view of the cause of my misery truly dispirits me and makes me pray for the end to my existence," he wrote Monroe.

"I now truly find myself a naked, castaway individual on a strange shore, without home, without friend, without resources whatsoever to command, deprived of all relations on whom I could call for assistance, and a debtor of several thousands of dollars."

When he died ten years later, his estate amounted to $45 in furniture and odds and ends.

But death wouldn't free L'Enfant from controversy. In life, he had battled with nothing more than real people; in death, his reputation would be pitted against the legends of American history.

This is the critical fact to keep in mind in weighing scholarly assessments of L'Enfant's contribution to the creation of the national capital: Every inch of originality granted him is an inch subtracted from George Washington, from Thomas Jefferson, from the Constitution, from the ideals that gave birth to the nation. Such ground is yielded very grudgingly.

Thus, for example, Julian Boyd's "Editorial Note"—"Fixing the Seat of Government"—that precedes his 20th Volume of *The Papers of Thomas Jefferson*.

It is a learned note, 72 pages long, gracefully written and exhaustive. To L'Enfant, it is absolutely unforgiving.

Was the Frenchman, as Washington wrote, the best planner known to him in the new nation? Not really. Washington was certainly familiar with Joseph Clark, who had made improvements to the Maryland State House. Besides, whatever L'Enfant's talents, he "lacked those qualities of character and professional discipline which Clark so evidently possessed."

Why was L'Enfant chosen? "He was available, he had some politically powerful friends, he was a war veteran who had been wounded in service, and perhaps most important of all, time was pressing."

What of the Mall?

L'Enfant's "Grand Avenue" was to be "400 feet in breadth, and about a mile in length, bordered with gardens, ending in a slope from the houses on each side"—a vast green adornment to the principal residential area of the city. At roughly the site of the current Washington Monument, the Grand Avenue would connect with the "President's Park," and at this merger of the city's north-south and east-west axes would rise the equestrian statue to George Washington.

By contrast, Boyd writes, "Jefferson's concept of extensive public parks and gardens along the waterfront . . . may rightly be regarded as the origin of what would eventually become one of the chief glories of the national capital."

The brief goes on for page upon page, always complicated by the fact that Jefferson was himself learned in architecture and familiar with the plans of the chief cities of Europe.

If nothing else, L'Enfant is generally acclaimed for the scope of his vision, his "*en grand*-ness." His plan went far beyond the relatively small area needed for the original government enclave. He saw in his mind's eye the city that was to be, not the one that was immediately needed. But Boyd doesn't grant him even that.

It was Washington's effort to accommodate landowners in both Carrollsburg and Hamburg that required the plan to be extended into both their domains. Jefferson himself had suggested something similar as early as the fall of 1790.

Nor does Boyd grant L'Enfant full credit for placing the Capitol on Jenkins' Hill, also known as Jenkins' Heights—that "pedestal waiting for a monument." The real reason lies, Boyd writes, "in the realm of conjecture," but evidence suggests that Washington himself had had the idea and the Frenchman was merely trying to flatter his patron. It's a remarkable charge from a scholar of Boyd's rank.

Nor finally does Boyd give L'Enfant full credit for the plan of the city itself—the one that bears his name, the one on which his reputation most directly rides.

Closely examined, the plan is full of erasures and additions. It was Jefferson who scratched out the monarchial "palace" of "President's

Palace," as L'Enfant invariably referred to the White House, and replaced it with the democratic "House"—a place where a regular American, a president, would live.

"In its final form," Boyd contends, the so-called L'Enfant plan is "a Jefferson document of considerable importance in the planning of the capital." L'Enfant not only must share the platform; he is pushed from it.

Worst of all from Boyd's viewpoint, L'Enfant seemed to have willfully misinterpreted the slight sketch of the federal city that Jefferson had executed and passed on to Washington—and Washington on to the planner.

"Such regular plans indeed," L'Enfant wrote back to Washington, "however answerable they may appear upon paper or seducing as they may be on the first aspect to the eyes of some people must even when applyed upon the ground the best calculated to admit of it become at last tiresome and insipid."

He might as well have called Jefferson a knucklehead.

"The obvious personal allusion," Boyd writes, "revealed a gross misconception of the mind and character" of Jefferson. L'Enfant had gone too far, and he would be made to pay.

"Of the projected plan, finally laid out in 1793," Boyd writes, "the only part of its concept which can beyond question be attributed to L'Enfant involves what he called the 'divergent avenues' cutting across the basic gridiron and resulting in squares, triangles, circles, and other irregularly shaped areas which have been praised beyond measure as if born of inspired genius."

One tries to imagine his apoplexy if L'Enfant could read it.

The evaluation presented in James Sterling Young's *The Washington Community: 1800-1828* takes a higher road—Young won the Bancroft Award for his work—but ultimately it is no less damning to L'Enfant.

"For the community plan, no less than the Constitution, is a blueprint for the governing establishment," Young writes. "No less than the Constitution, the community plan lays down principles of organization to be followed by the rulers of the nation . . .

"While authorship of the plan technically belongs to Major Pierre Charles L'Enfant, there is a certain hard justice in the relative obscurity to which history has consigned this unusual figure. For the real authors of the plan for Washington, in all but the narrow and technical sense, were the rulers themselves."

Thus, in the plan the Capitol and White House are set at such a great distance from one another—and imagine that distance in the terms of 1791, through thickets and marsh—not because L'Enfant thought of the two sites as becoming prominences and foresaw a splendid avenue connecting them; not, as Boyd contends, because he was merely dancing to George Washington's tune; but because the Constitution itself requires such a separation of powers. It is nothing more than the mere technical realization of a compelling idea.

And thus L'Enfant failed to allot specific places for the departments of the executive branch—State, Treasury, War—not because he simply never quite got around to it but because it is precisely within these departments, with their need to deal with Congress, that the separation of powers becomes most murky.

Thus, too, L'Enfant's radial avenues reach, like the foul lines of a baseball diamond, into eternity, into the very heart of the nation and in every direction, not because he found it a pleasing and useful design but because Washington was never meant to be an economically independent city. It was meant always to be dependent on such life lines to the nation's interior.

In all, it amounts to a neat dovetailing of plan and larger purpose.

"Here," Young writes, "was more than mere token allegiance to the Constitution. Here was an intention to carry the organizing principles of the Constitution far beyond the purposes for which it had been conceived."

L'Enfant, that is, was nothing more than the instrument of national will, a mere draftsman turning Constitutional principles into streets and building sites. One suspects that evaluation, too, would turn him apoplectic and maybe the more so. As much as he would have railed against detractors like Julian Boyd, L'Enfant would have despised being reduced to a cipher, a technoid.

The claims advanced for L'Enfant—the claims that brought him back from obscurity and caused his dust and bones 84 years after his death to be placed in state beneath the Rotunda of the Capitol—were as exaggerated as the charges leveled against.

L'Enfant was not merely restored to favor; he was very nearly deified.

As much as anywhere specific, that deification begins at the Columbia Historical Society on February 18, 1895, with a paper delivered by Dr. James Dudley Morgan: "Major Pierre Charles L'Enfant, the Unhonored and Unrewarded Engineer."

A descendant of the Digges family which had taken L'Enfant in in his penury—and of Daniel Carroll, whom the planner had irked by tearing down his half-finished house—Morgan would go on to become president of the Society. He also would devote some substantial portion of fourteen years of his life to seeing L'Enfant disinterred from the Digges estate and resettled in Arlington National Cemetery.

The report Morgan delivered to the Society in commemoration of that triumphant moment rings with idolatry:

"It was a lonely and unmarked grave more than six feet in length. A graceful, red cedar, drawing its vigorous life from the very earth which enveloped the ashes of the neglected Frenchman, his sole monument for eighty-four years, swaying and whispering with every breeze, carried the inspiration of his genius into never-ending requiem, while its pungent odor served as perpetual incense."

Indeed, the tree, which had been planted at the head of the grave when L'Enfant was first interred in 1825, was to give its last full measure of service at his disinterment. Cut down, a part of it would be hewn into the presidential gavel used by the Columbia Historical Society, now the Historical Society of Washington, DC.

At times, the idolatry of L'Enfant would slide into slapstick. One report to the historical society written in 1937 tells of a pen-and-ink drawing on deep pink paper, "generously supplemented by brushings of white water color," that L'Enfant supposedly had left to posterity.

In the foreground "an immense white marble shaft" foresees the Washington Monument (though L'Enfant himself had proposed an equestrian statue). At its base sits "a Grecian temple in general effect by no means dissimilar to the Lincoln Memorial."

One wonders if somewhere in the drawing, had it not again been lost to history, would have been found I.M. Pei's East Wing for the National Gallery or Philip Johnson's jewel-like pre-Columbian museum for Dumbarton Oaks. The drawing seems to have been that giving.

In truth, there is as much a utilitarian side to L'Enfant's deification as there is to his debunking. Dead men often serve larger causes than they ever intended.

Dr. Morgan was motivated by family connections as well as by his own interpretations of the city's beginnings.

The powerful McMillan commission authorized by Congress with planning "for the development and improvement of the park system of the District of Columbia" needed not only an original plan to hearken back to but an original planner of greater-than-life dimensions. If it was going to do what it proposed—rip the railroad tracks out of the immediate downtown, get rid of Andrew Jackson Downing's fanciful Victorian park on the Mall, impose a guiding logic on what more and more seemed like an illogical sprawl, it needed a L'ENFANT writ large, a towering eminence, a genius.

"The original plan of the city of Washington, having stood the test of a century, has met universal approval," the commission reported in 1902. "The departures from that plan are to be regretted and, wherever possible, remedied."

It was the stamp of official approval that L'Enfant had so desperately sought in life.

Other forces had a hand as well.

The eulogy delivered at L'Enfant's reinternment by the Reverend William T. Russell hints at a larger agenda:

"France—Catholic France—was our only ally, when we most needed friends. But for the ready financial aid with which Catholic France replenished our exhausted treasury . . . it may well be questioned how long our independence would have been deferred.

"This ceremony today reflects credit on the nation which thus speaks its gratitude, and honor on Catholic France and her heroes, who so rightly deserve it."

The first decade of the twentieth century saw the largest flow of immigrants to this nation ever, many of them Catholics of eastern and southern European origin. Perhaps L'Enfant's restoration was meant in part as a counterweight to the usual reciprocal xenophobia and anti-Catholicism.

Certainly, the French influence is undeniable.

Behind the scenes and in his writings, J.J. Jusserand, the French ambassador from 1902 to 1925, seems to have been nearly as influential as Dr. Morgan in elevating L'Enfant and maintaining his reputation.

The first complete life of the planner, Elizabeth Kite's *L'Enfant and Washington*, published in 1929, was funded by the Institut Français de Washington. Favorable on all the major issues, the biography is preceded by a lengthy introduction from Jusserand.

An architect and engineer in life, L'Enfant was to become a metaphor, a symbol in death.

What Pierre Charles L'Enfant had was an eye, a view, a way of looking at the world.

It's unfair to compare Thomas Jefferson's small sketch for the federal city with L'Enfant's plan. Jefferson was Secretary of State; he was drawing on the run. L'Enfant was engaged to do the work. Yet the Frenchman's plan is undoubtedly grander, in its particulars and, more important, in the imagination that underlay them.

Jefferson's plan was pragmatic; it dealt with what needed to be accomplished in the time and with the resources available. The White House and Capitol sit near each other along roughly what is now the line of E Street—the White House on the current George Washington University campus, the Capitol near 15th Street. South, across what was then Tiber Creek, the land falls away to the Potomac. The plan is tight, compact, rectilinear. The whole forms a nucleus of a federal city; the rest would grow from it.

L'Enfant's plan is anything but practical. It skirts reality. He began the project all wrong—not with a lock-step grid of streets, a tyranny of right angles, but with natural features, with the promontory for the Capitol. And yet his plan takes a barely tamed wilderness and makes of it a gleaming, civilized whole.

Perhaps L'Enfant was merely trying to please George Washington, or anticipate his desires, when we placed the Capitol and White House at such great distance from each other, but if so, one suspects that the placement neatly jibed with his own desires. He needed that kind of space to strut his stuff.

Perhaps the logic by which he tried to justify his system of radical avenues—that the squares where they intersect would form focuses of settlement; that as hypotenuses, they would shorten the real distance between two points; that they would open up the city visually—was an attempt to read reason into what he considered a pleasing aesthetic. But if so, he gave the city something unique and imposed a logic that carried beyond the space he planned and the time he lived in.

Washington is not Philadelphia or New York or any other place on the face of the nation. It is Washington, absolutely.

It is a city—the phrase is L'Enfant's—with "reciprocities of sight," a city where buildings look at one another and can be seen from multiple vantage points. Given L'Enfant's obsession with compensation and the speculative greed that nearly ruined the city in its infancy, it is probably only proper that the planner's greatest reciprocity of all—the sight line that joined the Capitol and White House—was destroyed by the new Treasury Department that Andrew Jackson had built beginning in 1838.

That, too, would have given L'Enfant apoplexy. The reciprocity was absolutely central to his vision. In any sense larger than mere law, destroying it was a criminal act.

Washington took seemingly forever to live up to L'Enfant's dream of it. The Portuguese Minister took to calling it "the City of Magnificent Distances."

Charles Dickens in his 1842 tour of America amended that to "the City of Magnificent Intentions": "Spacious avenues, that begin in nothing, and lead nowhere . . . ornaments of great thoroughfares, which only lack great thoroughfares to ornament." Dickens could turn a phrase, but attributing Washington's failure to grow to L'Enfant's vision of the city is no more justifiable than reading his personal lapses into the plan that person produced.

L'Enfant's soul, his spirit, his genius, were trapped in failed flesh. How many similar examples does history offer us?

L'Enfant thought big, and thought big of himself. He didn't want a little place of a federal city to celebrate his talent. A little place of a city was unequal to his self-conception and to his conception of what America should and would and must become, its manifest destiny.

But size wasn't his measure. He foresaw ultimately a city of about 100,000 people—Philadelphia already had a population of more than 43,000; his native Paris, more than half a million. L'Enfant's measure was a more subtle form of grandeur: the capacity of the capital to inspire.

The City of Washington in the Territory of Columbia—the name approved by the District commissioners—would be a place, L'Enfant wrote, where "the Youth of succeeding generations [would] tread in the paths of those sages or heroes whom their country thought proper to celebrate."

The architect Elbert Peets tracked L'Enfant's intellectual sources in a 1940 article for *House and Garden* magazine. Christopher Wren and John Evelyn both used radials in their plans for rebuilding London after the inferno of 1666. The great landscaping trends that emerged in Europe with the Renaissance found perhaps their highest expression in Andre Le Nôtre's design for Louis XIV's Versailles, "where the vista along the canal continues into the blue distance, giving the palace of the king dominance over the whole world." Herbert Stein-Schneider convincingly likens L'Enfant's street system to the paths of the royal hunting forest at Versailles.

Beyond much doubt, there is something of Versailles in L'Enfant's plan for Washington—a borrowing of its own reciprocities of sight, a monarchial model for the capital of a nation that was to teach the world another way of governing. It's irony, but it's not theft. L'Enfant was too proud for that, too.

He was what he was—a son of imperial France, invested with a cast of mind he never could quite overcome. To him, the White House was always the "President's Palace"; George Washington was always his "Excellency." But he had as well a great faith in the nation he adopted, in its future, its illimitable potential.

He fought for American independence, and he tried to deliver the nation that emerged from that war a capital city that would fit it when greatness arrived.

The miracle is that for all his flaws, all his "*en grand*-ness," all the roadblocks in his path—the ones put there by circumstance and the ones he put there himself—he managed to do just that.

—*Washingtonian* | January 1990

Street on the Hill

The residents of Acker Street like to think of their street as a microcosm of Capitol Hill, and of Washington in general. In some ways it is a microcosm of the future, as well.

By David Finkel

T he residents of Acker Street like to think of their street as a microcosm. It is a microcosm of Capitol Hill, they say, and of Washington in general, and in some ways it is a microcosm of the entire country, at least of its less-segregated parts. It is multiracial, multicultural, multi-generational and multi-class. It is black and white, old and young, working and jobless, frequent flier and frequent bus rider, affluent and broke. Only one block long, it is a street neatly contained, and on this day, October 31, 1991, as its two newest residents arrive in a rental van, it is one more thing: momentarily at peace.

The two people in the van are both men, both in their twenties, both white and both aides to a U.S. senator. One is named Tom Barnes, the other is Toof Brown. They pull over at 608 Acker, a town house, and begin wrestling furniture up the metal stairway that leads from the sidewalk to the front door. It is a nice town house—two stories, fresh paint, working fireplace, hardwood floors. The rent is $975 a month. Meanwhile, across the street at 617 Acker, where the front door is scuffed and the metal stairway is rusting through in parts, some black teenagers watch. It is a Thursday, early afternoon, time to be in school. And yet here the children are.

Now, one of them, a girl, maybe 13, crosses over to 608. As Toof Brown remembers it, she doesn't say hello. Neither does she say her name or introduce herself in any way. What she does do is mention that it's Halloween. "She came over and asked us if we were going to have any candy," Brown recalls. "I think we said no."

That's all that happened. A young girl crossed a street, asked a question, and went back to her house. There was something about the exchange, however, that Brown found disturbing, something about the way the girl sauntered, something about her tone.

"It just seemed awfully forward," he tries to explain one day. It is much later. It is after the murder of Tom Barnes, who was killed one evening while walking up Acker Street for coffee, and after another murder, that of one of the teenagers of 617, a 16-year-old named LaShawn Evans, who was found dead in Rock Creek Park. It is after Acker Street became a momentary symbol of this city's continuing chaos, and after some residents of Acker Street began thinking of themselves less as an uplifting microcosm than a modern-day parable, and a depressing one at that.

"Just one of those people you didn't want to get too friendly with," Brown goes on, trying to explain what was so off-putting about a child asking about candy.

He tries again, posing his thought as a question.

"You know—familiarity breeds contempt?"

On Acker Street, where the past few years have been defined by accusations and increasing polarization and calls to the police in the middle of the night, some residents will be understanding of what Brown is trying to say, and some residents will be offended, and that is the story of Acker Street at its core.

Two worlds.

One street.

Tom Barnes, 25, the second of the two murder victims, was the outsider here. He was born in Alabama and raised in Alabama, and the first time he left that state for any significant length of time was when he moved to Washington in 1990 to work for Sen. Richard Shelby (D-Ala.), an old family friend. His ideas of what he would find here came from books such as *Advise and Consent*, which meant he knew more about the image of Washington as a capital than the reality of Washington as a city. He lived here a year and a half. He died a year ago last month. He was shot once in the head on January 11—shot, according to police, by Edward Evans Jr., one of the teen-agers of 617—and when he died four days later it was a death that had an immediate, rippling effect.

His was the murder that caused Shelby to insist that Washington needed the death penalty, which led to impassioned debates over congressional meddling and D.C. statehood and expanding the parameters of home rule. It also led to last November's death-penalty referendum in the District, which became a referendum as much about race as crime and was decisively voted down.

It was a murder, in other words, that was pushed and pulled into a dozen different shapes. It was politicized locally and publicized nationally and achieved such status that it prompted thousands of expressions of outrage and grief, including a letter to Barnes's parents signed by George Bush that said in part, "Barbara and I were deeply saddened to learn of your loss. We know, firsthand, the tragedy of losing a child, and we pray that God will give you the inner strength to help you through these difficult days."

That letter, now wrapped in plastic, is in the Barnes home in Tuscaloosa where Sue Barnes, Tom's mother, constantly in search of that inner strength, is crying and apologizing at the same time. "I am not a crier," she is saying, unable to stop. "I was afraid if I ever started I wouldn't be able to control it. It's just I miss him so much it makes me sick."

LaShawn Evans, who was born and raised in Washington, died nine months before Tom Barnes. Like him, she was shot once in the head. Unlike him, she knew Washington as a city rather than a capital, and her death, typical of so many, galvanized no one. In the newspaper and on TV, the murder was a brief shrug noting that the body of a young black female had been discovered near a picnic area in Rock Creek Park, and on Acker Street the dominant reaction was less of sadness than relief.

"This is going to sound really awful," says one resident, Wendy Craine, remembering Evans and others who congregated in front of 617 as always outside screaming at people, always swearing, always taunting, at all hours of the night, "but we were so stressed, we said, 'Well, that's one down.'"

"A lot of us felt that way," says another resident, Patrick Smith. "She was a foulmouthed [girl] who came from no good and wasn't going to amount to anything, and basically, from the community, it was an attitude of 'good riddance.'"

"Even from her mother," he imagines, "it was probably a reaction of 'good riddance.'"

Actually, when Evans's mother, Lenita Burrell, learned that her daughter had been killed, she curled against her own mother's shoulder and, just as would happen with Sue Barnes in Tuscaloosa, couldn't stop crying. By that point, however, few people on Acker Street would have been moved by such a reaction, even if they had seen it. A lot of people, some of them white, some of them black, were tired of Lenita Burrell, and tired of her children, and wanted them off the street even though, as Burrell sees it, she was there first. Which is why she says of the place she has lived most of her life, "I hate it. Not the street. Just the people."

Acker Street is in Northeast Washington, on the very northern edge of the Capitol Hill Historic District. Police say it is far from the most dangerous part of the city, and their statistics, to some degree, bear this out. Last year, in an area that includes Acker Street and is composed of about 2,000 households, there were 30 violent crimes; the year before there were 42.

Within those numbers, however, are some of the city's most high-profile violent crimes—the mysterious shooting of former House of Representatives sergeant-at-arms Jack Russ; the violent robbery of Lucy Calautti, a U.S. senator's wife—and so a perception exists that Capitol Hill is becoming increasingly dangerous. And sharpening that perception, because of the Barnes shooting, is Acker Street itself.

In truth, police say, Acker Street is no worse than other streets within the historic district, but that is something they say only recently. Go back to the years leading up to Tom Barnes's shooting, and they say that they received more calls about Acker Street than any other street on Capitol Hill. "When I first got here in June 1991, some of the sergeants were saying, 'Have you been down on Acker Street? Have you heard about it?'" remembers 1st District police Lt. Cliff Wilson. "They just described the street as out of control."

How things got this way goes back to a time long before the murders, long before Tom Barnes and LaShawn Evans were born, back to the 1950s. It was when Lenita Burrell was growing up on Acker Street. The street then, as she remembers it, was all black. It was a wonderful street, she says, where everyone knew everyone else, children ran unrestrained from house to house, and summertime meant turning fire hydrants into sprinklers and playing into the night. "We could sit outside till the sun came up, and nobody bothered anybody else."

"Lord, all night long," says Dorothy White, who has lived on Acker Street 42 years. "In the summertime, after we put the children to bed, we would cook potato salad and some chicken, and someone might make chicken salad, and we'd drink a beer and stay out. This went on all summer. Then, when winter came, we congregated in my house."

Whether or not such reminiscences have sweetened with time, they are nonetheless the base line that both White and Burrell use for thinking about how the street has evolved since then, an evolution that has taken it from all black to black-and-some-white, to white-and-some-black.

"What was a good neighborhood changed," says White. "See, when I was coming up, the Negro would stop by, ask how I am, come in the house, visit. These people that live around here now, the White Man, they don't come and ask even though they know I'm here. They don't know me. They haven't bothered to introduce themselves to me. I guess they work all day, and when they come home at night they go in and close the door behind them."

"After they moved in, they put the trees in, they put the flower boxes in, tried to make it look better," Burrell says dismissively of some of the other changes.

"Now I got trees and leaves," says White of how the leaves blow up and down the street. "Who the hell needs it?"

The white people did in fact move in and plant trees and build flower boxes and pay one of the black people on the street to water and weed. They came in funky old Mercedeses and new Saabs and bright yellow Hondas; they hired painters and carpenters; they paid more than $100,000, $150,000, $200,000 for town houses that they thought needed fixing up. They were not just any white people, in other words, but a certain type that wanted to be in the city, and on Capitol Hill, and on an integrated street.

"Idealistically, I liked the idea of an integrated neighborhood from the time I was in school studying to be social worker and a supervisor said the best way to understand integration is to live it. So it appealed to me," says one resident, who moved to the street 15 years ago.

"It had an almost pioneer feel to it," says Wendy Craine, who came to the street four years ago. "We loved the idea of being in a community where everyone was represented. I thought that was an enhancing experience, and I still do." She remembers her first weeks on the street, when she was fixing up an old carriage house on her property and a neighbor, an elderly, very proper, very mannered black woman named Isabell Marsellus, would stop by. "She was so lovely. She would come over to the carriage house and peek in the window, and we'd be inside painting, and she'd say, 'Good morning. How art thou?' And we'd say, 'Fine. How art thou?'"

Nonetheless, Craine goes on, explaining how her idealism has dulled after four years of reality on the street, "when I get into the house, I lock my door immediately, I mean immediately, and I do not go outdoors at night. I get home and stay in the house. I have made concessions, and I am very angry about it."

The reason for the concessions, she says: the arrival on the street in 1989 of someone new. It was a woman who had grown up in Mrs. Marsellus's house, who lived on Acker Street until she was an adult, who moved away to marry and have children, who had five and got divorced, who lived in public housing in Southeast D.C. until a leak no one would fix caused a wall to fall in, who had nowhere to go at that point except the house where she had been raised.

This, of course, was Lenita Burrell. And just as the black people on the street felt everything change when white people began moving in, the white people felt everything change with the arrival at 617 Acker of a woman and her children who needed a place to live.

"My God, the frustrations," Wendy Craine says of what happened next, after friends of Lenita Burrell's children, and friends of the friends, began congregating in front of 617. "We were awakened a few nights by kids on the corner, yelling and screaming, jumping on cars, breaking off antennas, smashing bottles. We would call the police, and five minutes later they would be out there again."

"First it was obnoxious stuff, like riding bicycles over people's feet," says another resident, Peter Lefkin. "Then it went to name-calling. Then it was breaking windows, yelling at night, screaming. Then worse and worse people began hanging around. You just had a constant barrage of people going in and out of the house."

"Then, you see, when they weren't outside, they were inside the house, raising hell," says Craine. "There was incredible noise coming out from the house in the middle of the night."

Not only white residents felt this way: "The complaints came from both blacks and whites," says Kay Etheredge, a D.C. police sergeant who spent two years working with the children of 617 as part of a police effort to bring control to the street. Etheredge, who is black herself, remembers one neighbor who no longer lives there, "an old black guy on the street, he was crying one day, saying he couldn't take it anymore. He said, 'I just wish we could have some peace.'" Another neighbor, she says—a black woman who, because of safety concerns, didn't want to be interviewed for this story— "begged me to spend the night in her house, just to listen."

"They'd wake me up sometimes at 2 in the morning," says Dorothy White. "I was terribly upset because I never allowed it among my children. I raised eight, and they were inside, taking a bath, by 9 o'clock."

"I would hear them, but I never got up and said anything to them . . . It wasn't my business," says another of the longtime black residents, Georgia Campbell. "Sometimes I'd hear the noise and wake up and say, 'Hmmph. Children.' But I didn't bother. You might get in trouble going out and bothering a bunch of children. You don't know."

Other neighbors, however, particularly some of the younger, white ones, felt no such restraint:

"One of the first nights I was there, they were making a lot of noise, and I went out and said, 'Why don't you be quiet?'" says Patrick Jeffery, who moved to the street after Burrell and her children. "I went and got a piece of wood, a 4-by-4, and they ran inside, and I started whacking on the door with the 4-by-4 . . . "

"Dear Harold," began a letter, one of many, from Peter Lefkin to D.C. Council member Harold Brazil, whose ward includes Acker Street. "Harold, without intending to be dramatic, the situation on our block has deteriorated to a war zone . . . "

"Dear Sharon," began a letter from Brazil to D.C. Mayor Sharon Pratt Kelly. "The occupants of 617 Acker and their hordes of reportedly juvenile delinquent friends are terrorizing the neighbors in an almost 'Nightmare on Elm Street' fashion . . . "

"Things really reached a crescendo in spring 1991," says Lefkin. "That was the spring of hell."

"I'll show you," says a man named Pete. "I made a little videotape."

Pete, who didn't want his last name used in this article because of safety concerns, is now a former resident of the street. He says he and his wife, Laurie, first bought a weekend house in West Virginia to escape the noise; then, after Tom Barnes was killed, they decided they had had enough of Washington. They sold their town house for a profit, although not the profit they had imagined while they were renovating it, and moved away. Now, in their new home, they watch as an image of Acker Street comes onto their TV and the voice of Pete, on tape, narrating what he is shooting, says, "Let us start the parable of the Acker Street family portrait."

It is somewhat disconcerting what comes next: 20 minutes of video shot by someone so frustrated he has decided to use his camera as a kind of weapon; a video that unfolds in several disturbing, occasionally confrontational, somehow voyeuristic scenes.

Scene 1:

"Here's the infamous 617 Acker Street," Pete begins. The picture is of a few teenagers on the front steps who look up and see the camera pointed at them. A girl shrieks. "Smile," Pete calls. A boy waves and grabs his crotch, and Pete can be heard laughing.

Scene 2:

Now the view is from the window in Pete and Laurie's bedroom on the second floor of their house. A man can be seen walking up the street from the direction of 617. "What's the problem?" he says, stopping under the window. In the background, a girl can be heard screaming. Pete moves the camera around trying to locate the source of the screaming, but the only other person he finds is Peter Lefkin, sitting on his front steps. Lefkin says something to the man standing below Pete and Laurie's window. "Last night?" the man hollers back. "There was no problem around here last night." "There was a problem at 2:20 a.m.," Pete says after he has settled the camera back on the man. "Then again at 3."

Now a woman can be seen walking up the street. Her arms are folded, and her walk is slow. "There's Lenita," Pete says as she comes to a stop near the man. She listens to the discussion, then says it's not always her children making the noise, that it's often children from neighboring blocks.

"I think that anybody who doesn't recognize they live in a community where they can be heard real easily and wake people up in the middle of the night, they've got a problem," Pete says to her.

"I understand what you're saying," Lenita says, looking up to Pete's window, defending herself to this man pointing a camera at her, "but it's not all the time . . . " On goes the discussion for several more minutes, neighbor and neighbor, softer and louder, until, in the background, the screaming can be heard again, and now a child can be heard crying, and now three young women, girls really, one with a toddler, walk up the street, and one girl says angrily that she hates it around here, and they all walk away toward 617, none of them looking back except for the toddler who keeps turning around to look at the man with the camera. "Now why would they be so upset about being filmed?" Pete says sarcastically as he follows their retreat. "I just can't understand that."

Scene 3:
Now it is nighttime. The view, again from the bedroom window, is of the street, and the sounds are of earsplitting screams followed by a boy's voice shouting, "I'm gonna bust your ass . . . I'm gonna bust your ass . . . " Eventually, some police cars arrive and everything quiets down. "Typical evening activity," Pete narrates.

Scene 4:
"It's 4:30 in the morning," is how Pete begins this one. Two teenagers, both boys, are wrestling. "That's Edward," Pete says of one of the boys, referring to the oldest of Lenita Burrell's children. They fall against a car, push each other along the street, wrestle each other over the curb, go up and down the sidewalk.

Scene 5:
"It's 1:30 in the morning," Pete says as he focuses on a girl and boy standing in the street. "Get off me!" the girl is shouting. "Get off me! Get off me!"
"Let her go!" shouts a second boy. "Let her go!"
"Give me my [expletive] shirt!" the girl screams, breaking away, wearing nothing but slacks and a bra.
The two boys begin to fight. Other people stream up the street to watch. A police car pulls up. Then another. Then another.
"A person lying on the sidewalk," Pete narrates. "Police checking."

Scene 6, the final scene:
"It's five till 5 in the morning," Pete says, his voice ragged, as he focuses on two people leaning against a car. "There's been screaming, bottle-breaking at 617. We've been unable to sleep for an hour and a half." Now the two people seem to be hugging and kissing. "This is the kind of thing that just goes on," Pete says. "This is right out my bay window." He says nothing more as he continues to tape. For the

moment, there are no discernible sounds coming from the street. The only sound that can be heard is coming from the camera itself, the mechanical whirring of the zoom.

The tape ends.

Pete turns off the TV. He is visibly tense.

"Just thinking of it stresses me out," he says.

"Me too," Laurie says. "If I still lived there, I couldn't watch this."

"It was a clash of values," Pete says, trying to explain what went wrong. "Of neighborhood pride."

"Of respect," Laurie says. "And courtesy."

"Of peace and quiet," Pete says. "Of life itself."

"Always a feeling of violence and hatred, that's what I felt on the street," Laurie says. "It was a major clash of values."

One other thing about the videotape: It was made in spring 1991, mostly in April, the month LaShawn Evans was killed.

"Here's a picture of her," says Dora Prince, LaShawn's aunt and one of Lenita Burrell's sisters.

The picture, part of a memorial that hangs on Prince's wall next to a silk rose, shows a 16-year-old girl in blue jeans and a red sweat shirt and orange Etonics. "I loved her like she was my daughter," says Prince. "I'd try to get her to slow down, but I think I was too late. She was out with the wild crowd, staying out all hours of the night, sleeping all day. Sometimes we'd sit down, I'd say, 'Why are you out there?' She'd say, 'I got nothing else to do.'"

In fact she didn't go to school very often, didn't work, didn't do much of anything at all other than hang out. Sometimes this was on Acker Street, and other times it was at Prince's apartment several miles east of Acker Street, where LaShawn would show up in the middle of the night and fall asleep on the living room floor. "Sometimes I'd come in and put a blanket over her," says Prince.

This, then, is how the final months and weeks were spent in one 16-year-old's life: on the floor in her aunt's apartment, or on Acker Street filling the air at all hours with chatter and shrieks.

"She was one of those loud, boisterous kids, cussing a lot, using a lot of profanity, hollering up and down the street," says Kay Etheredge, the D.C. police sergeant. "I felt sorry for her. The profanity was just a way of language for her. It wasn't like an attitude. There was an innocence about her. She was a follower—if one of her friends hollered at her, she'd holler back, and maybe they'd run up and down the street. But really, she was like a baby. Sometimes, I think, she used to suck her thumb."

She also wore a wig from time to time, and tight shirts, and polka-dot spandex pants, and that's what she had on when Etheredge was called to the morgue to identify her body. "One of the officers called me . . . her mother hadn't been told yet," Etheredge remembers of that day. "I was looking at her clothes and thinking about the last time I saw her in that outfit. It was hard. I just talked to her two days before about riding along with me. I told her I was going to pick her up, and she was going to ride with me for eight hours and see everything I do, and she said okay. But like I said, that was two days before she was killed."

Etheredge, who spent so much time dealing with the children of 617 that she began thinking of herself as a kind of social worker, likes to believe she was a force in LaShawn's life. But there were other forces as well, including growing up in a family that Michelle Prince, another of Lenita Burrell's sisters, describes as "dysfunctional." This showed up in the children, who rarely went to school (at one point, says Etheredge, she was told by school officials that if LaShawn returned to school she would be placed in the equivalent of sixth grade). And it showed up in the parents—Lenita and her husband, Edward Evans Sr.—whose marriage, according to family members, steadily disintegrated into a relationship of physical violence.

"It was an all-right marriage, but he used to fight her a lot," says Dora Prince, who lived with the family for a while. "He used to hit on her. They used to argue. He would sometimes just smack her."

"True," Edward Evans says to that. "I don't have anything to hide. It was a very rough marriage."

And so LaShawn and the other children grew up around parents who often took things out on each other, and later, on Acker Street, after Burrell split up with her husband and returned to a place she thought she had left behind, the children began taking things out on her. Lenita says she and her children have always gotten along fine, that there have been no extraordinary problems, but Kay Etheredge remembers one day in particular with LaShawn that suggests otherwise. "It was about a week before she died," Etheredge says. "I was talking to her mother, and she came in and went berserk. She was yelling at her, cussing at her. She was making death threats, saying she was going to have her killed, that she hated her, and I took her outside and told her she can't do that . . . "

"LaShawn would yell at her. They all did," says Michelle Prince. "She tried to discipline them, they'd all curse her."

"Put it this way. The kids had no respect for her. They made it evident because they'd do what they wanted to do. Nobody could control them," says Etheredge.

"Her life is just messed up," Delores Burrell, Lenita's mother, says of her daughter. "Her life is miserable as hell."

That's how Lenita Burrell's family sees it. Along Acker Street, though, she was less a sympathetic figure than an irresponsible one, the mother of those children, and on April 27, 1991, an unusually warm spring day, a day for opening windows, when Kay Etheredge came to tell her about LaShawn, and Burrell said tiredly, "What did she do this time?" and Etheredge told her that LaShawn was dead, it must have sounded like business as usual at 617, another person screaming for no particular reason. But behind the door, Lenita Burrell was folding herself into her mother's lap and curling against her shoulder.

"Just like a child," says Delores Burrell.

"Like a big baby," says Dora Prince.

"She kept saying, 'Why?'" says Delores Burrell. "I said, 'Okay, get yourself together.'"

Later, Lenita was taken to the morgue where she was shown a photograph of a girl with a badly swollen face and a bullet hole near an eye. The body had been discovered in a section of Rock Creek Park between the golf course and Picnic Area No. 6, halfway down a wooded slope, face-down in leaves that had survived the winter, lying next to her wig. Yes, Lenita said, the girl in the photograph was her daughter, and with that she was taken back home.

Three things happened next:

There was a funeral, paid for by the city, in which LaShawn was buried in an unmarked grave.

There was a police investigation that, so far, like so many in Washington, has produced no suspects, no arrests, no motives, no results of any kind.

And Wendy Craine got a call from Kay Etheredge.

"'I cannot believe I'm asking you this,'" Craine recalls Etheredge saying, "'but if there's anything you could do financially . . .'"

"I said, 'Sure, we'll take up a collection.'

"And so we did."

Some neighbors gave without hesitation, including Peter Lefkin, who gave $75, and Georgia Campbell, who gave because "you help when you can," while others, such as Pete and Laurie, decided not to give at all. "There was a lot of pressure from the white people on the street to contribute," he says, "and my feeling is that it was being done out of guilt, that it was a false gesture. That it wasn't coming from the heart."

In the end, $300 was collected, which paid for flowers and a limousine to the funeral. Etheredge remembers telling Lenita the money came from neighbors and Lenita saying, "I'm surprised." Craine remembers Lenita never saying thank you, not directly, "but a reaction came in a different way. There was a softening. I was able to go up to her and pat her on the back and say, 'How are you doing?' And she said, 'You know how it is.' And I said, 'No, I don't know. I can't possibly know how it is.' She was grieving. She was sad. She had little tears coming down that she quickly wiped away."

Soon, though, Lenita seemed sealed off once again, and Pete was back in his window videotaping, and the street turned its attention to the other children of 617, especially Edward, the one many of the neighbors found even more troubling than LaShawn.

"Edward presents as an intellectually limited young man who might be eligible for the support of the mental retardation system," a court-appointed psychiatrist would write in July 1991, after Evans had been placed on probation for unlawful use of a motor vehicle. "He is vague and superficial in describing people, especially the members of his family. In response to who loves him the most and whom he loves the most, the answer is 'nobody.'"

"Edward is confused about himself," a court-appointed psychologist would write in a second report. "He says his nerves are [a] wreck and that under pressure he destroys things. He feels hatred for his family and other people. Edward's self-control, especially emotional control, is poor. Under stress he may react violently without realizing the consequences of his actions."

This is the street to which Tom Barnes came.

Of course he knew none of Acker Street's history or anything about the family across the way. Like Lenita Burrell, he came to Acker Street because he needed a new place to live.

He had been in an efficiency a block from Sen. Shelby's office. Early on, as he worked his way up from intern to legislative aide, he decided it would be a good thing to have cable TV, especially C-SPAN, but when the installer came he left about 12 inches of wire dangling exposed in the hallway before it disappeared into Barnes's apartment. The efficiency was in a condominium, and in a condominium rules are rules, and one of the rules prohibits dangling wire, and soon there were complaints. Barnes called the cable company, the cable company didn't show up, the complaints continued. This went on for months. Finally, Barnes decided to move, and on October 31, he and Toof Brown carted his furniture out of the efficiency, through the lobby and past a glass-topped table by the mailboxes, which, in a few months, would hold a card addressed to Barnes's parents that people would sign, "Our prayers are with you," and "He was always the perfect gentleman." At one point, one of the residents told Barnes to be careful, that he was moving to a more formidable part of the city. Barnes said he would keep that in mind, got in the van and went to Acker Street, a half-dozen blocks away.

Such is city life, particularly on Capitol Hill. Life changes by the block; extremes are juxtaposed; variety is the desire. "He definitely wanted to be on the Hill," Brown says of Barnes. "There's no question." He worked so hard, though, he was rarely on the street at all. He left early, came back late. Two and a half months later, when he was found lying at the end of the street, the neighbors who discovered him didn't know exactly who he was.

This was on January 11, 1992. By then, there had been numerous meetings about 617, sometimes with the police in attendance, and with each one it became apparent that there were some significant differences in attitude between black families on the street and newer-to-the-street whites. Many of the black residents, mindful of how long Isabell Marsellus had been on the street, which is to say how long they had been on the street, seemed more tolerant of 617, while some of the white people were designing a plan to somehow purchase 617 and push the family out. From all this, a chilliness seemed to descend, which Toof Brown felt soon after he and Barnes moved in. "Acker Street never had that feeling like the rest of the Hill," he says. "Very few people sat out on their stoop, except for the people at 617."

Still, even during the worst moments of all, Acker was a street where some neighbors continued to socialize, and on January 11, John Costanza was looking out his living room window, watching for the Romeros, who were coming over for dinner. Just after 7:30 p.m., he saw them cross the street; a few seconds later they rang the bell and Costanza's dogs began barking; a few seconds later Costanza's roommate, Patrick Smith, was guiding the Romeros upstairs to look at some renovations; a few seconds later Costanza looked out the living room window again and saw someone in the street. "We figure less than a minute," Costanza says of how long all of this took. "All of a sudden, there he is," says Patrick Smith of the sight of Tom Barnes, "as if he's a mirage that appeared."

He was in the street, lying face up. By the time Costanza ran out, Patrick Jeffery, who had been driving up the street when he saw Barnes in his headlights, whose first thought was that it was a scam, that he was being set up by someone who wanted to steal his Saab, was already standing over Barnes. "I think he's been hit by a car," Jeffery said, and Costanza ran back into his house and yelled for Charlotte Romero, who was an emergency room nurse. She ran out, heard Barnes choking, put a hand under his head to steady him. She too thought he had been hit by a car, but then she knew it was something worse. "Because I lifted up his head," she says, "and part of his head was gone."

There was only so much to do. He was bleeding heavily, and the bullet had passed from a point behind his left ear into his jaw. "I told him to be still," she goes on. "I tried to bring his head in alignment, keep his neck straight, his body straight. I checked to make sure he was breathing okay. I checked his pulse."

And then along this fractured street something striking happened: One neighbor after another came outside, some black, some white, some to gawk, but many more to see if they could help. "I was amazed at how many people showed up," says Romero. "At least 15 people. It was a chilly night. I said, 'We've got to get blankets for this guy,' and blankets came from everywhere. Blankets, coats, there was so much cooperation it was fabulous."

The police came. The ambulance came. Eventually, the people of Acker Street drifted back to their town houses, and Tom Barnes was taken to Washington Hospital Center, the very hospital where, in one of those strange coincidences, Edward Evans Jr.'s first child had been born the night before. The child, a boy, was still in the hospital as the ambulance carrying Tom Barnes arrived.

Meanwhile, at John Costanza's, Charlotte Romero began washing up. It took her a long, long time. She stood at the sink, kept scrubbing, couldn't seem to stop.

"You feel like 'MacBeth,'" she would say later. "You just can't get clean. You can't get rid of it. Not the blood, the feeling. That such an evil thing had taken place."

Some things in life are mysterious, and some are predictable, and darkness is one of the things that is both. In January, days always darken early, but sometimes it is the kind of darkness that doesn't so much widen slowly through the light as descend suddenly upon it. It is this way in Washington, where people walking in such darkness can be shot in the middle of a street, and it is this way in Tuscaloosa, where a family couldn't truly imagine such a thing occurring, not until, on one such night, Sue Barnes answered her phone. Don, her husband, was in the shower. John, her other son, four years older than Tom, was rattling around downstairs.

"Mrs. Barnes, it's Toof."

"Hey darling, how are you?" she said.

"Tom's sick," he said.

"How sick is he?" she asked.

And with that, the Barnes family began to fall apart.

It is a family unlike any on Acker Street, one of suburban rhythms and southern courtesy in a house surrounded by a yard. The neighborhood, of bricks and columns, is white, but that's not the point. More important is its stability, and its sameness of desires and ideals. The Barnes house is one of the more modest ones, not at all pretentious, one in which wall after wall is covered with family photographs. It is a house of one family's history. Don, Sue and John Barnes moved there in July 1966, and five months later Tom was born.

He was a Boy Scout. He was captain of the safety patrol. He was vice president of the student body. He was chairman of the prom. Just like 617 Acker, his was the house where the neighborhood children gathered, but unlike at 617 the neighbors never complained. Once, when Tom was in fifth grade, he fell out of a treehouse, and his face swelled, and his eye closed, and a few weeks later when the eye opened it could distinguish only between dark and light. The damage was permanent. But this is a family that lived on the positive side and had every reason to; his other eye was fine; they moved on. "Nothing bad ever happened to us," says Don Barnes.

And so Tom went to college and became president of his fraternity. And graduated from the University of Alabama in August 1990. And eight days later was on his way to Washington. "Dear Mom and Dad," he wrote a week after his arrival, "Everything is wonderful here and I can't begin to describe how I have fallen in love with this town."

A year later, he called to say he and Toof Brown were thinking of moving to Acker Street, and Sue Barnes, on a whim, headed north with a suitcase, a camera, three eye-round roasts, a jar of spaghetti sauce and three custard pies. "I was just aching to see him," she says. The first day she stayed in his efficiency and fixed him supper. The second day it rained, but she walked over to Acker Street anyway to see it for herself. "He didn't know. He had a fit later," she says. "He said, 'You're not supposed to go anywhere alone in Washington.'" She, in turn, didn't tell him what was on her mind after her walk, that "as I got closer, I got a prickly feeling," that "I thought, 'Oh, I like where you are so much better.'"

She entered Acker from Sixth Street, the opposite end from where Tom would be found. "I walked to the end and turned back," she says. "I was amazed it was such a short street. Then the rain got harder, and it was getting pretty late, so I started back."

She went home to Alabama. Tom moved. He came to visit over Christmas. Then it was January 11 and Toof Brown was on the phone.

Now, nearly a year after that, Sue Barnes, sitting in her dining room, is going through some photographs. Here's one of the Washington Monument, which she took from the plane on her trip to check out Acker Street. Here's one of 608 itself: bars over the windows, dried leaves on the sidewalk, a flower box with pansies. Here's one of Tom. It's a close-up. A profile. The left side of his head. The side he was shot in.

"I can't look at those," Don Barnes says, walking away.

"I know," Sue Barnes says, continuing to stare.

They have boxes of photographs, and boxes of letters too. They got 1,800 letters in all, and $25,000 in contributions for a scholarship fund in Tom's name, and so many flowers that the flower shop still hasn't delivered them all, and so many hams that the freezer is still full. It is said that parents of children who die go through periods as if they are sleepwalking, and that is how it has been for the Barneses since Sue Barnes hung up the phone.

They remember only so much. "You have to understand—this period is pretty much a blur," says John.

They remember calls being made that night, a dozen calls, back and forth. They remember the house filling up with people who came automatically as soon as they heard, and they remember John at one point severely injuring his hand when he smashed his fist into an oak door. "This rage just came over me," John says. "In retrospect, it was a stupid thing to do, but I almost see it as a badge."

"I took a shower," is what Sue remembers. "I was so hysterical."

They also remember wanting nothing more than to be in Washington, but it was too late, the commercial flights were done for the day, and so a call was made to a charter company in Birmingham, which sent a jet to Tuscaloosa, and soon Sue, Don and John were in the air, sealed in quiet, hooded in darkness, too sad to talk even to each other. "I remember coming into Washington, all the lights," Don says. "He loved the city. He was so defensive about it. That's the irony of it, how much he loved it there."

Then, the hospital. There was Toof. There were the doctors. It must have been 3 a.m.

"Before they let us go back, I remember leaning against a wall and sliding down it," says Sue.

"I remember Sue just sitting on the floor," says Don. "And, of course, the news was terrible."

"They would not let us go back until they explained things," says Sue. "They said, 'This is what you're going to see. This is the machinery.'"

"And someone said, 'We have to clean him up a bit,'" says Don.

By that time, Tom was out of the Medstar unit and in intensive care. He had IVs in both arms and a breathing tube in his nose and monitor wires on his chest and restraints on his ankles and wrists. The bullet was still in his head and his eyes were closed, and that's what the doctors prepared his family to see.

"His color was good," says Sue.

"I thought his lips were swollen," says John.

"Well, that was from the bullet," says Sue. "Of course we all touched him," says Don. "Hoping he would respond. But he didn't."

He was alive. But unconscious. But alive nonetheless, and he would remain so for three more days, until the doctors suggested it might be compassionate to simply turn off the machines.

There was a meeting about this. The doctors made their case. His kidneys had failed. He was turning rigid. "He will never be Tom again," John remembers one doctor saying. "You have to make a decision." They left the Barneses alone, and somehow the three of them distanced themselves enough to decide that the doctors were right. "We went and told him goodbye," says John, and then "we had to get out of the hospital."

They were gone an hour or so. The doctors had told them it could be a day or it could be a week, but he was dead by the time they got back.

Now, many months later, so many things have happened, both publicly and privately. There was the fight over the death penalty. There was a request by the hospital for Tom's organs, and Sue, struggling to remain polite, declined, saying, "This town has gotten all it's going to get from me." There was a period of time when Don, an artist, was unable to work because he couldn't stop shaking. Sue, for a while, taped a note over the doorbell that said, "We're resting"; and Don, learning that Tom was going out to get a can of coffee when he was shot, couldn't stop thinking about how he had meant to send him a three-pound bag of his favorite blend in the mail, "so I have to live with that"; and John, whose own grief was unbearable at times, learned what it was like to have parents whose sadness seemed to have no bottom. "To lie in bed in the middle of the night and hear them sobbing in bed was a terrible thing," he says. Tom, of course, was always in the house, in photographs on the walls, in conversations real and imagined, but the one thing the Barneses have been unable to do is talk about the moment they learned he had died.

"I think he lived 40 minutes after they turned off the machines," Don tries. "We went to see him, and he looked pretty good. He really did."

"And John, he didn't, well, none of us wanted to leave him," Sue begins, but then she closes her eyes and can say no more, and Don reaches out for her hand, and John gets her a tissue and gives it to her and kisses her, and Don says something about how good it was to get back to Alabama, how much better he felt "when I saw that red soil," but then he can say nothing either, and in a declining afternoon he takes a sip of beer from a glass, and Sue keeps crying, and Don keeps holding her hand, unable to talk until he finally finds the voice to say, "We've had some horrible days."

One street.

Two children.

Two mothers.

One day, one of the mothers goes to visit her son.

"This is Marc Ray Clement, he lived catty-corner to us," Sue Barnes says, walking through a section of Tuscaloosa Memorial Park.

"Here's Dick Lollar. A wonderful man ... "

"Buford Boone, he owned the Tuscaloosa News. He won a Pulitzer when they integrated the university ... "

"Pug Newton, he owned a restaurant, it was right down from my father's bookstore ... "

"These were all friends," she says.

"This is my grandparents, my mom's parents.

"This is my aunt and uncle over here.

"We picked this spot because it backs up to Daddy," she says. Now she is standing by the outline of a rectangle in the grass. After all this time, the ground is still a little higher and the grass is a little lighter. There, at the base, is Tom's name, carved into a white marble marker. His is one of eight plots, six of which have yet to be filled, all surrounding an obelisk that says Barnes on it.

"I feel like it's a neighborhood," Sue Barnes says contentedly of this place. "I really do."

Another day:

The other mother goes to visit her child, though not the daughter who died. "She's my daughter. I love her. Yeah, she's on my mind, but I block it off," Lenita Burrell says of LaShawn. "You lose a child, you don't want to keep saying goodbye." And so she hasn't been back to the cemetery since the funeral.

Instead, she is at the D.C. Jail to visit Edward. This is in November, two months before his arrest for the Barnes murder. He is in jail on another charge at this point, a pellet-gun shooting of a man walking near Acker Street. During a later court hearing, Evans will testify that the shooting was accidental. The testimony of an eyewitness— the driver of a car that Evans was riding in—will be that Evans aimed the gun and pulled the trigger. The testimony of the victim will be that he felt a pellet pierce his chest and then heard someone in the car laugh.

This day, Lenita has come with a surprise for her son: one of his children. It is a girl, 2 months old. She is his third child. There is another girl, born of a different mother nearly the same day as this one, a twin actually whose brother died at birth. And there is the boy who was born the night before Tom Barnes was shot. So, three. Lenita has this baby bundled in a pink flannel snowsuit, and she holds her against her shoulder as she waits to go through the metal detector and upstairs to the room where she will see Edward through glass and talk to him on a phone and show him his baby girl. She tries to remember when Edward was that small. "He was calm. He was no trouble. He was okay," she says. "He grew up too fast." She tries to remember when LaShawn was that small: "Shawn was no trouble either."

It is 1 p.m. As always, the wait is long. Fifty people crowd into the small lobby, then 75, then 100, so many that no one can move. At 3 o'clock, the jailers announce they are beginning a count of the inmates, and no visitors will be allowed in for at least an hour. At 4:15, another announcement is made: Something went wrong, the count didn't add up correctly, "it will be another hour." With that, Lenita knows she won't get upstairs before 6, won't get home until after 8.

"If it wasn't my son, I wouldn't do this," she says. "Got to keep his spirits up. It's something I got to do."

She gives the baby a bottle. She wipes the baby's mouth and pats her on the back. She holds her close. Kisses her. Smiles at her. Doesn't smile. Waits.

Upstairs, far from Acker Street, far from his family, far from everything, is Edward, sitting calmly in a room one day where he has been brought for an interview. He is talking about the death of Tom Barnes:

"When I first seen the murder, I was coming home from the hospital," he is saying. "My son had just been born. My son was born January 10th, the murder happened the 11th. I just got off the bus, I seen all these people running up and down the street, I didn't know what was going on. I went in the house and told my mother something was happening on the street. I grabbed my bike, went up the street, checked what was going on. I saw a dude lying on the ground with a cover over his head, blood coming from under his head. That's all I seen . . . "

And now he is talking about the effect that such a sight could have on him:

"I see it all the time on TV, so it didn't bother me. I watch a lot of gang flicks, like 'Colors,' 'Boyz N the Hood,' flicks like that. I see a lot of people die. I just think of it as that, and just let it be."

Evans is 19. He has a baby's face, which makes him "look younger than his age," according to the psychologist who saw him last year. He has a smile that shows up even when he is trying to be serious and an IQ measured at 70, which is on the border between normal and slightly retarded. According to the psychiatrist who saw him, Evans could name no states, could do no math beyond adding and multiplying two and two, and "although unclear in his explanation, he claims to hear, only at night, 'like a mouse in the corner,' someone calling his name. He thinks it might be 'my conscience.'"

The psychiatrist went on to describe Evans as a "wise guy," but on this day he is rather subdued. On Acker Street, he is said to be abusive and loud, but this day he is neither.

The subject of the interview is supposed to be Acker Street, which Evans describes as a place where people were "afraid to come outside, afraid we were gonna rob them, beat them up, do things like that . . . Capitol Hill wasn't made for black kids, I'm going to put it like that. It's not made for black kids, certain parts, because you got a bunch of white people on the block, and you got a bunch of old people, and all they want is peace and quiet. I'm from Southeast. I'm used to loud noise, staying outside, hearing people screaming up and down the street, guns going off. I'm used to that."

Soon, though, Evans is talking less about the street than about other things in his life, particularly school and family. These, of course, are the stabilizing aspects of a young life, but with Evans, what he says suggests something else entirely.

"Okay, I have a problem with people laughing at me," he says at one point. "That's why I didn't stay in school, because kids were always laughing at me, and I'd get mad. I got mad at the principal once and tried to burn the school down."

As with everything else he will say during a lengthy conversation, Evans seems neither angry nor apologetic. "I'm slow, okay?" he continues. "I can't read, I can't count, I'm not good in math. Everybody'll finish first, and the teacher will call on me, and I'm not finished yet, and then she'll just take my work. So when she calls on me in class and says, 'Mr. Evans, what's this?' and I can't read, I try to read and I miss a word. And kids used to laugh at me. I used to get mad because I feel bad . . . I just got mad, walked the halls, ran from the principal, and all that. I'd get suspended, go home . . . I'd go back to school and do the same thing, over and over. So I figured like this: Instead of going through that pressure every day of them kids laughing at me, I started hanging with my friends and left school alone."

That was school. As for his mother, he says, "Let me tell you, I ain't never listened to my mother. She said something to me, I just took it as in one ear and out the other. I'm going to put it like this: If I had a man in my life growing up, I'd be okay. I'd be straight. Because women ain't going to discipline you. Women gonna be soft with you, and a man gonna be rough with you. My mother, she was soft on me."

And his father?

"My father, he ain't do too much for me," he says. "He came around, gave us money, most of the time he came in, checked on us, went back out the door. He hung with his friends more than he hung with us. That hurted me. Because a father is supposed to be there, like a role model. But I didn't have a father as a role model because he wasn't there for me . . .

"Most of the things I was doing with my friends, I was seeking attention," he goes on. "That's the thing, I was seeking attention from my father. You know how a kid always grows up and says, 'I'm going to be like my father'? Instead of me growing up being like my father, I grew up being like my friends. I let them raise me, and then I became like them."

Among his closest friends, he goes on, was his sister LaShawn. He remembers the photograph of her he saw at the morgue.

"Her face was all mushed up," he says. "Her eyes, I think, were open. It's hard to think about, but I don't mind telling you I sit in my cell and talk to her. I tell her about how much I miss her, how much I wish she was here. If she was here, I'd change my life and all that. I dream about her. I see her sometimes. I dream about her, I see her, I feel her. I ain't never gonna let her go."

"Me and my sister, we was like that," he says, "and ever since she died, I've been having a little mental problem with it."

One other thing Edward Evans says, this about Tom Barnes: "The dude, he was big. He was on top. My sister, she was bottom. A dude like him get shot, he dead, he dead, he dead, he in the paper, he in the magazine, he go on posters, everything else. But she get shot, they don't care. They ain't sweating it."

While John Barnes, speaking about LaShawn Evans, says, "Their family, I'm sure they hurt as much as we do. The loss of a child is the loss of a child."

Top and bottom, affluent and poor, black and white, alive and dead, child and child. If suburbs are defined by their sameness, a city is defined by its extremes, and sometimes the differences between two people are as extreme as things can get. Two people lived on the same street and died in the same way, but other than that they had nothing in common at all. Now, a year after Acker Street became a symbol, those differences are still causing currents of distance and mistrust.

"I've heard people talk about burning his house down," Patrick Jeffery says one day of Edward Evans Jr. "I've heard people talk about killing him, how to have him beaten senseless or thrown in the river. You would be amazed at what people say. I'm amazed that the guy is still around."

"Let me tell you this, and you can put it in bold letters," Edward Evans Sr., who lives in Southeast D.C. but says he owns a house around the corner from Acker, says unprompted another day. "If anything happens there, I have a house that's paid for on Sixth Street, and I can tell you that the people Edward associates with are a lot calmer than the people I associate with. So if something happens to any of them, I'm moving back to my house, and I'm bringing the worst elements of Washington with me. I know robbers, I know rapists, they would love to be on Capitol Hill."

So there are still tensions, still things to work out. But the theory is that everything recovers over time, even a grieving parent, even a rectangle of grass, even a skinny street, and so there have been changes too. These days along Acker Street, the feeling is that some kind of ending to all of this is in sight. In D.C. court earlier this month, after hearing a detective say that two unidentified friends of Edward Evans Jr. witnessed the Barnes shooting, a judge concluded there was probable cause for him to be charged with the murder. Meanwhile, along Acker Street itself, the crowd that once gathered in front of 617 has moved on. "Acker Street is so quiet now you can hear a pin drop," says police Lt. Cliff Wilson. "We've gone from hell to heaven as far as I'm concerned."

Several nights a week, there is even what passes in modern times for unity. In the old days this might have meant sitting on a stoop and drinking a beer and watching children run back and forth in the dusk; now it is built on the knowledge that on a street thought to represent everything, everything can go wrong. It is a unity of suspicion, in other words, and because of it, some of the residents of Acker Street get together with flashlights and dogs and go out on patrol.

The patrol covers much more than Acker Street and includes many more people than just its residents. But Acker, of course, is the one street everyone knows. This night, a cold, overcast evening, the approach is from Seventh Street, and as the patrol makes the turn onto Acker, one woman comes to a stop in the middle of the street and says, "This is where Tom Barnes was shot."

She stands there, bouncing up and down against the cold, telling what happened next:

First, someone painted the outline of a body on the spot where he had fallen.

Then someone splashed red paint across it.

Then someone painted the whole thing white.

Finally, some people on the street hired a man to remove all the layers of paint, and he brought out paint remover and a scraper and got it all up except for a few streaks.

It is on these that the woman stands and says no one knows who painted the outline or splashed it in red, that it is just one more mystery of city life. She shrugs. "It's a deceptively quiet little street," she says, and with that the patrol moves on.

It goes past the trees planted by the white people, and past the home of Dorothy White, who has watched another year of leaves blow past her door, a door where her neighbors have yet to appear to ask how an aging woman is getting along.

It goes past the home of Charlotte Romero, who says, "I don't want people to think this is an evil place. There are a lot of evil things that go on here, but I think they're solvable problems"; and past the homes of Patrick Jeffery, Wendy Craine and Peter Lefkin, all of whom continue to own houses but, at least temporarily, have moved.

It goes past 608, where there's a new tenant, Maureen Gawler, in from the suburbs, who says, "I really love this neighborhood"; and past 617, where Lenita Burrell wonders what happened to her daughter, and what will happen to her son, and how, without money or a place to go, she can move away from this place she hates. "I know he's being framed," she says of Edward. "I know how people are around here. They don't like black people. Especially kids. They're afraid of black kids. That's the whole thing. They're afraid."

On this night, everyone is inside, shades are drawn, doors are locked. There is no one breaking bottles, no one yelling insults, no one screaming threats, no one calling the police, no one standing in a window with a camera, no one asking about candy. There is no one on the street at all except for the people in the patrol, and now one of them says something, and now the others laugh, and now they turn the corner, and now they disappear, and now on the microcosm that is Acker Street there is nothing except silence and peace and a few streaks in the asphalt that have yet to go entirely away, and, for the moment anyway, it's a lovely night in the heart of Washington, D.C.

—*The Washington Post* | Feb. 27, 1993

GARY HART IN EXILE

The personal and political lessons of Gary Hart's career paved the way for Bill Clinton's victory, but the former Senator is still paying for his own defeat.

By David Remnick

It was freezing in the mountains, about ten degrees below zero. All across Colorado, drifts of snow swept halfway up the sides of the barns and the cabins. Without waking his wife, Gary Hart got up before dawn and walked downstairs to his living room, a cavernous place with a vaulted ceiling, high windows, and walls of lodgepole pine. It is a mountain house out of a plutocrat's fondest four-color dream. Hart could sit by the fire that morning and see deer, elk, mountain lions, and red fox move through the woods as the sun came up over the foothills of Kittredge. Lately, a Corsican ram had been climbing around the rocks near the house, and the dogs barked up at him. Hart built the house a couple of years ago for his wife, Lee, he said the other day, "because Lee had never had anything like this and Lee deserved it."

Hart was making real money now, as a lawyer and an international businessman. Born to Nazarene evangelicals in Kansas, he confessed to sometimes feeling "a little funny" about all the opulence: the poolroom, the sauna, the walk-in closets, the state-of-the-art appliances. It seemed sinful somehow. But the unease of living here was more severe than a passing case of guilt; it was endless and deep.

This was not the house that Gary Hart had thought he would be living in. At the start of the 1988 Presidential campaign, he had been headed, as if on a greased chute of destiny, for the White House. But out of vanity, it seemed, and stubborn refusal to curb his extra-marital liaisons for the purposes of high politics, he threw it all away long before the first primary. He could rage at the press for its blithe savagery, its puritan hypocrisy. But he should have known. In fact, he did know: he knew the risks and he ignored them. In May of 1987, he even invited the press to "follow me around" during the campaign. "I don't care. I'm serious," he told the *Times*. "If anybody wants to put a tail on me, go ahead. They'd be very bored." In the end, Hart paid for the sins of the flesh as no one else had done in two hundred years of American political history.

Hart's exile was immediate and absolute. To venture from the mountains of Colorado was to open himself to further humiliation. When he went to the 1988 Democratic Convention, in Atlanta, the only way he could enter the arena was with a Colorado dele-gate's pass. When he reached the Convention floor, the Democratic chairman, Paul Kirk, put a few security men between him and the television cameras. Hart's sense of martyrdom and piety was acute. "All our heroes are dead," he told Maureen Dowd, of the *Times*. "John is dead. Bobby is dead. And I'm dead—walking dead."

Now, five years on, Hart dispensed with self-pity and stuck to a handful of pitiful jokes. "Sometimes I'll be walking down the street in Washington and someone'll come up to me and say, 'Aren't you Gary Hart?' And I give 'em this little joke. I say, 'Yeah, I used to be.' And they laugh—'Ha! Ha! Ha!'"

After the Convention was over, Hart had wanted to get on with his life. He was constantly on the road, especially in Russia, trying to set up business projects—seaports, airports, banks, phone systems—that would enrich his clients and connect him, in some marginal way, to public life. But the 1988 bruises still hurt. Hart was convinced that he would never have lost to George Bush, that his fall was "an accident, a car crash in history." When his friend and adviser Paul Tully died, last September, Hart ran into Richard Gephardt, the House majority leader, at the funeral. The election was only weeks away, and Gephardt, ever the Eagle Scout, could barely keep a cap on his fizzy enthusiasm.

"I think Bill's gonna do it!" Gephardt said.

"Yeah," Hart said darkly. "But Bush never should have won in the first place."

When Bill Clinton finally did win, Hart tried not to betray his mixed feelings. "He was glad Clinton won," his daughter, Andrea, said. "But he does have that feeling—'It could have been me, I could have done as good a job as this man.'" In 1972, when Hart was in charge of George McGovern's campaign for President, he had hired Clinton, a law student on summer break, to help lead the Texas organization. "My impression was of a guy with a lot of enthusiasm and a lot of hair," he said. Now that kid was President, the savior of his party. But didn't anyone see that Hart, and not Clinton, had reinvented the Democrats? He had been preaching military reform, national service, and economic investment as a senator from Colorado when Clinton was still getting to know the precincts of Arkansas. But no one much cared. Hart had lately sent memos to the White House but had got no answers.

Hart's frustration in exile was not just a matter of failed ambition—nothing as vain and petty as that. Take the winter of 1990-91. The Harts were moving into the new house, on Troublesome Gulch Road—just up the path from their old log cabin—but Gary felt no great happiness. Like everyone else in the country, he was spending hours in front of the television watching the bombing raids over Baghdad. In the press, many of the armchair analysts were predicting that when the land war finally began thousands of American soldiers would die. Hart reflected that if he had been in the White House he would have gone the "sanctions route" a good deal longer. "I was terrified we'd lose a lot of people," he said later. "If thousands of American lives had been lost, I would have felt personally responsible."

Personal responsibility for thousands of dead—all for a weekend trip to Bimini on the good ship Monkey Business. This was what it was, at times, to be Gary Hart. "When you talk about Gary Hart now, people don't focus on anything except that here was this guy who got out of the race and the Donna Rice episode," Billy Shore, one of Hart's closest aides from the early days, said in February. "If he'd been hit by a bus the week before all that happened, the *Times* would have written an obituary paying tribute to 'a legislators' legislator.'" Now he was a living punch line.

"I don't like 'feel' questions," Hart said as we drove in his Jeep from Denver west to Kittredge. Over and over, in Kittredge, in Denver, and in Washington, Hart would dip lightly into the waters of the personal and then suddenly yank himself out. "It's all part of my death struggle with ego," he said.

Rarely has an American ego been more thoroughly probed, indulged, and, ultimately, destroyed. After his weekend became public knowledge, Hart quickly toppled from the pinnacle of public life, to join that shadowy population of Americans who are ready fodder for "Where Are They Now?" columns. They are figures first of irony and then of trivia; after a while, the game is guessing whether they are alive or dead. But Gary Hart's story will prove grander than that. His rise to prominence and fall from grace rings of Hawthorne and Dreiser, and it played a critical role in the election of Bill Clinton.

Hart, whose parents forbid dancing, movies, alcohol, and the indulgences of the flesh, marries Lee Ludwig, a Nazarene girl from a good family, and they head east to New Haven. It is the age of John Kennedy, and Hart, at Yale Law School, is swept up in Kennedy's charisma and call to public service. In 1972, he runs McGovern's children's campaign against the demonic Richard Nixon. The loss is overwhelming, but is eventually redeemed somewhat by Watergate. In 1974, Hart is elected to the Senate, where he gains a reputation as an innovative advocate of reform, the best of a new generation of "neoliberals." In 1984, he runs for President and stuns the experts by placing second in the Iowa caucus and winning the New Hampshire primary. One estimate has him suddenly gaining three million supporters a day. "Not since the Beatles had stormed onto the stage of the Ed Sullivan Show twenty years before had any new face so quickly captured the popular culture," Paul Taylor, of *The Washington Post*, writes. Hart is told by Warren Beatty, "Watch out. You've become famous too fast." If it hadn't been for the Democratic Party machinery and a botched campaign in Illinois, Hart could well have won the nomination in 1984. He finishes the race with a string of victories, but loses narrowly to Walter Mondale. In 1987, Hart is the odds-on favorite to win the Party's blessing and challenge George Bush in November. But then, in May of 1987, he vanishes under the wave of scandal as the Miami *Herald* stakes out his house and *The Washington Post* snags a detective report commissioned by a jealous husband. Hart quits the race. In December, he reënters it, but he can never regain his footing. In Iowa, he gets less than one per cent of the vote and finishes last. Five weeks later, he goes home to stay.

Hart still has the rangy, handsome look that his handlers always hoped would be seen as a Colorado version of "Kennedyesque." In deepest winter, he still wears cowboy boots with his business suit, and no overcoat. Aware that his tag has come to be "aloof," or "imperious," Hart makes an effort to charm. As we drove through the foothills of the Rockies, past one old mining town after another, he told some familiar Nixon stories in a dead-on Nixon voice. His set piece is about the day he found himself seated next to Nixon at the funeral of Jacob Javits.

"All of a sudden I feel him tapping me on the knee. . . . Whap! Whap! Whap! . . . And he says, 'That music. Is that Bach or Brahms?' . . . Bach or Brahms? . . . I said I didn't know. And he says, 'Bach is much better than Brahms. Because Bach is *tougher* than Brahms.'"

Hart is fascinated by Nixon—by his cynicism and his uncanny ability to remain in the political limelight. Though Hart would be appalled by the idea, he and Nixon are historical partners. Both men were always remarkable analysts of everyone but themselves. Their downfalls were successive chapters in the history of the media and American politics. Watergate represented the apogee of investigative reporting on the Presidential level; the Hart scandal took the public's right to know beyond any previous framework. It was Nixon who acknowledged this strange kinship when he wrote to Hart in 1987:

> Dear Gary,
>
> This is just a line to tell you that I thought you handled a very difficult situation uncommonly well. . . . What you said about the media needed to be said. They demand the right to ruthlessly question the ethics of everyone else. But when anyone else dares to question their ethics, they hide behind the shield of freedom of speech. They refuse to make the distinction that philosophers throughout the centuries have made between freedom and license.

Hart drove slowly along the road that cuts through his property, of a hundred and seventy acres. He pointed to a spot where he had seen a fox the week before and to the gate outside which, in 1987, hundreds of reporters and TV trucks had hunkered down, waiting for another glimpse of scandal. The Harts haven't had many reporters at their house since those days. They had invited me for dinner and to stay the night, and, in a clumsy attempt to thank them, I'd bought flowers in Denver and brought them as a gift.

Getting out of the Jeep, Hart smiled thinly at the bouquet. "It's gonna take a lot of flowers to make Lee feel any better about reporters," he said. "Lee was pretty brutalized, you know. I think she's all right now."

As we walked through the snow toward the house, we were greeted by the barking of dogs and then by Lee Hart, standing in the doorframe. She looked eager and nervous at the same time. Since "the events of 1987," as her husband often calls them, Lee Hart has kept out of the public eye. Even some of the Harts' closest friends are bewildered by the endurance of their marriage.

"Babe, why don't you give him the tour, and get that over with?" Hart said.

"That's what I was going to do, Gary."

Perhaps the thing that struck me most about the house, besides its sheer splendor, was how few signs there were that one of its owners had been so close to becoming the most powerful person on earth. Politicians usually keep several dozen grip-and-grin photos around—self-gilding memorabilia from the old campaigns or the trips abroad. At the Harts', just a few black-and-white pictures had been tacked up—familiar images from the campaign trail, with both Gary and Lee all smiles and looking a bit younger.

We sat by the fire and talked about "The Good Fight: The Education of an American Reformer," a book that Hart was getting ready for publication. "I really wanted to title the book 'The Diary of a Failed Reformer,' but they wouldn't let me," he said. "My editor had a fit. They give no credit to people for a sense of irony. The truth is, I don't think I was a failure. I just wasn't a success."

Hart's is a willfully soulless book. Throughout, he uses "the reformer" in place of the first person—a device that was intended to make the book seem less self-conscious and succeeds only in making it seem more so. Instead of paying tribute to Henry Adams with this device, as Hart had intended, he summons Norman Mailer's old alter ego, Aquarius. That might not be so grating if Hart had written openly, bravely, even angrily, about his own experience. He has not. His reticence is at constant war with his sense of injury, and the conflict produces a tinny, self-righteous effect.

Hart wrote with far more passion in a number of letters to his editor at Random House, Jonathan Karp. One reads:

> You must condition yourself and your colleagues to the fact that nothing short of suicide will satisfy the skeptics and the cynics or even the asinine acquaintances. The reason simply is this: a newly aggressive and intrusive press establishment, never comfortable with my refusal to be categorized, exploited (and possibly created) an incident very near the bone. . . . I will never escape from this event, as you say, simply because the press cannot afford to let me escape it and because social and political exile is

demanded to sustain the hypocrisy. *Nothing*, I repeat, *nothing*, I say in the foreword would solve these two problems. It would require an act of utmost contrition, which I am incapable of making.

In "The Good Fight" Hart writes a skeletal history of various reformers in America and the ways they have been stifled, thwarted, or killed. Although he propounds no grand conspiracy theory, he is fascinated by the conspiratorial elements in the murders of Martin Luther King, Jr., and the Kennedys, and in the defeats of McGovern and the reformer. A prominent Washington journalist once told me that Hart, after a couple of drinks on an airplane five years ago, described his own fall in 1987 as a conspiracy of power élites: the military establishment, the energy industry—in short, all the institutions he planned to reform as President.

I told Hart I thought there was an acute sense of conspiracy running through the new book linking his own trials with those of the Kennedys and King.

He seemed genuinely surprised. "If you think that a paranoid sense of conspiracy runs through the book, then you're misreading it, or maybe I should rewrite it," he said. "And I may put myself in line with reformers, but it doesn't mean my loss was in any way equal to their losses. You can be a good Christian or a follower of Christ or Paul and not think you are Christ or Paul. My own impression of my experience in politics is that it was very minor. Virtually none of the things I wanted to get done got done."

Lee Hart called us in to dinner. She had prepared an elaborate salad of greens, bacon, cheese, and fruit, and then chicken breasts with wild rice and, for dessert, the richest chocolate cake this side of Lyons.

"This wine's a little tart, though, isn't it, babe?" Hart said. "Musta been a lemon vintage."

Lee Hart looked mortified. "Maybe another bottle . . . "

Hart smiled. "Don't bother, babe. This'll do."

I asked Lee Hart how the two of them had managed to pull themselves together after the disaster of 1987.

There was a pause. Then Lee said, "We were redoing the kitchen in the old house, where Andrea's living now. And Gary cut a lot of logs. Some were the Miami *Herald*, others were *The Washington Post*—"

Gary Hart's face turned the color of claret. "Now, babe," he said, in a voice freighted with anger and meaning.

"I just meant—"

"Babe, speak for yourself. Sure, it was hard. And if it was a career it was the tragic end of a career. But if you take it as public service, the way I did, then it's just the end of that part of your life."

"That's true, Gary. You always said that."

"The key thing is your attitude going into it. When I was elected to the Senate, I was eager to be there. But I never thought that this would be it, senator for life, or climb the ladder to the Presidency. I just decided in the eighties that the Democratic Party had to be the party of change. And 'up or out' became my attitude. I just could not stand to look at the lack of courage in the Senate. And then after I lost in '84—well, you really can't go back to the Senate after running for President, and rejoin those silly, inane discussions. I'm against the two-term limit, but people should leave voluntarily. They have to avoid being coöpted by the permanent Washington crowd—the journalists, the friendship. They get coöpted after a couple of terms. I want to go back to an earlier time, when politicians didn't hobnob with the press, and they saw themselves as public servants for a time. I was made fun of, even ridiculed, because I always said 'Mr. Koppel' or 'Mr. Brinkley' when I was on TV. My staff and family gave me hell about it . . . "

"I didn't," Lee said.

"Now, babe. C'mon. But for me it was an important thing. I thought I should be businesslike. Chumminess on television, the 'David' and 'Ted' stuff, was symbolic of the problem."

I tried to get back to the question of how the Harts went on with their lives in 1987.

"I left the Presidential race at noon Friday and I was back in my law office at eight o'clock Monday morning," Hart said. "To prove something to everyone—that life goes on. Being President isn't everything in the world. If you are a mature adult and you have your values straight, you just go ahead and do the next thing. The hardest thing to deal with was the continual drumbeat of the press. I was out of politics, but it kept coming. I mean, how many times can you kill someone? How many times can you be dead?"

"Gary, don't make it seem as if—"

"Speak for yourself, babe," Hart said.

"Well, O.K.," she said. "A lot of people have the idea that you just didn't want to be President."

"Well, that's just . . . Look. We are at the stage where we think that you've got to be all-consumed by the idea of becoming President. But it's nonsense. Thomas Jefferson gave his Inaugural speech and then walked home through the mud to his boarding house. Now they think that your life is ruined if you fail. The danger of running for the Presidency is that if you don't make it—and that's the case for almost everyone who tries—then you are considered a failure."

After dinner, we had coffee in the living room, and I asked the Harts about the '92 race.

"When Clinton began to pick people for his team, there was a moment of elation for me when I saw Eli Segal, John Emerson, and those people—people who had been with me once—getting serious jobs in the Administration," Hart said.

I asked him whom he had supported initially in the race.

He seemed embarrassed, and Lee broke in, saying, "I supported Tsongas in the primaries. Clinton's idea of a middle-class tax cut was just pandering to voters. I also didn't like the Japanese-bashing. Gary, you said the same thing."

Hart reddened once more.

"Just let me recollect, babe," he said, and then, "Tsongas's famous little book looked like a lot of my stuff. When he called me and said, 'I'm going to run for President,' I started laughing. And he did, too. It was like an unspoken thing on how crazy it is to run for President."

"I remember you said, 'Paul, I knew you weren't feeling well, but I didn't think you were sick in the head.'"

"Maybe, babe. Maybe. But we went on laughing for three minutes or so, and then, a few days later, he announced."

Hart said he was tired and ready for bed, but before he left I asked him what he did now on a typical day when he was not travelling abroad.

"It's very boring," he said. "I sit behind a desk. I make telephone calls, draft proposals. I give speeches. I negotiate proposals for airports and seaports. I'm an advocate. In '88, I tried to figure out a way to maintain a link to the private sector, to do something in the private sector related to what my goals had been in the public. I went to Taiwan, to Argentina, but it didn't lead to anything."

"You got to play a lot of tennis," Lee Hart said.

"Yeah, babe. And to Czechoslovakia, Japan. When I travelled, I discovered there was a lot of bewilderment out in the world about why I hadn't succeeded. They still thought I had something to say, even if no one at home did. That was very vivid."

Lee Hart and I stayed up and talked awhile in the kitchen. I was grateful to her for the trouble she had gone to. No matter how much the Harts steered away from the "events" that Hart had ruled out of bounds, the presence of yet another reporter could only have been painful to both of them.

"You know, it's different for Gary from what it is for me," she said. "He was the one running for office, and, contrary to what some people might have thought, I really never fantasized about being in the White House. That was putting the cart before the horse. I did think Gary should have been President. I didn't fear the White House. There were all sorts of things I would have worked on. But I had no long-standing ambitions. Maybe that was a mechanism of self-protection. You protect yourself against disappointment. I'm delighted with Hillary. Early on, she made a few faux pas, which happens, but she's a good speaker and doesn't have a lot of mannerisms that drive you crazy."

I said it seemed strange that the Clinton Administration had asked Mondale, Hart's 1984 opponent, to be the Ambassador in Moscow—an appointment that Mondale eventually turned down, and that went to Thomas Pickering. Friends and family had told me that Hart, who wrote a book on *perestroika*, and travels to Moscow several times a year, was particularly galled by the Mondale appointment.

Lee Hart's face tightened into an expression infinitely sad.

"I'd have been stunned if he had been asked," she said. "But it tells you something. Gary has never, ever, abused the public trust. And when we know the garbage that's come out of that city . . . The truth is, Gary is trashed anytime there's anything negative brought up about anyone else. Clinton would never have been President had it not been for what happened to Gary. The Clinton people know that they got off easier than Gary did. Clinton also had the support of the Democratic Party people, who hung in there with him, which Gary never had. I was just very happy that they survived. The press seemed to have learned—or I hope so, for the sake of the country. Otherwise, who would ever run for office?" Lee Hart's eyes widened and filled. "In many respects," she said slowly, "our situation was just so simple, but it was not what they thought it was or said it was. It never was."

While Gary Hart was still running for President in 1988, he mapped out in his mind the first months of his term. The first thing he would do was invite Gorbachev to the Inauguration, and then he'd get a quick arms-control treaty on strategic arms and nuclear testing. "I may flatter myself, but I think Gorbachev sensed in me a dramatic figure who was like him, at least in some small way," he said. Then he would get started on the Middle East, break some of the old molds on defense policy, the economy, energy policy.

Some of Hart's former aides found themselves wandering through the Inaugural events in Washington this year and thinking, This should have been us—four years ago.

Hart had hoped that Clinton, as President, would make a bold gesture to the Russians, as he said he himself would have done. He told some of Clinton's aides that they ought to invite Boris Yeltsin to the Inauguration, as an indication of support for democratic reform. "I got back mumbo-jumbo about who was where last, the protocol of it," he said, rolling his eyes. "They missed the whole point."

But even if Clinton didn't ape Hart's Inaugural strategy, the political debt of the new President to the exile is undeniable. For one thing, the White House is stocked with former Hart people: John Emerson, the deputy director of personnel; Eli Segal, the head of the fledgling national-service program; David Dreyer, the director of planning; Jeremy Rosner, the counsellor and director of legislative affairs at the National Security Council. And Larry Smith, who was Hart's key aide on defense policy, is now the counsellor to Secretary Les Aspin, at the Pentagon.

The influence goes beyond mere personnel. In Denver, Hart and I watched the State of the Union speech together. He spent some of the time laughing at the standing ovations and the primping of his old colleagues, and the rest of it, and he nodded paternal assent to the policy initiatives coming from the podium: a stream-lined defense, an economy based on investment rather than on consumption, a program of national service. In Hart's time, all this was known as neoliberalism, the sharp break with the ideological orthodoxy of the Hubert Humphreys and Walter Mondales of the Democratic Party.

"In 1984, Hart fired the first shot at the fortress of the Democratic Party and lived to tell the story, which inspired a bunch of others who might have been scared off," Bruce Reed, a domestic-policy adviser to Clinton, said recently. "To the extent that he made the world safe for new ideas, Gary Hart made his mark."

Where Hart and Clinton differed profoundly was in their style of personal politics. Hart's was cool, intellectual, while Clinton's is more that of a populist, a hugger, a figure of almost preternatural resilience. The joke about Hart among his aides during the 1984 and 1987 campaigns was that the candidate would go to a reception for five hundred people, and after it was over his aides would ask, "Well, did he meet any of them?" The joke about Clinton last year was that the duty of the Secret Service was to protect the people from the candidate.

But Clinton's edge didn't consist only of his natural warmth toward people and crowds; he had history, and Gary Hart, to learn from. In 1987, when the press first started asking Hart questions about his marriage and his sex life, he knew there was static in the Washington air. At the same time, he had faith—an unwise and luck-less faith—in precedent and the secrets that the press had always kept. Hart's staff members were far from ignorant about "the Issue." They had prepared explanations in 1984, too. But they continued to suspend disbelief. They wished away disaster. Then, in April of 1987, just two weeks before the scandal broke, Larry Smith went to Colorado for a "blue skies" meeting with the campaign leadership. He asked the group what they intended to do about rumors of Hart's womanizing. "One of the campaign's leaders laughed, and said, 'We never talk about it,'" Smith recalled. "I said, 'Well, you'd better think about it.'"

Reporters might whisper, but what would the papers actually print? Just look at what had gone on before, they said. Andrew Jackson was married to a bigamist. Grover Cleveland supported an illegitimate child. Wendell Willkie had an affair with an editor of the New York *Herald Tribune* at the very time the paper was promoting his candidacy. Franklin D. Roosevelt and Dwight Eisenhower had affairs, and the Homeric catalogue of John Kennedy's afternoons of leisure surely needed no recounting.

But, as Hart well knew, the atmosphere had changed immeasur-ably after the Watergate scandal. The press had become adversarial, wary of being duped or of being seen as "in the tank" for a public official. And the truth was that reporters never really warmed to Gary Hart. They found him imperious, aloof, reckless, a little strange. Somehow, that made it easier to bring him down.

"It's like with George Romney in 1967," I was told by Richard Cohen, a *Washington Post* columnist who travelled with the Hart campaign in 1984. "The press knew that Romney was an idiot, but the question was: How do you write it? So along come his comments about being brainwashed, and—*wham!*—they take him out. He's history. Same with Hart. There was always this sense among the press that he just wasn't—well, right. That he was weird. But how do you write it? And then along comes Donna Rice."

After the Miami *Herald* rushed into print with the results of its stakeout of Hart's town house, on Capitol Hill, "Hell Week" began for the campaign. Nothing like this had ever happened in American politics. The rules had suddenly changed, and the Hart cadres, young, and scattered across the country, were utterly confused. The newspapers and the television stations were in a mad dash to win the race to nail Hart. "I thought the whole system had gone awry," says Kathy Bushkin, who was once a close aide of Hart's and is now an executive at *U.S. News & World Report*. "For whatever reason, Gary Hart showed bad judgment and, for whatever reason, the press seemed determined to get something on him. Inside the campaign, people were stunned, frightened, frustrated. These were people who had come to politics out of great idealism. They weren't prepared for things like spin control and damage control."

John Holum, who worked with Hart in both Presidential campaigns, told me, "When the story broke, Gary called me. No one else was talking to the press. We needed to do something. I said, 'What's going on?' He said, 'John, I'm not crazy.' So I said, 'So it's not true.' He said, 'Right, it's not true.' So I went on television and got hung out to dry saying that I had known Gary Hart for seventeen years and I believed him. Now I think he did lie. I was very angry. What really made me angry is that he could let all those people pin their hopes on him and then not have the personal discipline to make his candidacy viable."

While Hart struggled to keep his candidacy alive—while he faced unprecedented questions from the press on the order of "Have you ever committed adultery?"—editors and reporters at *The Washington Post* looked into a detective's report they had been given which provided evidence that Hart had been carrying on an affair with a Washington lobbyist. When *The Post* called Hart and said that it was preparing to run a story on the subject, Hart quit the race and went home to Kittredge.

"No one looks back on that with great memories, but the rules evolve," says Dan Balz, a political writer at *The Post*. "We're in a period like that now, with babysitters and nannies sinking Cabinet appointees. What Hart did was wrong, because he misrepresented his own marriage and life in a way that became fatal. For a lot of people in this country, the simple fact of infidelity is disqualifying.

Also, his actions were contemporaneous with the race. He stretched the limits."

David Dreyer, who was a key Hart aide in the Senate and is now a member of Clinton's staff, naturally sees it otherwise. "I think he was treated shabbily by the press," he says. "His privacy was invaded. The trials he went through after the campaign were disproportionate to what he had done. He was treated as a non-person, almost as a political prisoner in a totalitarian system. He's off the political radar screen."

While Hart always denied to his staff that there was a problem, Bill Clinton acknowledged from the start that there would be questions, and he intended to act before the press did. In September of 1991, John Holum and other Democratic activists went to a meeting of an exploratory committee of the Clinton campaign at the Quality Inn on New Jersey Avenue in Washington. "Clinton himself brought up the question of the marriage," Holum told me. "Clinton said, 'I know you are all concerned about this. Here's the situation: There were problems in our marriage and we've worked them out.' I was so gratified. No, I was *thrilled* that he was doing this."

To compare Hart's shock and his steely defensiveness at his press conferences during Hell Week with Bill and Hillary Clinton's command of the same subject in the early stages of their campaign is to see consummate politicians learning from the foibles of a deeply flawed teacher. Hart made himself into a martyr. He went before his supporters and the cameras and said that his campaign was a "crusade," and that "if I'm right about that, it really doesn't matter if the leader is struck down in battle or with a knife in the back, because the case goes on and the crusade continues."

Clinton and his aides watched Gennifer Flowers unleash her unholy confession in the *Star* and went immediately on the counter-offensive, charging her with profiteering and saying that taped conversations with the candidate had been doctored. On January 26, 1992, just after the Super Bowl, Clinton and his wife went on "60 Minutes" and seemed to speak past the host, Steve Kroft, and straight to the voters, in a way never seen before in Presidential politics. When Kroft asked for the specifics of the problems in the marriage,

Clinton replied with a combination of frankness, indirection, and a knowing vocabulary which was designed to admit imperfection and, at the same time, shield him from further assault.

"I think the American people—at least, people that have been married for a long time—know what it means and know the whole range of things it can mean," he said. "You go back and listen to what I've said. You know, I have acknowledged wrongdoing. I have acknowledged causing pain in my marriage. I have said things to you tonight and to the American people from the beginning that no American politician ever has. I think most Americans who are watching this tonight, they'll know what we're saying; they'll get it, and they'll feel that we have been more than candid."

And then, perhaps even more important, Hillary Clinton echoed her husband, and did so without apology or embarrassment: "You know, I'm not sitting here—some little woman standing by my man, like Tammy Wynette. I'm sitting here because I love him, and I respect him, and I honor what he's been through and what we've been through together. And, you know, if that's not enough for people, then, heck, don't vote for him."

The Clinton campaign had it easier. If there had been extramarital affairs, they were not going on during the campaign. Hart had not given voters reason to believe the same of him. And Clinton was not taken by surprise. His young campaign handlers, some of whom run the White House communications office today, were no longer fooled by even the friendliest of reporters.

"The Clinton cadre had no illusions about what the press was capable of doing, while the Hart people were stunned by it," a Party activist who worked in both candidates' campaigns said. "With the Hart episode, people on the Democratic side began to understand about reporters. 'O.K.,' they said about the reporters, 'they may be our age, they may look like us, and even vote like us, but they are not us. They are another political force, an adversary.' The Clinton people hated the press even more than the Hart people."

On a clear, cold evening this winter, I went out to the Pentagon and was led to Larry Smith's office. Like so many offices around

Washington this year, Smith's rooms were newly painted and bare. "We're just finding out where the coffeepot is," Smith said by way of greeting. Smith worked as Hart's top aide in the Senate from 1978 to 1982, leaving the office just as the other aides were discussing strategy for the first Presidential race.

"Let me begin by saying this," he said. "Gary is a truly tragic figure. Though I love him, I left him in the late spring, early summer of 1982 because I lost confidence in him. I believed he felt himself in a way to be divine."

A mixture of anger, dismay, and real, lasting affection was characteristic of every former Hart aide I had met, but Smith was the one who was most willing, or able, to display his feelings.

"There is a theology that says that if you sin you are cast into the outer darkness, called Hell," Smith said. "If you are mortal, like most of us, you have to deal with the fact of sin, so when you do sin you are in your own mind condemned to Hell. That is, if you are human and do not deny that fact. The only other way is to insist that you are above the usual rules. I came to believe that Gary Hart felt that the fate of Gary Hart was that he was destined to be President of the United States and he was not bound by the disciplines that impinge on the rest of us. In the end, the guy broke everybody's heart.

"Look at what Clinton did. He signalled that he had come short of the glory of God. But he looked into the camera and acknowledged it and said he still felt worthy of support. In other words, he is like us. He is human. That was a powerful political act."

I interrupted Smith to say that Hart had told me he could not have stayed in the race, because "other lives" would have been dragged through the press and ruined.

"Maybe so, maybe so," Smith said. Then he said, "But before you go, I want you to hear something."

Smith crossed the room and found a hardbound copy of the collected poems of Yeats, a gift from Gary Hart. He leafed to one of the later poems—"Come Gather Round Me, Parnellites," an ode to the Irish hero and statesman whose political career faltered when he became a co-respondent in the divorce case of his mistress, Kitty O'Shea.

"I can't read this without thinking of Gary," Smith said. And he read:

> The Bishops and the Party
> That tragic story made,
> A husband that had sold his wife
> And after that betrayed;
> But stories that live longest
> Are sung above the glass,
> And Parnell loved his country,
> And Parnell loved his lass.

Larry Smith's eyes filled with tears as he closed the book. "That's the tragedy," he said. "But with Gary it's worse. He didn't even love the lass. Now he is walking around like a ghost. What I want for my friend is to have a fine peace on this earth."

Gary Hart is in Washington looking for work at a new law firm. He sits by the window of a trendy Washington restaurant, i Ricchi, drinking cappuccino.

"Clinton was a watershed," he says. "There was the scandal, and it was dealt with for a couple of weeks, and then it went away. It wasn't just how he handled it. I hate that word 'handle.' They say Clinton handled his situation better than I did. Poppycock. It wasn't the decision to go on '60 Minutes.' It was the editorial decision not to pursue it any further. I didn't see editors this time sending reporters halfway around the world to peek in a politician's window. And that was good for the country. The wife of a very prominent Washington journalist told me the other day that everyone in Washington thinks Bill Clinton never would have been elected President without Gary Hart. Maybe. The idea is that I somehow carried away the burden of scandal. Maybe she also means that I plowed new ground on the Party and the issues. If that's the case, I'm a happy man. You don't always have to win to win. You don't always have to achieve the highest office to succeed.

"The hardest adjustment was having a platform for twelve years and then having it disappear overnight. See, you don't have to be President to have a platform, but when you lose you've lost your platform. Even if you are speaking in an empty Senate, when it's a sea of mahogany, you can feel you are contributing. That urge doesn't end overnight. Imagine a writer told he could not write. A painter. It was a way of expressing myself, my convictions. One day, you're speaking ten times a day, and then, suddenly, you're not. I was in London, and one of the papers sent around a reporter to interview me. They also sent over a photographer to take my picture. I'd met her before, and we started talking to kill time while she set up. I kind of interviewed her. She said she was married, but the marriage wasn't too happy, and someone had suggested she get involved in photography. And now, she said, her camera had become her whole life. 'If someone ever took away my camera,' she said, 'I'd be lost.' Then she started asking about my life and my situation. And I said, 'Well, you know how you would feel if someone took away your camera? You'd be completely lost. Well, that is how I feel. I've lost my platform, my chance to influence things and contribute.' And when she turned around there were tears streaming down her face.

"So now I have no public role. I don't have a platform. You are limited at the *Times* Op-Ed page to one appearance every six months or so. I tell them that doesn't seem to apply to Henry Kissinger, but that doesn't matter. Every time I call there with something to say, I get a new young thing on the line. Very nice, smart, but they just don't want to hear from me. This is not an American ethos, it's an American journalistic ethos. There are a handful of people who decide who is going to have a platform and who will not. The golden Rolodex. My category—my place in the Rolodex—is the Privacy Issue for Public Officials. Which is the only thing I won't talk about. My friend Billy Shore gets on me to write about Yugoslavia, and I say, 'For whom? Who cares what I think about Yugoslavia?' The young thing at the other end of the phone says, 'When were you last in Yugoslavia?' I'll bet they never ask Nixon that."

—*The New Yorker* | April 19, 1993

Rosetta's Legacy

For four years Dash, a reporter at *The Washington Post*, followed the lives of DC resident Rosa Lee Cunningham, her children, and five of her grandchildren, in an effort to understand the persistence of poverty and pathology within America's Black underclass. An excerpt from the book that grew out of the story, winner of the Pulitzer Prize and the Robert F. Kennedy Journalism Award.

By Leon Dash

Rosa Lee is so weak she cannot get out of bed.

I cradle one of her limp arms while Richard grips the other. Gently, we lift her up and support her as she tries to stand. She rocks unsteadily, groaning and whimpering from the exertion. We slowly lean her back against a tall wooden chest of drawers to brace her, but she slumps against it, banging the chest into the wall. We hastily return her to bed.

It is clear she needs immediate medical attention. She has been growing weaker and weaker since her release from Greater Southeast

Community Hospital eight days ago. Rosa Lee's youngest daughter comes into the bedroom to dress her while Richard and I step out into the living room. I tell Richard that I am taking Rosa Lee to the Howard University Hospital emergency room. "An excellent idea," Richard declares.

Later that day, doctors began searching for the cause of her dangerously weak condition. After a blood test, the mystery unraveled.

Rosa Lee was a victim, it turned out, of her inability to read.

The blood test showed that she was overdosing on Dilantin, a medication that helps prevent seizures. She had twice the recommended level in her system.

She had been taking Dilantin only a few weeks. Doctors had prescribed it for her after a seizure in February—her fourth since October—had landed her in the Community Hospital. When they sent her home, they gave her written instructions on how to take four medications they had prescribed for her. Under the word Dilantin, the instructions read "100 mgs 3X daily."

"No, I didn't tell the nurse I couldn't read," says Rosa Lee defensively. "She didn't ask me if I could read. I wouldn't have told her if she'd asked."

Rosa Lee didn't know that "100 mgs" meant 100 milligrams or that she was supposed to take one 100-milligram tablet three times a day. She thought she could take more than one pill if she wanted, as long as she took them three times a day. "Sometimes I would take two of them," she said. "Sometimes I'd get up in the night and take them."

It became an unending cycle: The extra Dilantin doses made her feel disoriented and weak; as she grew weaker, she would add another pill, thinking it would make her feel better. "I didn't know, Mr. Dash," she says, her voice reflecting pain and embarrassment. "I was trying to get well."

Rosa Lee can recognize certain words—enough to fool strangers—but the pages of a book look to her like a mass of gray, encrypted code. She can decode bits of it, spotting a word here and there that she knows, but she cannot make sense out of the sentences.

She often asks me to break the code for her. One morning at her favorite McDonald's, she asks me to explain a letter she has received from Washington's public housing agency. We are having breakfast after her daily visit to one of the two nearby drug-treatment clinics.

She rifles through the rolled-up sheaf of tattered papers she always carries in her pocketbook. The filing system I had set up for her a few months earlier has been abandoned. She scrutinizes each piece of paper for the housing agency's recognizable letter-head. The bulky stack is her portable filing cabinet, the place where she keeps all her documents, some dating back years. She never throws anything away, because she can't read well enough to decide what she needs and what she can discard.

Finally, she finds what she is looking for and hands it to me.

"This is the wrong letter," I say.

"No, it isn't!" she retorts. "Read the letter. It's from public housing!"

I shake my head and point to the date at the top of the letter: 1989. "This refers to public housing you lived in on Blaine Street two years ago," I say, "not to the application you have filed for a new apartment."

"Are you sure, Mr. Dash? Read it and make sure."

"This is not the letter. I've read it. In fact, you can throw this away."

"Don't you dare!" she says, snatching it. "I might need it."

It is infuriating that someone with such a sharp and quick mind is shut out from much of the world around her. She cannot find an unfamiliar street on a map of Washington, but she skillfully navigates the complicated bureaucracy of the city's public housing agency, repeatedly securing apartments for herself and her family ahead of other applicants who have been on waiting lists for years. Balancing a checkbook is out of the question, but she successfully handled large sums of money when she was dealing drugs in the 1970s and 1980s, satisfying customers and wholesale suppliers not known for patience.

She tries to hide her illiteracy by going on the offensive. Anyone spelling a name for her is ordered to slow down while she prints each letter in big, bold capitals. Sometimes, she casually hands over pen and paper and asks the person to write it for her, as if she were too busy to be bothered. She's so good at covering up her illiteracy that I find myself forgetting that she can't even read the few words on a medicine bottle label.

Saturday is my birthday. I stop by Rosa Lee's hospital room in the afternoon, dropping off a bunch of black seedless grapes for her, before going to celebrate. Since our visit to the Pepco office the previous September, this is the first time she has seen me in suit and tie.

"Where ya going all dressed up?" she asks, smiling, after we greet each other.

"I'm going out later. It's my birthday," I tell her.

"How old are you?" she continues. "Forty-seven," I answer.

"Oh, you're an old, tired man. Over the hill." Rosa Lee laughs.

"Thank you," I reply with feigned anger. "I really need you to tell me that I'm an old, tired man and over the hill. On your birthday, I say, 'Happy Birthday, Rose.' But you talk about how old I am. I'll remember that. I seem to remember you being upset that no one remembered your birthday one of the last times you were in here. You wait 'til your next birthday comes around. I'll fix you good! In fact, I think I'll take my grapes back."

Rosa Lee continues to laugh at my empty threat. "There's nothing you can do can hurt me, buddy."

She's back to her feisty self.

I expect the same bouncy frame of mind when I call her Sunday morning. Instead, Rosa Lee begins crying into the telephone. "Richard's going to get me put out of here, Mr. Dash." This is just incredible, I think. It never stops. Rosa Lee remains stuck in perpetual turmoil and pain holding on to her adult children.

Richard had brought Rosa Lee's grandson, the boy she had taught how to shoplift a flight jacket, to visit her in the hospital on Saturday, shortly after I left. Rosa Lee was happy to see the boy when he walked into her room alone. She asked him how he'd gotten to the hospital. He told her he'd come by bus with his uncle Richard. In the hospital lobby, he continued, Richard gave him instructions on how to get to Rosa Lee's room and told the boy he would meet him there. "I got something to do," Richard announced.

Rosa Lee asked her grandson whether Richard had a tote bag with him. Yes, he replied, a big one, collapsed and folded up under his arm. Twenty minutes later, Richard walked into Rosa Lee's room holding the full tote bag by its handles.

"Richard, I hope you haven't been doing what I think you've been doing," Rosa Lee said, annoyed.

Richard played dumb. "Whatcha mean, Mama? I came here to see you. How are you feeling?"

Rosa Lee didn't say any more. She didn't want the patient in the bed next to hers to know that Richard had gone quickly around the hospital, slipping into empty rooms and stealing telephones.

In a dinner interview with Richard four days later, he insists that he has gotten off crack and, because of that, has dropped his practice of stealing from Washington's hospitals and office buildings. It's our second lengthy interview in a month and I'd rather he tell me the truth about his life, so I decide on a little shock treatment.

"Tell me how many telephones you got out of Howard on Saturday," I say.

Richard stops spooning up his seafood gumbo and sits back in the booth. "Great God almighty!"

"In a big tote bag," I continue.

"You know, I feel so bad about it, I'm not going to ever, ever do that again," he says, picking up his spoon.

"Tell me how many telephones you got," I repeat.

"Five," he responds. Normally, he says, he can sell them for forty dollars apiece.

"How much did you flip them for?"

He earned only forty dollars for all five telephones. He had to move them fast. He needed to buy some crack. "I sell them to people that I know. Beauty parlors. I got customers out there, Mr. Dash. Liquor stores. Restaurants. Chinese stores. They buy them."

It's clear Richard will soon be going back to prison. "The last time you went down to Lorton, you got busted over at the Washington Hospital Center stealing telephones," I remind him.

Richard keeps his head bowed over his gumbo and nods, indicating yes, he knows.

On the afternoon after her release from the hospital—a blustery March day that makes us welcome the warmth of her apartment—Rosa Lee and I are sitting on the plaid couch in her living room. Howard Hospital has given her a new prescription schedule, and she has asked me to help her take the medicine correctly this time.

I have a legal-size notepad of white, blue-lined paper. I intend to write up a schedule in bold print using her physical descriptions of the medications with words she says she can read.

I pick up one of the amber-colored plastic containers. "This is the phenobarbital. I notice they reduced the amount down to thirty milligrams. When you left Greater Southeast, they had you up to sixty milligrams." I shake several into my hand. "Now, do you recognize this tablet? What do you see it as?"

Rosa Lee squints at it. "The little white pill. That's the kind that makes me drowsy."

I print "LITTLE WHITE PILL" on the paper and hold up a different pill. "Tell me what you see this pill as. This is the Dilantin."

"Is that one of the seizure pills?"

"Yes."

"A white-and-orange pill," she says. "That's the one I took so many of."

"Right," I say. "That's what made you sick." I write "WHITE AND ORANGE" on the list.

"Now this one," I say, displaying a folic acid tablet that she takes as part of her HIV treatment.

Rosa Lee studies it. "Little white pill," she says tentatively.

"No, no, no. That's the phenobarbital. This pill is the yellow pill. Here, look at it again."

"The yellow pill," she repeats, staring at the tablet.

"All right," I say, moving on to the last container. "This is the retrovir, the AZT. This is for your condition of being HIV positive. Now, you tell me how you see this pill."

"My blue and white."

I show Rosa Lee what I am writing. "I'm putting down the times you are to take each pill."

"Okay," she says, "but please put the P.M. and the A.M. for me."

"I am. Now read this to me."

She read each word slowly, carefully, like a rock climber ascending a cliff. "Little white pill: 8 A.M., 1 P.M., and 6 P.M. The white and orange pill: 8 A.M., 1 P.M., and 6 P.M. The yellow pill: 8 A.M."

I interrupt. "You only take that once."

"Once. Okay. Blue and white pill: 8 A.M., 2 P.M., and 8 P.M."

"Right," I say. "Now, will that work for you?"

"Yes," she says.

Rosa Lee taped the list to the wall outside her bedroom so that her grandchildren, who read better than she does, could help her. As her strength returned and she spent more time away from home again, she took the medication schedule from the wall and stuck it in her pocketbook. After several weeks, she memorized the routine, and the list became just one more out-of-date item in her portable filing cabinet.

Rosa Lee has no trouble remembering when she began hiding her illiteracy.

It was 1953, and she was sixteen years old, separated from her husband of a few months and raising three children in her mother's house near Capitol Hill. It was the last place she wanted to be. Living in Rosetta's house meant living by Rosetta's rules, and those rules were choking Rosa Lee.

Rosetta and her family had come to Washington in the mid-1930s, seeking refuge from their harsh lives as sharecroppers in North Carolina and Maryland. While Earl was alive, and even more so after his death in 1948, Rosetta's domestic work brought in the household's most dependable income.

Just as Rosetta's mother had prepared her to be both a share-cropper and a domestic worker, Rosetta schooled Rosa Lee in domestic work. Long before Rosa Lee turned ten, her mother taught her to scrub laundry on a washboard, to wash a floor so it shined, to make a bed so it looked crisp and neat. Rosa Lee's apartment is a monument to those lessons; no matter how many people are living there, it is always tidy, clean, and well organized.

As the eldest girl, Rosa Lee was expected to do laundry for everyone in the house: by the time she was in the third grade, she was spending hours at the scrub board every week, washing sweaters and shirts. "My mother didn't ask me did I have my homework done," Rosa Lee says. "When she came home from work, she'd say, 'Betcha didn't pull those sheets. Betcha didn't wash those clothes.' School wasn't important to her, and it wasn't important to me."

That was what Rosetta Wright's generation always called "training," says the historian Elizabeth Clark-Lewis. "It was a very bad reflection on the mother, the family, the broader community for a young woman not to be well trained. Training is reflected in what you can do with your hands, be it cleaning the house, washing expertly."

Since the early 1980s, Clark-Lewis has interviewed more than 120 black migrant women from the South. Eighty-three of them were of the same generation and out of the same southern rural traditions as Rosetta Wright. They came to Washington from all over the South in the 1920s and 1930s to work as domestics. About twenty, like Rosetta, were from rural North Carolina. "The reality of domestic work was all pervasive for black women of that generation," Clark-Lewis says.

As I spoke with Clark-Lewis, it became clear why education was such a low priority to Rosetta Wright. She had grown up in a time and place where hard work was the only way rural black sharecroppers could survive. What little education Rosetta managed to get in the segregated schools had not given her the wherewithal to sustain herself and her family. Especially not in Washington. Work did that. And if you were a black woman, work meant domestic work.

Rosetta's parents, Thadeous and Lugenia Lawrence, never had a school to attend, so they did not learn even the rudiments of reading, writing, and arithmetic. Both grew up in the isolation of the forests and swamplands of the Bishop and Powell Plantation near the hamlet of Rich Square, North Carolina, before marrying in 1916.

When the white renter of the plantation, Joe Purvis, went broke in 1925, the Lawrences and their children moved to another farm ten miles north, where they sharecropped for its white owner, Charlie Lane, for four years.

Rosa Lee knows little about her grandparents or their experiences. She knows that they picked cotton in North Carolina before coming north a short time before Rosa Lee was born in Washington, but she doesn't know much else. "I don't know if my parents and grandparents came together or not," she says. "No one ever told me about that stuff and I never asked."

Thadeous Lawrence was a big man who almost never smiled. Rosa Lee remembers that, as a child, she thought her grandfather's serious demeanor was strange. "He wouldn't laugh or nothing, Mr. Dash," she recalls. "I just remember him sitting in a chair on his porch all day not doing nothing and not saying nothing." She once asked him why he never laughed, and she still remembers his reply. "We've had such a hard time down in them sticks" in North Carolina, he told her, "I don't see much to laugh about."

She didn't understand his response and still doesn't. "What do you think he meant by that, Mr. Dash?" she asks. "That's all I remember him saying."

I respond that her grandparents and parents lived in the South when segregation was rigidly enforced, rural blacks received little or no education, black men were routinely lynched, blacks had no legal rights, and their labor was exploited.

Rosa Lee says she understands what I've said. "I heard them talking sometimes about North Carolina and what they had to put up with, but I never really understood all of it," she continues. "Just bits and pieces."

On the Lane farm, the Lawrences settled into a ramshackle, weather-beaten two-story sharecropper's house on the northern edge of Quarter Swamp. The house is still occupied today, although it has been added on to and covered with dark green aluminum siding. The Lawrences sent their children, Ozetta, Rosetta, Joseph, and Jean, to the two-room schoolhouse at Cumbo, the nearest school available for black children, on the south side of the swamp.

The four Lawrence children were allowed to attend school only when two circumstances converged: when there was no work to be done on Charlie Lane's farm and when the water in Quarter Swamp was low. That did not mean many days at school.

When the water was "up," the children could not use the two-mile-long footpath—a route cut by the longer-legged adult boot-leggers—which enabled them to get to school in little more than half an hour. The only alternative was to walk along five and a half miles of dirt road, which took them almost two hours—each way.

The water in Quarter Swamp was often up year-round, even in the cold of winter when there was little farmwork to be done. Rotting swamp vegetation keeps the bogs warmer than the surrounding land, and the running stream agitates the water so it won't freeze. Sometimes, Lugenia Lawrence sent her children along the longer dirt-road route, but most of the time she did not, according to Mamie Barnes, now in her mid-seventies, who attended the Cumbo School with all the Lawrence children. "That swamp didn't freeze over in the winter like you might think it would," remembers Barnes. "The water would be up from melted snow and ice."

Barnes's late husband's first wife was Lugenia Lawrence's sister. She knew all the Lawrences well and is close to Rosa Lee's brother Ben. She's never met Rosa Lee.

Compared to the Lawrences, Mamie Barnes was fortunate. She lived south of the swamp and did not have to contend with crossing the soggy morass at all. She was able to attend classes many more days than they did. She completed the seventh grade when she was fifteen, ending her education to take care of her ailing mother.

"We all went to that school together," says Barnes. "We all was in the same class." The Lawrences "didn't come to school too much 'cause it was too far to walk. And they didn't go to school too much in the winter. When it snowed, they had to stay home for a long time. If it rained, they stayed home."

Although Barnes was six years younger than Ozetta, and five years younger than Rosetta, the two Lawrence sisters missed so much school "that I went by them in grade. They even stopped school before they moved from Charlie Lane's farm" in 1929.

The white landlords of Rich Square had no interest in encouraging the black sharecroppers to send their children to school. Education was a threat to the sharecropping system that dominated much of the South when Rosetta was growing up in the 1920s; sharecroppers who could read and write might take their labor elsewhere. If they could do math, they might be able to tally up their own debits and earnings, and come to a different reckoning at the end of the harvest, a reckoning that would not leave them in debt to the white landowner.

The Lawrences were in the bottom tier of the three new post-Civil War class formations among African Americans in Northampton County, according to local amateur historian Samuel Glenn Baugham, who knew Thadeous Lawrence. The social hierarchy operated within the rigid confines of racial segregation and discrimination that affected all blacks.

The Lawrences were extremely isolated sharecroppers known as "river" or "swamp" blacks, who lived and worked on the plantations bordering the swamps along the Roanoke River. The river blacks were descendants of the slaves who had worked on the same plantations and, until the Depression, were cut off from even the small flow of humanity that passed through Rich Square. Generally, they had limited or no access to education.

Earl Wright came out of the "piney woods" blacks, the African American sharecroppers from around Rich Square who looked down on and generally ostracized the river blacks. Also the descendants of slaves, they lived in and among the pine tree lots far back from the meandering Roanoke River. They had easier access to education at an all-black school in Rich Square.

The descendants of the African Americans who were "free coloreds" before Emancipation were at the top of this hierarchy. They were better educated and had craftsmen's skills, such as carpentry and masonry, which the two lower groups lacked. Those among them who were not landowners were also the first to migrate North when urban factory employment opportunities first opened up for blacks during World War I.

By the time her son Ben was born in 1932, the fifteen-year-old Rosetta had worked in the cotton fields for a decade. The countless hours spent in the fields changed her body and shaped her soul, and taught her the importance of discipline and stamina. She developed quick, powerful arms and a tough, stern demeanor—a younger version of the grim, brooding woman in the photograph in Rosa Lee's bedroom.

There is no available record of the Lawrence "share" in 1932, no way to know whether the family earned enough to repay the white landowner for the money he had advanced them over the course of the year. According to family lore, Thadeous had a hidden source of income that kept the family from falling into irredeemable debt: a moonshine still. "My grandmother said my grandfather did a lot of bootlegging," says Ben. "He had plenty money! She said sometimes she would not see him for three and four months at a time. By bootlegging, he was able to pay off everything he owed" the white landowner.

Many sharecroppers, however, remained perpetually in debt, unable to make their share, yoked to the same landowner year after year. Most could not read or write, add or subtract, so they had no way to challenge the landowner's tally at harvest time. The Lawrences and Wrights were no different. Ben says his grandparents and father could not read or do arithmetic, but his mother could read a little.

Sharecropping for black farmers was a particularly harsh life, made even harsher by the effect the Depression was having on cotton farmers around Rich Square. In the space of three years, the price of a bale of cotton dropped from $500 to $250. So when Joe Purvis returned to Rich Square after the 1932 fall harvest and offered the Lawrences the opportunity to work with him on a dairy and tobacco farm in St. Mary's County, Maryland, the family decided to leave their friends and relatives and the land they knew so well. Rosetta, her six-month-old son, Ben, and her new husband, Earl Wright, joined the Lawrences on the journey.

Ben and Joe Louis vividly remember the stories that their mother and grandmother told them about their harsh life in southern Maryland. They had almost no money. Meals frequently consisted of whatever they could pick or trap. "They were eating a lot of muskrat and watercress," Joe Louis says. Watercress grew abundantly in the clear springs nearby, and muskrat was then a popular regional dish that the family never got used to. "My mother would say, if she ever got a job and made any money, she was never going to eat another muskrat," Joe Louis remembers. "Had to eat it, because that's all they could trap."

After the 1935 harvest, like thousands of other sharecroppers during the 1930s and 1940s, Rosetta and Earl Wright gave up rural life and headed for the city. The Lawrences stayed behind with three-year-old Ben, afraid that the boy might starve if his parents couldn't find work in Washington. Ben spent his entire childhood with his grandparents. "I was the oldest grandchild and a boy. They favored boys in those days. It was a different time. My mother was a fifteen-year-old teenager when she had me. She was still living at home. I used to call my grandmother 'Mama.'"

Six months after Rosetta and Earl moved to Washington, the Lawrences followed. The family's sharecropping days were over.

Washington in the 1930s was no land of opportunity for black migrants from the South, especially poor sharecroppers. It was a segregated city, but within the black community was a well-established and educated middle class that traced its roots to the freed slaves who stayed after the Civil War. Over the years, these families had built an extensive network of churches, schools, theaters, and other institutions. It wasn't a closed society, but neither did it reach out to embrace poor migrants from rural areas.

Some of the more fortunate newcomers had friends or family in the city to help them through resettlement. Others, like the Lawrences and Wrights, were on their own. Finding a job, any job, was a challenge.

Most of the jobs then open to blacks—as Post Office clerks and federal agency messengers and cafeteria workers and railroad station porters—went to middle-class blacks who had connections or education, says Portia P. James, the chief researcher at Washington's Anacostia Museum, one of the major repositories of black Washington's history. "You had to have certain resources to get those jobs," James told me. "Those jobs were very competitive.

Low-level civil service positions were for the elite of black people. Those weren't considered just regular working-class jobs. Those jobs were considered highly desirable jobs." Middle-class blacks "knew how to take advantage of opportunity," she says. "That's how they got where they were."

For those migrating out of the rural South with farming skills and almost no education, employment opportunities were extremely limited. Thadeous and Earl became general laborers on construction projects, while Lugenia and Rosetta became domestics. This fit a familiar pattern, according to Elizabeth Clark-Lewis. "The middle class was not standing waiting for these people with open arms," she says. "There was a great deal of resistance to them. They had unrefined ways. There were color issues. There were all kinds of class issues. Education issues. Very few men could come in and get a government job, and for most poor, rural women, domestic work was the reality."

As the family grew—Rosetta gave birth to twenty-two children, ten of whom died before reaching adulthood—Rosa Lee became accustomed to bedrooms crammed with too many people and living rooms with no place for private conversation. But one thing that Rosa Lee could never understand was why her brothers could not chop the wood needed to heat the water to wash the endless tubs of sheets and clothes. "Why did I have to do all the work when my brothers could go out and play? I could see them in front of the house. My mother favored my brothers. It was like I was already a day worker and cleaning up behind them. They didn't have to do NOTHING! It used to make me mad! Mr. Dash, I didn't understand it." And she still doesn't understand it all these years later.

"They worshipped boys," agrees Clark-Lewis, explaining the values of Rosetta Wright's generation. "They absolutely adored sons. Sons are their joy." Women like Rosa Lee's mother, she continues, believed that "daughters are to be trained. They are to be worked. They are to be reared! But they are not to be indulged because life is not going to allow them to be indulged. It's part of being African American and female."

Rosa Lee remembers complaining to her mother about the number of chores she had to do and how young she was. "I was still in Giddings [Elementary] School when she gave me the whole house to clean, all the clothes to wash. Mr. Dash, it was just not fair! I told her, too. I stood out of reach of her arm when I did. Like on the other side of the room with something between us. Like a bed or something."

Rosetta Wright would look at her eldest daughter and shake her head, saying, "You're going to find out. This is the only kind of job we can find for black people."

As the first-born girl, Rosa Lee's role was set by the southern traditions that had shaped her mother. "For the older daughter, in particular," says Clark-Lewis, "the mother is so dependent on her carrying the household that the younger ones will have opportunities that the older one just won't have. By the time you are four, there are clear expectations that people have of you. By *eight*, you are considered dull or dim-witted if you cannot carry on almost all the functions of a household. Period!"

While Rosa Lee was still in the early years at Giddings, her smoldering resentment caused her to silently reject her mother's vision of her future. She was determined that domestic work was not going to be the way she survived. "I didn't tell my mother—she would have smacked me in the mouth—but I told myself that I wasn't going to work in white people's houses like she did. I didn't trust white people. I had never heard but that they had done us harm. Why would I want to work in their houses?"

The first-grade classroom at Giddings Elementary School that welcomed six-year-old Rosa Lee in the fall of 1942 was a long way from the Cumbo School that Rosetta Wright had first gone to seventeen years earlier in rural North Carolina. But there was one similarity between the schools that Rosetta and Rosa Lee attended: Both were part of the South's segregated school systems.

Rosa Lee's difficulty with reading and writing began in first grade. She does not remember getting any special help from teachers. "If you didn't learn it, you just didn't learn it," she said.

Then one morning at the beginning of fourth grade in 1946, nine-year-old Rosa Lee saw that school could be something more than a place of idleness and frustration. Although Rosa Lee's classroom was on the second floor, she followed a boy up to his third-floor classroom. "His name was Herman. I went up there and sat in the back. I meddled with the boy, but I saw he wasn't paying me a bit of mind. Then I got my mind off of him and started looking at how Miss Whitehead was teaching." Rosa Lee had heard Miss Whitehead did things differently in her classroom.

Within a few hours, Rosa Lee felt as if she had stumbled into a new school. On the second floor, she and her classmates rotated among four classrooms every day. But Miss Whitehead's students stayed all day in the same classroom and Miss Whitehead handled all the subjects. The students in Miss Whitehead's class had paper and pencils. Downstairs in her classroom, Rosa Lee was not required to write much of anything most of the time.

In Miss Whitehead's classroom, "the students didn't make a lot of noise. They didn't be in the back messing with each other. They were doing their work. I actually sat there and looked around. 'Well, I'll be derned.' This teacher acted like she really cared about her students."

On the second floor, the teachers seemed to spend a lot of time in the hall, talking to each other, while Rosa Lee and her classmates played and "meddled with each other." The teachers would "come back into the classroom if we got too loud. Tell us to be quiet. Then they went back out into the hallway." By contrast, Miss Whitehead's class seemed calm, orderly and exciting.

For three straight days, Rosa Lee climbed the stairs to Miss Whitehead's classroom and sat there, undetected. For the first time in her life, she found school fascinating. "She was teaching!" she told me. "She made you feel like you were learning something." Rosa Lee planned to stay upstairs forever.

Why weren't the children downstairs taught like that? she asked a girlfriend. The friend told her that the second-floor class was for "slow learners."

No one had told Rosa Lee that she was a slow learner. She remembers angrily cutting her friend off. "I don't want to hear that shit!" Rosa Lee forever felt the sting of the phrase *slow learner*. It was not true that she was slow, but no one ever told Rosa Lee anything different.

It seems difficult to believe, but Rosa Lee went unnoticed in the class for those three days. On the fourth day, she raised her hand to ask a question. Miss Whitehead asked, "Who are you and what are you doing in my class?" She asked Rosa Lee to stay behind during recess.

After the other students left, Miss Whitehead asked Rosa Lee where she was supposed to be, and Rosa Lee told her the name of her assigned teacher, adding that she preferred to be in Miss Whitehead's class. "But that's not the way we do things," Miss Whitehead told her. "You have to pass to my class."

Rosa Lee told her, "'I can't read, but I can do number work.' I showed her my paper."

Miss Whitehead insisted that she return to her regular classroom.

"But I like the way you teach up here," Rosa Lee said. "Why won't you let me come up here?"

"You're not supposed to be up here," she remembers Miss Whitehead saying. "You're supposed to be downstairs."

Rosa Lee retreated to the second floor. "That was the most painful thing. I really wanted to stay up in her room. She was teaching and she made you feel like you were learning something."

Later that school year, Rosa Lee began skipping school frequently. When her teacher would turn her back to the classroom, "I would go right out that side door, Mr. Dash," Rosa Lee tells me one day as we stand inside her second-floor classroom at Giddings, which is now an adult education center. "I would go and get some other kids out of the room. Mr. Dash, I was a bad girl. We would hang on the back steps." On many mornings, she left the house as if she were going to school, but she spent the day roaming the streets of her Capitol Hill neighborhood instead. Rosa Lee says her mother was never notified about her absences. And despite her inability to read, she was promoted to the fifth and sixth grades.

At the end of her sixth-grade year, Rosa Lee's class was called to the assembly hall for its graduation ceremony. She knew she was not graduating so she sat in the last row, trying to hide. "I cried and cried, Mr. Dash," she recalls, sadly. "I didn't know what to do."

It was the spring of 1949 and Rosa Lee had been held back twice during her elementary school years. After the graduation ceremony, a schoolteacher came by her house. The teacher told Rosa Lee and her mother that Rosa Lee would be allowed to attend junior high school in the fall. "She told me I was being passed on account of my age," Rosa Lee said, "not because I had passed any of my classes."

Rosa Lee isn't sure how she made it as far in school as she did, considering her reading problems. Though she would have been allowed to return to seventh grade after Bobby was born, she never did go back to school. She had Ronnie at fifteen, and then, weeks after her sixteenth birthday, she married the father of Alvin, her third child.

Rosetta had insisted that Rosa Lee marry twenty-year-old Albert Cunningham. She told Albert if he didn't marry her daughter, she would report him to the police "on account of I was underage," says Rosa Lee. "I was only fifteen when I got pregnant by him." Rosa Lee didn't love Albert, but she was thrilled anyway. Marriage meant she could leave her mother's house forever. Four months after they married, she was back: her husband beat her after he found out that Rosa Lee had been sleeping with a neighborhood boy who lived in the house next-door to her mother's.

"My face was so swollen my mother didn't recognize me coming in the door," says Rosa Lee. "She told me, 'You don't have to go back to that man.'" Albert came by Rosetta's house that evening looking for Rosa Lee. Rosetta met him at the door and told him Rosa Lee was not ever going back to his house.

Yet those few months of independence made it hard for Rosa Lee to return. She and her mother argued often about Rosa Lee's welfare checks. Rosa Lee wanted the money to come to her, but Rosetta said she was too young. "What are you going to do with it?" Rosa Lee remembers her mother saying. "You don't even know how to pour piss out of a boot."

"I never saw a penny of it!" recalls Rosa Lee. "If I even asked for ten, fifteen dollars so I could have something, I didn't get it."

Rosa Lee craved her mother's love and affection, but she also feared her. She looked at her mother's broad back and powerful hands, and could think only about how to avoid the stinging slaps Rosetta often delivered during their arguments. "My mother classified me as very dumb," Rosa Lee told me one day. "It was almost as if she was making fun of me. I never felt that my mother loved me."

The friction between Rosetta and Rosa Lee, the quick smacks and harsh beatings for any infraction, was not something unique to them; it was a common tradition from the rural black South. "Especially between mothers and daughters," says Portia James. The way Rosetta raised Rosa Lee "seems to be a very typical [southern rural] upbringing," as opposed to what would be expected in an urban culture.

Rosa Lee saw public housing as her escape. With the help of friends, and without telling her mother, she found her way to the public housing agency one afternoon. She asked a clerk there for help, telling him that she could not fill out the application by herself. The memory of his sneer still causes her mouth to tighten and her voice to thicken. "Back in those days, they didn't give you any sympathy when you said you couldn't read," she says. "It was like, 'So what? It ain't my fault.'" Humiliated, she trudged back to her mother's house. She vowed never again to reveal her illiteracy to someone she didn't know.

"Can you read?" she asked her then-current boyfriend, the boy who lived next-door to her mother. Of course he could read, he told her. Couldn't she?

No, Rosa Lee said defiantly. She sat next to him, brooding silently, while he filled out the applications to switch the welfare payments to her and to get Rosa Lee into public housing.

The showdown with Rosetta came four days later.

Rosa Lee was relaxing on the front porch, feeling good that she had completed her chores for the day, when she felt Rosetta's strong fingers jab her in the shoulder.

"Why didn't you tell me that you went and applied for welfare?" Rosetta demanded.

Rosa Lee had forgotten to check the mailbox. Now it was too late. She decided it was time to stand up to her mother. "I wanted to get me and my kids out of your hair," she remembers saying. "It seems like my kids were getting on your nerves."

Her mother's response was tinged with anger. "They're not the only ones getting on my damn nerves!"

Shaking her head at the memory, Rosa Lee stops narrating the scene for a moment. "My mother was very hard!" says Rosa Lee, before continuing.

Rosetta went on, "I don't know what this is going to prove. I've got to sign that I'm no longer taking care of them."

Rosa Lee had her response ready. "Mama, you're not taking care of them. *I'm* taking care of them. I take care of them all the time. Not only my children. I take care of my brothers and sisters. It's time for me to take my children and leave."

Rosa Lee was praying that this was as far as their conversation would go "because I was scared. She was ready to hit me because I was taking income from her."

Rosetta wanted to know more. Who helped her? How did she know where to send the application?

"I got somebody to help me! You wouldn't help me!" Rosa Lee retorted.

"Who are you talking to like that?" Rosetta said in the tone that Rosa Lee knew well.

"Mama," Rosa Lee pleaded, "you would not help me fill it out."

"How am I going to help you fill it out when I can't even read it myself?" Rosetta shouted.

Rosa Lee was stunned. She had assumed that her mother could read, and did not know that Ben helped Rosetta whenever there were any forms to fill out.

"Why didn't you tell me you couldn't read, Mama?" asked Rosa Lee.

"'Cause I thought it was none of your damn business!" Rosetta said.

It is a January morning and Rosa Lee is fretting over her telephone bill. She stares at the eight pages, trying to figure out how her bill could be $241 when her monthly service costs $15.38.

She thrusts the bill into my hands. "Read it for me, Mr. Dash," she says, her lower lip trembling as it always does when she's upset.

As we talk, Ronnie, Richard, and Ducky are in the living room. They are watching a movie on cable, which Rosa Lee had installed for them. Patty is asleep on the couch after an all-night crack cocaine binge. None of them is working at the moment, and no one is helping Rosa Lee to pay the sixty-four-dollar monthly rent, the electricity and phone bills, or the cable.

Rosa Lee has the only steady income. The legal part is the $437 a month she receives from the Supplemental Security Income program for the disabled poor; the government considers her disabled because her medical problems and lack of skills limit her job prospects.

Money never lasts long in the Cunningham household, so when the phone bill arrived in late December, Rosa Lee was frantic. The words on the first page—"Message Units" and "Federally Ordered Subscriber Line Charge"—meant nothing to her. The subsequent pages, each showing totals and subtotals, confused her even more. She couldn't check the numbers, much as her sharecropping grandparents could not check the landowner's math when he added up their share after each harvest.

She put the bill aside. Three days after Christmas, the phone company disconnected the line. When her disability check came after New Year's, Rosa Lee paid $140 and the service was restored. But with $101 unpaid, Rosa Lee is worried. Her worries grow when D.C. Cablevision threatens to cut off its service as well.

I'm not eager to get caught up in her personal affairs again. I suggest she call Alvin. She can trust him to take care of it.

"NO, NO, NO!" Rosa Lee screams at me, tears trickling down her face. "Alvin's going to be angry and fuss at me for letting these grown-ass children live off of me! No! You've got to help me! You've got to call the phone company. If I call them, I'll only get flustered, and they'll find out I can't read. These bills are kicking my butt, and I'm not getting any help to pay them. *Please? Please?*"

"Okay, okay, okay," I reply, my head pounding, "but they won't be able to hear me if you're crying."

I scan the bill, which shows a balance of $137 from November, and quickly notice several problems.

Someone has been making calls to 900 numbers that charge four dollars a minute for sexually explicit conversations. After checking with Rosa Lee, I ask the phone company to put a block on the line that will prevent any more calls to 900 numbers.

There also are thirty-eight calls to directory assistance, at a cost of $9.88. That makes sense: Only Richard reads well enough to use the printed phone book, so everyone else uses directory assistance to find phone numbers.

And there are 511 message units for local calls outside the District—to phone numbers in Maryland and Virginia. This is a mystery: Rosa Lee, who didn't realize that she had to pay extra for such calls, says she doesn't know who might be making so many calls.

As I get an explanation of the charges from the billing office, I look at Rosa Lee accusingly. The 511 message units were all calls to the *same* number in Prince George's County. This was on top of 340 calls made to the number in November. What is going on? I ask.

Rosa Lee looks both surprised and sheepish. She has been letting a young woman down the hall use the phone to call her boyfriend in Prince George's County. The woman's phone has been disconnected for several months. But Rosa Lee had no idea the woman has been making so many calls.

It doesn't make sense. Why would the woman call her boyfriend 511 times in one month, an average of seventeen calls a day? And how does she do it without Rosa Lee's knowledge?

The answer, it turns out, is drugs. Rosa Lee finally tells me the woman's boyfriend is a crack dealer, and the woman has been relaying orders for neighborhood teenagers who work for him. She makes most of the calls during the day, when Rosa Lee is out. One of Rosa Lee's children lets her in.

Rosa Lee is upset to learn the woman has taken advantage of her. But she is reluctant to cut off her use of the phone.

"What?" I say. "Why?"

"Sometimes I need some bread," Rosa Lee says. "Sometimes I need some sugar, or something . . . and I ask her to get it for me."

When Rosa Lee's arthritic knee is too painful for her to walk to the store, she would rather send her neighbor than one of her own children. "They spend my money on crack and don't come back with my change or my food," Rosa Lee says.

She gets up and begins nervously cleaning up her spotless bedroom, aimlessly opening the drawers in her bureau. Her bottom lip trembles, and tears begin to fall. I've been through this scene more times than I can count, so I get up to leave. "NO!" she shouts. "Don't leave! Stay with me a little while!"

She picks up the large brass crucifix that she keeps on top of her television, clasping it to her chest. "I need somebody to stand by me!" she says loudly, her voice reverberating off the walls. Her bedroom door is open. I know her children in the living room can hear every word. "I don't have nobody. I don't have nobody. I can't do it by myself."

For more than an hour, Rosa Lee continues her monologue, interrupted occasionally by a question from me. "I stick with my children. I try to do everything I can. I even give them my money, give them a place to live. I don't care what I do for 'em. It seems like they still walk over top of me."

I speak to her very softly, trying to get her to calm down again. "You don't have to shout."

She shouts again. "I WANT THEM TO HEAR IT!"

I finally get up to leave, telling Rosa Lee I'm exhausted. She says she understands and she won't wear me out like that again.

When I step into the living room, Richard is sitting in a chair watching television. He avoids eye contact with me. Patty is snoring on the couch. She's slept through all of Rosa Lee's shouting. I ask Richard where Ducky is. "Ducky left when Mama started crying," he replies. I walk back to the kitchen. Ronnie is in there cleaning it, although it is spotless.

—Excerpted from *Rosa Lee*, Basic Books, 1996

The Heiress and the Gaucho

She was the daughter of a Monaco billionaire. He was the son of an Argentine farmhand. They met in Virginia horse country and became passionate teammates on and off the polo field. Now she's been charged with his murder.

By Eddie Dean

I t was a bright September Sunday, a perfect afternoon for a friendly game of polo. A breeze gently ruffled the shiny tresses of thoroughbreds and trophy wives alike as a high-society crowd gathered on the grassy field at the Gone Away Farm, one of the pampered patches of green in western Montgomery County. The air was spiked by a musky blend of fresh dung and perfume—the unmistakable smell of money.

Clothes by Ralph Lauren, cars by Volvo and Cadillac, horses by a benevolent creator and the world's top breeders. Polo is known as the sport of kings, and many here at least looked the part. Joe Muldoon

Jr., a lanky, gray-haired patrician in riding boots and white breeches, ambled about his place like Peale's portrait of Gen. Washington come to life. The 63-year-old head of the Potomac Polo Club was hosting the afternoon's marquee event, a charity match that pitted his U.S. team against Argentina. Despite the ideal weather, an unforeseen cloud threatened the proceedings: The match was scheduled to begin shortly, and one of the Argentine players, Roberto Villegas, still hadn't shown up.

It wasn't like Villegas to be late for a polo match. A dedicated and dependable polo professional, the 38-year-old veteran usually spent hours before an event preparing his ponies. Unlike many pros, Villegas often served as his own groom and reveled in the gritty work. Muldoon assumed that Villegas's trailer had broken down on the drive up from Warrenton, about two hours south in Virginia horse country. Just the day before, Muldoon had played in another charity event with him in Pittsburgh, and Villegas had vowed to attend the match at Muldoon's farm.

This wasn't just another polo exhibition to Villegas but a matter of patriotism and pride; the event marked the end of a nasty international stalemate over food imports. After nearly seven decades, restrictions on Argentine meat were finally being lifted. To celebrate, the Argentine embassy had brought to the farm the first official shipment of prized beef. Now, more than 300 pounds of pampas-raised tenderloins—as thick around as logs—smoked on an arsenal of grills outside Muldoon's mansion on the other side of the ridge. This carnivore's feast was the main attraction of the asado, or Argentine barbecue, to follow the match.

No expense was spared at the "Taste of Argentina," as the event was billed. There were 1,000 bottles of fine Mendoza wine, and a storied tango troupe had been brought in from New York. The crowd was filled with Argentine big shots, many of whom had jetted up from Buenos Aires for the big day. The new ambassador to the U.S., Diego Guelar, a dapper gent who sported a carved walking cane, was among the many shiny dignitaries.

For Villegas, the event was a long way from home, and not just in miles. He had grown up in a village in the boondocks of Argentina;

the son of a farmhand, he had begun his career as a stable boy on a neighboring ranch. In his teens, he had accompanied an Argentine polo star to the U.S. to work as a groom. After almost two decades on the circuit, he had become one of the most respected club polo players in the country. Beyond bringing together his two loves, polo and asados, the match would mark his arrival: The former farm boy breaking bread with the ambassador himself. What would the gauchos back in the provinces say?

"It was something that Roberto wanted to do desperately," Muldoon says later. "It would have been a great honor for him to play before the ambassador and all his countrymen, especially considering his poor background."

Muldoon checked the phone messages at his house. Still no word from Villegas. Fortunately, the club was able to find a last-minute replacement. After the match, as the asado began under the canopy of trees in Muldoon's yard, the bad news arrived in a murmured whisper: The reason Villegas couldn't make it was he was dead.

That morning, his patron and girlfriend, Susan Cummings, had shot Villegas four times in the throat and chest; authorities found him lying in a pool of blood in the small kitchen of Cummings' 18th-century mansion outside Warrenton. Nearby, on the hallway floor, was a Walther semiautomatic pistol, one of the best-selling guns from InterArms, the weapons business owned by her billionaire father, Sam Cummings. The 35-year-old heiress says she was defending herself from a knife-wielding Villegas. She claims she wanted to end a two-year relationship that mixed business and pleasure, and he wouldn't take no for an answer. Friends of Villegas prefer another version: A jealous, possessive Cummings tried to prevent him from leaving her.

At the asado, news of the slaying was kept quiet in order not to disturb the festivities.

The tango show went on as scheduled; as darkness fell, torches were lit among the tables. The dancers whirled and stomped to the slashing bandoneón and the crowd's delighted applause. At the end of every number, punctuated by bitterly danced recriminations, the couple always reconciled in a swooning embrace.

A month later, many in attendance that afternoon can't shake the sadness brought by the violent death of Villegas, who was regarded as a local hero in Washington polo's tightknit scene.

An aspiring amateur, Fabian Koss is a weekend warrior who started playing polo just a few years ago. A native of Buenos Aires, he works at the Inter-American Development Bank in Washington; he is keenly aware of the uphill struggle Villegas faced in one of the world's most elite pastimes, typically handed down from generation to generation. "Roberto wasn't born into a wealthy polo family," says Koss in his downtown office. "He came from the provinces, from a very humble background, and he pulled himself up by his bootstraps. He was a self-made guy, and that was the beauty of it. He made it."

Indeed, many confirm that, in spite of his background, Villegas moved with grace in the wealthiest of social circles—the word "gentleman" is used often. Those who fund the sport, known as "patrons" in the polo world, include the world's richest man, the Sultan of Brunei, and former Villegas patrons include Australian tycoon Tim Gannon, founder of the Outback Steakhouse chain. A charismatic man, Villegas was known for his quick smile, a Cheshire Cat grin that lit up his dark, rugged face.

From young grooms in barn jeans to businessmen in tailored suits, the entire polo community packed St. Stevens Catholic Church in ritzy Middleburg for Villegas' funeral service. William Ylvisaker, founder of the Palm Beach Polo Club and another former patron, gave the official eulogy ("He loved the sport of polo and everybody loved him"). Later, at a local funeral home, there was an open-casket viewing, as is the Spanish custom. All afternoon long, mourners filed silently past Villegas' body, which was dressed in a polo uniform over a turtleneck sweater that covered the gunshot wounds. On the foot of the flower-strewn coffin rested an arrangement of crossed polo mallets next to a ball signed by his teammates: the fallen horseman, armed and ready for his final match.

The memorial service wouldn't have been possible without the aid of Villegas' friends and countrymen. He was rich in compañeros and little else. In a sport in which top pros earn six-figure salaries, he was a journeyman player and just got by living day to day. Villegas' widowed mother and his sister couldn't afford to have his body flown back home, so the Argentine embassy footed the bill, and a fund was established to pay for his burial in his hometown of Chaja in the province of Cordoba.

Susan Cummings was not part of the public outpouring of grief that enshrouded horse country. Authorities charged her with first-degree murder and held her on a $75,000 bond. At a hearing at Fauquier County courthouse in Warrenton, several locals spoke on her behalf, describing her as a gentle, trustworthy person. With the help of a local businessman, she posted $2,500 bail, surrendered her passport and weapons, and pledged her extensive real estate holdings as collateral. After a night in jail, she was free to await the pretrial hearing at her 350-acre farm, where she lives with her twin sister Diana.

In Argentina, newspapers had a field day, blaring such headlines as, "Polo player's slayer paid her bond and is free." The implication was obvious: If Villegas had shot Cummings, he'd be behind bars and probably facing the death penalty, while the rich American was getting away with murder—at least for now. Likewise, the U.S. media jumped on the case, from *Time* ("Murder in Pololand") and *Newsweek* to *Inside Edition* and *People* ("Death of the Hired Man") to the supermarket tabloids. It's one of the oldest traditions of a free press: There's nothing more deliciously scandalous than the sins of the rich. A local woman watching the frenzy at the courthouse summed it up: "There wouldn't be all this fuss if her daddy didn't have all that money."

Indeed. There was another shooting shortly before the Villegas slaying that's more typical of local homicides: A man gunned down a dude nicknamed Gator outside a country store; they were squabbling over a $50 debt. The incident, which had begun as a tussle in the bed of a pickup truck, rated only the obligatory mention in the local papers.

That sort of pedestrian gunplay pales next to the polo killing, which recalls the '76 slaying of ski star Spider Sabich by French actress Claudine Longet, who was exonerated. And whatever the Cummings-Villegas incident lacks in the celebrity quotient, it makes up for on the irony meter: The daughter of the world's largest small-arms dealer—expertly wielding a James Bond-style handgun, no less—kills her polo-player lover, an Argentine charmer who allegedly threatened her life. Her friends say the shy, reserved Cummings is an animal lover who wouldn't swat a fly; his recall a good-natured, gregarious soul incapable of being rude, much less abusive. Add the hotshot lawyer who successfully defended Lorena Bobbitt. Now that's a story.

The Willow Run Polo School lies at the foot of a small mountain off U.S. 17 a few miles outside Warrenton. Through the lush pastures winds a creek hugged by the massive, graceful willow trees that give the farm its name. It's an almost absurdly picturesque scene, and it was in this storybook setting that Susan Cummings and Roberto Villegas met.

During the long days of summer, Willow Run bustles with activity, as novices flock to learn the game of polo. On this fall afternoon, though, the place is quiet, and the setting sun casts long shadows. It's the end of the polo season, and instructor Jean Marie Turon is preparing to head south for the fall and winter. A small, wiry man with a trim mustache, he's one of about three dozen Argentine pros whom the locals call "Argies." These nomads travel the East Coast circuit depending on the season, but most spend the summers in Virginia horse country.

A longtime friend of Turon's, Villegas often visited Willow Run, which doubles as a popular hangout for Argies. Though not an instructor, Villegas would lead practice matches with students, cook an asado, play cards, or just socialize. The asado pit under a corrugated roof is just a pile of ashes now, a sad reminder of good times past. In the distance, an Argentine groom walks a pair of ponies on their afternoon paces. Now the only excitement at Willow Run is provided by a large, dusky horse raising a ruckus in the stable. "Look at my new gray," says Turon proudly. "His mother is Argentinian and his father is an American. He has a lot of potential, but he's a mean son of a bitch—and that's what I like."

Like Villegas and many of the Argies, Turon has found a home in the U.S. He's been here for years, speaks English quite well, and makes a good living; he even married an American. In the summer of '95, a shy, slim woman came to Willow Run for lessons. She pronounced her name "Suzanne" in a thick European accent, and she had a reserved manner that bordered on the morbidly taciturn, her dour expression seemingly frozen in a gaze of puzzled concern: our lady of the perpetually raised eyebrows. From the very beginning, she had an interest in the game that was anything but casual, especially compared with the hordes of newcomers taking up polo in search of instant status.

Unlike those nouveau rich, Cummings was born into relatively old money, and she could be counted among the international jet-setters who retire to horse country to live quietly among their own. Indeed, the area boasts so many big-money sorts that millionaires are a dime a dozen. It is the billionaires who own the really lavish spreads here, family dynasties like the Mellons, the Curriers, and, of course, the Kent Cookes.

In many ways, Cummings is as much—or more—of a foreigner in the U.S. than Villegas was. Born in Monaco in 1962, she is one of fraternal twin daughters of billionaire Sam Cummings and his Swiss wife, Irmgard Blaettler. Sam Cummings' firm, Interarms, was founded in 1953 and was for decades the world's leader in the small-arms trade. According to Patrick Brogan's 1982 biography, *Deadly Business*, the Philadelphia-born, Washington, D.C.-bred Cummings "has sold more guns in the past 30 years than any other private individual in history." The former CIA agent has equipped citizens and armies, dictators and rebels, wars and revolutions all over the globe, often supplying opposing sides in the same conflict: "It's based on human folly," he said of the arms business in a 1996 interview. "And the depths of human folly have never been plumbed."

Cummings launched the company in Alexandria, where an Interarms warehouse still sits in Old Town on the banks of the Potomac. Interarms flourished during the Cold War, and today the $100-million-a-year company is based in Manchester, England; Cummings is a British subject and has lived for decades in the tax haven of Monaco.

Susan and her twin sister Diana (pronounced Dee-Ana) were

schooled in France and were raised in the ultrararefied world of Monte Carlo, but theirs was a sheltered upbringing away from the casinos and nightclubs. In *Deadly Business*, Brogan presents Cummings as a devoted family man—doesn't smoke, drink, or gamble—who just happens to be the world's wealthiest weapons tycoon: "There is nothing of the merchant of death about him . . . . He spends the spring and autumn in Monte Carlo, when it is at its sleepiest and most provincial. In the high summer he and his wife are in Villars, a mountain resort in the canton of Vaud high in the Swiss Alps, where children are sent out of their parents' way to enjoy the clean air and unrelenting dullness of the Swiss . . . . His routine is somewhat changed by his daughters, who may insist on spending the summer in Monte Carlo instead of boring Villars, and drag their reluctant parents down the mountain into the cosmopolitan humidity of the Riviera."

When they were 9, Susan and Diana gained dual citizenship (American and British), and Susan eventually attended Mount Vernon College in Washington, where she earned a B.A. in arts and humanities. In recent interviews, Susan has said her "real interest was caring for animals." Like many a young girl she was fond of horses, and in different circumstances she might have become a veterinarian. But she was the daughter of Sam Cummings, so there was no pressing need to pursue a career. If it was country life she craved, all she had to do was ask.

In the early '70s, Cummings bought a factory at an abandoned airport near Midland in southern Fauquier County. He chose the site not because of its "snob appeal," writes Brogan, but "because it was cheap, convenient, and there are no unions in the South." The factory opened in 1976 and was soon cranking out some 25,000 guns a year.

On his frequent trips to the Midland factory, Cummings fell for the scenic hunt country, and he apparently decided to find a place suitable for his daughters to indulge their passion for rural pleasures. In '84, he purchased the historic Ashland Farm, a 350-acre estate on U.S. 211 between Warrenton and the Blue Ridge Mountains. The main house is a faded stone mansion built in the late 18th century;

it was used by Union troops during the Civil War. For the past 13 years, the sisters have lived on the property, though not exactly together. Through whatever agreement exists between them, Susan stays in the main house, and Diana resides in one of the estate's guest cottages. Sam Cummings and his wife were frequent visitors at the farm until recent years, when his health began to fail. (The 70-year-old is seriously ill in Switzerland and reportedly has not been told of his daughter's predicament.)

During their residence at Ashland Farm, the Cummings sisters have gained a reputation as, if not full-scale recluses, then certainly as quiet, unassuming members of the wealthy gentry. They have no servants, employing only a few hired hands to help with the horses and cattle on the farm. They work in jeans and boots, and compared with flamboyant high-society butterflies like Marlena Cooke, a former neighbor down the road, the Cummings twins are homebodies.

Even so, Diana is more outgoing and social, while Susan is aloof and reserved. Besides their differences in temperament, the twins share little physical resemblance. "They look different, but they both have a great elegance about them," says an acquaintance. "They're quite striking."

Despite their differences, the sisters found a common love in horses. On her arrest warrant, Susan gave her occupation as "horse-woman," which around these parts can be a calling as much as a career. Out here, where farms boast names like Houyhnhnm Acres (for the talking horses in *Gulliver's Travels*), it's sometimes unclear who the real masters are, as indulged as some of these thoroughbreds often are. Certainly, the collective obsession for horses makes for a great social equalizer, where heiresses like the Cummings nonchalantly work side by side with hired help.

"When you are passionate about horses, it's easy to cross those boundaries," says a local who boards her horses at Ashland Farm. "The people that are really snobby we kind of laugh at, because they're the people who've just moved out from McLean and they don't get it. They don't get the whole horse thing. It's like having a child. Maybe you can afford five nannies, but maybe you don't want

five nannies. Maybe you want to take care of the horses yourself."
The comparison of horses to children is more than apt; Susan has
been known to bottle-feed animals.

Local businessman John Pennington has known the Cummings
sisters since they first moved to Ashland Farm; he was leasing part
of the property when they arrived, accompanied by their own live-in
governess. He has seen the sisters mature into self-sufficient, unpre-
tentious women. "Both have a lot of dignity, but they don't dress up
and they don't spend a lot of money on clothes," he says. "They're just
a couple of farm girls, and I think that's what Sam had envisioned
for them—a very simple, down-to-earth life, away from Monte Carlo
and all that."

For years, Susan limited her equestrian activities to "hunter
pairs," a cross-country event that trains horses for fox hunting.
Diana competes mostly in jumpers and other show-horse competitions. Local resident Louisa Woodville boards her horse at Ashland
and often rides with Susan at the farm and at charity events; they
have been friends for nearly a decade. "She's a lovely, gentle person,"
says Woodville. "I would say she's a little bit shy, but I find her to
be very warm and kind—she'd do anything for you. She's gracious
and compassionate, and she wouldn't hurt a flea. She really loves
animals." A neighbor says that when the sisters had to get rid of
some pesky groundhogs, they hired a firm that trapped the vermin
humanely and set them free elsewhere.

In the summer of '95, Susan discovered a new pursuit that
would disrupt her routines and expose her to an entirely new social
milieu. "When she started doing polo, I didn't see her as much," says
Woodville. "Because I'm not interested in polo."

Cummings undertook her new venture with the utmost seriousness, a devotion that was not lost on her polo instructor. "She was
coming almost every day to ride," recalls Turon. "I have different
groups, and she was jumping into any group. She was kind of
following me around, so some of the people joked about it."

It's not uncommon for students to have crushes on their riding
teachers, and Turon says he brushed it off as no big deal. He had
enough problems just trying to converse with his new pupil. Her

emotionless, icy exterior unnerved the laid-back Turon, who was more accustomed to the boisterousness of his fellow Argies. "Susan has a weird personality," he says. "She doesn't really show any feelings. You don't know if she's happy or sad. She's just there." She was a decent rider, Turon says, but like most beginners showed little of the athletic skill it takes to whack a tiny white ball while riding at full gallop.

According to Turon, Cummings soon turned her attention to a Mexican groom, but a steady relationship never developed. She forged on with her polo lessons, hooked by a sport that some devotees compare to drug addiction.

But Cummings apparently didn't want to remain just another bumbling beginner or Willow Run groupie. According to Argentine pro Rodrigo Salinas, Cummings told a female novice that taking classes wasn't enough: If you want to become a good polo player, she advised, you have to date a professional. Everyone knows the best players around are the Argies, and the most charismatic, friendly Argie was Roberto Villegas, star of the local polo scene.

"She wanted to get into the polo world," says Koss. "And what better way to get into the polo world than to buy herself a polo pro?"

It wasn't long before Cummings and Villegas were a couple, on the field and off.

A week after Villegas' death, the Great Meadow Equestrian Center in The Plains is packed with spectators. Every Friday night, the club hosts twilight polo, and this is the final match of the season, a charity fundraiser known as the Last Divot. It is also a memorial of sorts to Villegas, who as much as anybody made the weekly ritual so popular.

This event features arena polo, a faster, higher-scoring game than traditional open-field polo. Despite its name, arena polo is an outdoor event held in a circular paddock much smaller than the playing area in field polo. There are three players per team instead of four, and each game has fewer chukkers, or periods. Because it requires fewer ponies, arena polo is less expensive and more accessible to newcomers who don't have a million bucks to blow.

For the last several years, Villegas was an undisputed star of the twilight matches, thrilling fans with his flamboyant, aggressive horsemanship and flashy scoring. The last two summers, he played here nearly every week, either for Cummings' Ashland Farm team, which included Susan, or the host club, Great Meadow. According to club president Richard Varge, Villegas was the major attraction that pulled in the crowds. "Everyone wanted to watch him play because he was such an exciting, outstanding athlete. He was extremely quick on the horse, always making spectacular plays. But he was also a great sportsman and a gentleman. He never discriminated against lower-level players. He was their mentor," says Varge.

Villegas helped revive a sport that had fallen out of favor. In Washington, arena polo has its roots in the Potomac, Md. area, where it enjoyed immense popularity from the late '50s into the '80s. "It was the largest outdoor cocktail party in the Washington area, every Friday night all summer long," says Joe Muldoon.

Led by Villegas, the arena matches at Great Meadow made polo a hot sport again in horse country, and the twilight events are the pinnacle of horsy hip. Groups of young professionals hold tailgate parties just outside the paddock walls. Many have struck it rich in the computer industry, and they smoke their overpriced, trendy cigars and try to emulate some half-baked fantasy of the country life. Meanwhile, packs of young women known as polo groupies (or polo sluts, depending on whom you talk to), clomp through the grass in high heels and miniskirts eager to meet a player or patron.

A local winery has set up tables tonight to fete the weekly singles crowd. For most, the cocktail chatter under the stars proves far more enticing than the action in the arena; the majority pay attention only during an awkward moment of silence in Villegas' honor. Not that they're missing much, at least tonight. According to a player in the audience, the match is desultory and barely resembles competitive polo. The reason is simple: Villegas wasn't there.

"You can't have decent polo without Robertos," says Muldoon. "At this low-level [club] polo, if you put four businessmen against four businessmen, it's like killing snakes. Nothing happens. All you need is players of Roberto's ability and two sponsors on each team, and then you get something happening. Then the game moves."

It's not as if Villegas was the best ever to pick up a mallet; he was simply impressive in context. Just as the top golfers travel on the PGA tour and the rest work at local clubs, Villegas was a solid, low-level pro who never reached the international stardom attained by some Argies. His four-goal handicap, while high at a club like Great Meadow, isn't much next to the eight-, nine-, and ten-goal champions who rule hallowed venues like Campo Argentino de Polo in Buenos Aires, where the best polo in the world is played.

By most accounts, Villegas was happy with his lot as a journeyman pro, living the nomad's life and sharing the field with a succession of patrons. "Roberto always seemed to be on the endless trail, but he always enjoyed himself, and he enjoyed life, and people enjoyed him," says Bill Fallon, a former sponsor who played on a national championship club team with Villegas in '90. "The guy could ride absolutely anything, whether it was green, broke, or made. He was just an incredible horseman. He'd been riding horses all his life. He thought like a horse."

Villegas had come a long way from a dusty farm in rural Argentina. "He was from the fuckin' ass of the world," says a fellow Argie. "So he was happy just to have a nice roof over his head. In his kind of polo, if you're a three- or four-goal player, you're gonna have a good life, eat a lot of asados, have fun doing what you like— but you're not gonna get rich." To make the top ranks of polo is a tricky business, and it depends as much on riding better and better ponies as it does on your ability with a mallet. Friends and former teammates say that Villegas was satisfied to remain at the club level, playing a sport that sponsors spend their vast fortunes to make possible. In the '80s, he worked his way up the polo ladder, mostly based in Sarasota, Fla. By the early '90s, he was playing for top clubs in Virginia, including Ylvisaker's Middleburg team, Cotswold Farm, and Fallon's Rappahannock Club.

But the years on the circuit took their toll, and Villegas told friends he was ready to settle down, for a while at least. He accepted Cummings' offer to become resident pro on her new Ashland Farm team; though he apparently received no salary, she paid the upkeep on his ponies, covered his expenses, and gave him a place to stay. In

Cummings, the longtime bachelor found a patron and a love, both of which he'd had more than his share. ("Roberto loved to party every day," says one Argie.) She in turn had found her polo pro, and soon she found herself thrust into a scene beyond her country estate.

"Roberto was really her entree," says Peter Arundel, founder of Great Meadow Polo Club. "He gave her a lot more social activity than she had ever had. They held hands everywhere, and in social circles they stood arm in arm, wrapped around each other. He was always very gregarious and had a great sense of humor, and she was always very reserved and remote."

If they seemed an odd couple—the billionaire's daughter and the farmhand's son—friends say they complemented each other quite well. "She's European, so she was more suited to him than if she'd been an heiress who grew up here," says a local woman. "She wasn't the typical girl from here who'd gone to Foxcroft or National Cathedral and had her debutante ball in Washington. Somebody like that might have been more inclined to turn up their nose at a professional horseman."

For his part, the extroverted Villegas helped her come out of her shell, however tentatively, while she seemed to assert a calming influence on the former playboy. Though not a smoker and no longer a drinker, Villegas was still an inveterate partygoer, and years of asados had given him a middle-age paunch. After embarking on a diet recommended by the health-conscious Cummings, he slimmed down.

After six months of dating, they were a tight couple. In the winter of '95, Villegas went to Florida for the polo season, and Cummings visited him. During the next summer, they played together again on the Ashland team and apparently lived together on the farm as well. "They were inseparable," says Varge. "Wherever you saw Roberto you saw Susan, and vice versa. They did everything together. They didn't have a groom; they did it themselves, and she was very fastidious about the care of the horses. We used to kid Roberto all the time that he was already married—it was like husband and wife."

Certainly, they were getting more serious about their relationship. Last winter, Villegas stayed in Virginia rather than head south with the other Argies. Even now, though, he was by no means a kept man, and apparently he enjoyed little charity from Cummings, whom some say is a notorious tightwad. He told his friends he was taking a break from polo, and he worked the cold months at an apple orchard called Sunnyside Farm in nearby Rappahannock County.

In the spring, Villegas took another step away from his former independence when he sold Cummings his truck, trailer, and string of horses—his sole worldly possessions. Some of his Argie pals claim he only made the deal to get plane money to attend his father's funeral in Argentina, because Cummings was too miserly to pay his airfare. Others say he was broke and more than glad to be rid of such an expensive responsibility. "I remember him telling me how much better he was going to play this year because the financial burden had been lifted and he was going to be able to focus on being a good player," recalls Arundel. "And he definitely was more confident and happy as a player."

The couple sometimes entertained friends at Ashland Farm. After a match, they would have an asado and a party. Some visitors were surprised to find the main house so under-furnished, as if only part of the place were being lived in and the rest was simply museum space. Turon recalls Cummings proudly showing guests her gun display, an entire room filled with weapons of all sorts, from ancient muskets to shiny handguns. It was a sort of mini-arsenal, courtesy of Interarms. Turon says that Villegas often bragged about what a sharpshooter Cummings was, and that he once joked that she had shot at him in the middle of the night when she had mistaken him for an intruder.

Cummings' fondness for guns is nothing special in hunt country, where many women carry pistols in their purses and keep shotguns in their houses. "It's not a weird thing to have a gun if you're a woman here," says a local horsewoman. "I have a lot of friends who carry guns. But if you're a woman and you get a gun, the thinking is, make sure you know how to use it."

As the summer polo season began, Villegas and Cummings seemed the happy, smiling darlings of the twilight polo matches. Villegas often mentioned to friends that they were talking about marriage.

But beneath the perfect picture of intercontinental romance, cracks were beginning to show.

Villegas had rented a room in a house on the edge of Warrenton. Though he still worked at Ashland Farm and played for the team, the new living arrangements signaled some sort of change in the relationship. Maybe Villegas felt he needed some breathing room; maybe the domestic life wasn't for him after all. Or maybe Cummings had kicked him out—at least, out of her bedroom in the big house. She may have grown tired of Roberto the boyfriend, even though she still needed Roberto the polo star.

There were other subtle changes. Some recall that the couple were often absent from the post-match cocktail circuit. Rodrigo Salinas noticed it was Cummings who now drove the truck to polo matches; before, Villegas had always been behind the wheel. To Salinas, this was her way of making it clear to Villegas that she was the boss—still a rarity in polo, the most male-dominated of all horse sports. "She controlled the money, the horses, everything," Salinas says. "She had the power."

Cummings' attorney Blair Howard dismisses such talk, saying it was Villegas who controlled the relationship, albeit behind the scenes. In an interview shortly after the shooting, Howard says Villegas had a dark side that he showed only to Cummings. "Everybody thought that O.J. Simpson was the most charming man, that he was mild-mannered and always smiling," he says. According to Howard, his client was trying in vain to end the romance. "It's like every other relationship in the world, whether you're a princess and heir to the throne or not," he says. "Relationships go bad, and people go their separate ways." Despite Cummings' efforts, Villegas allegedly had his own plans, says Howard: "There was a psychological dominance, or at least an attempt to psychologically dominate and control her with threats of violence."

At least one former girlfriend, Kelli Quinn, says she saw no semblance of an abusive person in Villegas. During their four-year relationship in the early '90s, the couple traveled the East Coast circuit; she helped take care of the ponies while Villegas played in polo matches. It was not an easy life, but Quinn recalls it with fondness. "He was a nice person, and he was good to me," she says. "We were together pretty much all the time. It wasn't a perfect relationship, and sometimes we argued like normal people do." Quinn dismisses Cummings' allegations of a domineering Villegas as so much hogwash.

Likewise, friends and acquaintances say that Villegas was the same good-natured person off the field he was on: the perfect gentleman. "Polo is a sport that brings out the best and worst in people, because it's so physical," says Muldoon, who competed against Villegas in countless matches. "Gen. Patton said it was the best training for war outside of war. It's the kind of thing where if you're going to lose your temper, that's the place to do it, but Roberto never did."

Locals who aren't part of the polo community have a less sympathetic view of Villegas and his fellow Argies. One deems them a "band of gypsies who invade Fauquier County" every summer to score—in polo and in romance. To them, the Argies fit the stereotype of Latin lady-killers who prey on smitten Southern belles. "A lot of them are lacking morals to the worst degree," says a long-time resident. "I know some of them have wives, but they also date other women while they're here."

Villegas was by no means refined. "He had a [peculiar] sense of humor," says Alex Roldan, an Argie who knew Villegas for years. Roldan compares Villegas to a cowboy whose idea of a joke is watching someone fall off a horse—slapstick, definitely not cerebral stuff. "Maybe a joke in Texas would be considered rough in New York," he says.

But attorney Howard maintains that Villegas was all too serious, and that Cummings grew fearful of her boyfriend. On Aug. 20, she went to the Fauquier County Sheriff's Department to get a restraining order against Villegas. In a two-page statement, Cummings detailed the alleged threats in her neat, schoolgirl's cursive handwriting: "Within the last six months, he has begun to show signs of aggression toward me with threats to kill me. His words are: 'I will put a bullet through your head and hang you upside down to let the blood pour on your bed.' This is only one example of such strong destructive language. Drowning me was also mentioned several times and it seems this is becoming a daily discussion. These various threats always follow after a very minor disagreement on my part. For example, I will say I do not have time for you today, Roberto, I have a lot of work to do. He always reacts negatively to my demands or personal duties. He is overpowering, short-fused, nontolerant, changes his moods quickly and admits that [he] is the 'crazy type.'

"He insists on marrying me and wants two children because he says, 'The world needs more people such as himself to teach everybody a lesson' (what lesson I do not know). His words are also, 'I will show you and all these little rednecks over here what a real man is. I will teach them who is the boss and after you go, Susan, I will kill a few cops and the rednecks before I put a bullet in my head . . .'

"Roberto Cerillio Villegas, as far as I know, is struck with a mental condition, one that can be very dangerous for the people surrounding him at a critical moment. I have offered to let him go, not to be involved with me anymore, I have tried to be his friend and understand him. He refuses to let go. The game of polo is what associated us."

Villegas' friends say these angry declarations (and use of terms like 'rednecks') sound nothing like the man they knew, while supporters of Cummings say the words ring all too true, especially concerning Villegas' allegedly one-sided interest in marriage. "I have never heard Susan or Diana speak of that relationship being that serious as far as them talking about marriage," says John Pennington. "Normally, you hear a lot more from the girls than the guys when it comes to getting married." Nuptials are not something to be taken lightly by heiresses of a billionaire. "Marriage for either one of those girls is a very complicated thing," says Pennington. "It's almost a business proposition as well as a romantic one, because of their assets."

A sergeant from the sheriff's office told Cummings to file a complaint with a magistrate and post "no trespassing" signs at her farm. She refused, and friends say they're not surprised. Both the sisters were known for their self-reliance and downright stubbornness in refusing to ask for help. One neighbor recalls that during a blizzard one winter the sisters were snowed in for days before they asked ("almost apologetically") for help plowing a path to the barn so they could get feed for their animals.

Instead of seeing a magistrate, Cummings scheduled another appointment with the sergeant for Sept. 8, the day after the shooting. Even though Cummings felt frightened enough to go to the authorities, she apparently never tried to simply fire Villegas (instead of "offering to let him go") and bar him from her property. After all, she was his employer, and firing him could have perhaps made a restraining order unnecessary.

Nonetheless, despite the apparent internal friction, the couple continued to attend polo matches, and the rare social function, as hand-holding lovebirds. Still, there were occasional lapses of decorum, as when Villegas was spotted with a date at some local watering holes, Mosby's and Fiddlers, a week before the shooting. "I went up and gave him some shit," says a friend of the couple. "I said, 'Ohhhh, Roberto, where's Susan?' And he basically just gave me a smug little grin and didn't say anything." People were starting to talk, and it became prime gossip that the Argie was playing the field once again. A question still hangs: Did Cummings know or care about his alleged extracurricular activities?

A few days before the killing, Villegas stopped by Willow Run for an evening visit. He, Turon, and two other Argies played some truco, an Argentine card game similar to poker. According to Turon, Villegas spoke enthusiastically about various plans that he and Cummings were busy making together: looking at some land in Montana, building a polo field on the bigger, more level Cummings property known as LeBaron Farm, still discussing the possibility of marriage.

Villegas' visit wasn't just a social one, though. He wanted Turon to accompany him to the exhibition match up at Muldoon's club that Sunday. Turon had already told him he probably wouldn't be able to fit it into his schedule. Villegas made a convincing argument, though, especially when he reminded him about the asado after the match. No self-respecting Argie could pass up an asado, especially this one, with beef from the home country. Turon promised he would try to make it, and Villegas told him he would stop to pick him up on the way to Muldoon's.

What he didn't tell Turon was that Cummings wasn't pleased about Villegas' plan to attend the Sunday match and that she had no intention of letting him take the ponies there. One of the main points of conflict between them concerned the treatment of the horses. Cummings cherished them as pets to be pampered and indulged, while Villegas considered them work animals whose purpose was polo, plain and simple. "Roberto was a real gaucho, like our cowboys out West," says polo patron Jack Whittemore. "He was a tough player and he was hard on the horses, because that's the way they handle them in Argentina."

There were other problems: Villegas was also scheduled to play in another charity match that Saturday in Pittsburgh, and Cummings had tried to bail out of that as well. But the sponsor told her it was too late to find a replacement for a four-goal player like Villegas, so she reluctantly agreed to attend. Her lawyer Howard says that this trip was not a sign that she was still interested in him romantically, merely a byproduct of Cummings' desire to fulfill a social commitment.

They eventually made it to the Pittsburgh event, but tensions were high. Muldoon, who helped organize the charity match, says the couple stayed in separate motel rooms. But others saw them holding hands during the event, just like old times. Before everyone headed home, Muldoon offered to put the couple and their ponies up for the night at his place, but Villegas politely declined, assuring him that he would see him the next day for the "Taste of Argentina."

At 8:51 a.m. the next morning, a Fauquier County dispatcher received a 911 call from Cummings. Speaking in a calm but hesitant manner, she told of a shooting at her house at Ashland Farm. "I need to report a shot man, and he's dead," she said softly in her thick French accent. She gave the victim's name, carefully spelling "Roberto Villegas," then blurted out, "He tried to kill me." "Did you shoot him?" asked the dispatcher. "I had a gun, yes," replied Cummings. The dispatcher repeated his question. "I need to talk to my lawyer," said Cummings.

The 12-minute tape was played in its entirety at a recent pretrial hearing at the Fauquier County courthouse. During the playback, Cummings sat silently at a table, facing a life-size oil portrait of Chief Justice and Warrenton native John Marshall, which hangs above the judge's seat. The century-old courthouse is a musty stone building that breathes history—Confederate hero John Mosby practiced law here after the war. Without bathrooms and lit by a quartet of chandeliers hanging from the ceiling, it has high windows and a gallery of rickety wooden pews that held more journalists covering the case than spectators.

For the better part of the morning, Cummings sat quietly and still, hands resting on her knees, in a row awaiting her hearing. She was dressed in tight black jeans, a black pullover, a cashmere sweater, and black tennis shoes—not so much casual as simply functional, as if she'd barely finished feeding the horses before catching a ride to court. In person, she appears thin and fragile but oddly alluring. She has a bony, classically attractive face and heavy-lidded eyes underneath flowing brunette curls, more like an anorexic Botticelli heroine than a murderer.

As the court docket dragged on—mostly baggy-trousered teens pleading guilty to marijuana possession—Cummings stared expressionless at the proceedings. Surrounding her in two pews were nearly a dozen supporters (among them her sister Diana), all of whom but one were women. During the wait, a pair on either side rubbed Cummings' back and thighs and stroked her hair, a mobile support group lending comfort. Meanwhile, only one friend of Villegas' attended the hearing, a former patron from Fairfax named Travis Worsham. He explained that the polo crowd had headed down to Aiken, S.C., for the fall season, but he simply had to be here. "Roberto was like a brother to me," Worsham said.

During a break, a *Vanity Fair* reporter conversed gaily in French with members of Cummings' entourage. Meanwhile, Cummings remained in her pew staring ahead as if she were preparing her final walk to the guillotine. In fact, she had little to fear, at least at this stage in the legal process. No pleas are entered in a preliminary hearing; the judge simply rules on whether there is enough evidence to send the case to a grand jury for possible indictment.

After the 911 tape finished playing, Howard went into high gear, eloquently arguing self-defense. Howard is one of the most dramatic and effective lawyers you'll ever see. In Manassas back in '94, he successfully defended Lorena Bobbitt, just one of many clients he has kept out of prison in his career. When you get into trouble in these parts, you call Howard. He lives in nearby Marshall, and he is an avid fox hunter.

The morning of the shooting, Howard was at the house in Ashland Farm less than an hour after the incident, a point he brought up repeatedly to Judge Charles Foley. When he arrived, he said, he saw raw, red slashes on Cummings' wrist, and he cited photos that showed "blood running down her arm."

The scenario presented by Howard is a clear-cut case of self-defense: In the kitchen of the stone mansion, Villegas was making good on all his threats, putting Cummings in mortal fear for her life. He attacked her repeatedly with a bone-handled knife he'd won at a polo match several years earlier. The weapon was found on the floor near his body. He was dressed in a work shirt and blue jeans, lying face down in a pool of blood. Howard maintained that only after she had fired four shots into his neck and chest with the Walther semiautomatic could she finally stop the raging bull.

Howard said the autopsy implied that the fourth and final bullet was the actual cause of death. "This man was advancing on her with a knife in her home on a Sunday morning, and she kept firing until he dropped," he bellowed. Then Howard invoked the memory of "our forefathers" and their hallowed "defense of the castle" law handed down from olden times. "We're not talking about the usual self-defense," he said, his voice echoing in the high-ceilinged chamber. "We're talking about something that happened in her home on a Sunday morning."

"The irresistible conclusion here is that she was being assaulted," Howard said in his final statement. "She was assaulted. She was cut. And in defense of her life, in her own home, she had a right to take this man's life. That's the law."

But the prosecutor presented a drastically different version of what happened that Sunday morning in the kitchen at Ashland Farm. Commonwealth's Attorney Kevin Casey said he had proof that Villegas was shot while he was seated at the table, not the most strategic position from which to assault Cummings with a knife. "This is our photograph of Mr. Villegas lying on the floor," said Casey. "It's a wider angle than the one offered by Mr. Howard. You will see Mr. Villegas' legs under the table and the chair, and you will also see on the chair itself blood. And the autopsy shows that Mr. Villegas was shot four times by Ms. Cummings while sitting at that table, not advancing on her."

In the commonwealth's version, Villegas is no wanton attacker but an unsuspecting house guest settling in for a morning cup of coffee—and getting blown away. As for the knife, it's a common enough tool for equestrian work, and all the Argies have one. Then there's the fact that Cummings pulled the trigger four times on a Walther, a powerful, double-action semiautomatic pistol. According to the prosecution, this wasn't self-defense but premeditated murder, with a couple of extra bullets added to make sure the job was done properly: "No. 1 [bullet] was chosen as the cause of death in the autopsy report," said Casey in his closing zinger. "The one that tore through Mr. Villegas' neck, tore out his carotid artery, struck his spine, and burrowed 10 inches down his back. That shows you the cause of death."

Foley praised both performances from counsel and then ruled that the case be turned over to the grand jury, scheduled to meet Nov. 24 in Fauquier Circuit Court. Howard seemed pleased and even buoyant, as if he'd already won. Outside the courthouse, he held court for a throng of reporters, as Cummings was whisked away in a waiting car.

"You haven't seen anything yet," said Howard. "That was their evidence we were looking at today. Wait until you see what we've got."

Shortly after the hearing, on a bluff near the edge of town that faces the Blue Ridge, an old woman kneels in the dirt and digs in her front yard garden, planting her fall crocuses before it gets too cold.

A tiny, sprightly lady, she is the landlady who rented a room to Villegas during the final months of his life. She's perturbed when she finds out she missed the hearing this morning. A local paper erroneously reported that the court date had been postponed. She mutters that she'll be sure not to miss the trial, that's for sure.

"I was the last person to see him alive," she announces almost with pride, squinting in the midday glare.

The landlady says she knew Villegas quite well and had coffee with him every morning before he went to work at Ashland Farm. She was very fond of Villegas and deemed him a good, honest man. Otherwise, she wouldn't have rented him a room in her house in the first place. She's had many a boarder, so she knows how to size people up. Villegas was one of the best, she said, on time with the rent and good-natured to boot. He kept a photo of Cummings by the bed and spoke of her constantly.

Through conversations with Villegas, the landlady got to know Cummings intimately, and she even met her several times. "I liked both of them," she says. "But she lived in a fantasy world. Sometimes in the fantasy world and sometimes in the real world. She could do both, you see."

It's clear with whom her sympathies lie. She sounds like a mother describing how a beloved son got his heart broken by some lowdown, bewitching femme fatale. "She had him buffaloed," she says. "She took everything he had."

Then the landlady kneels to resume her digging: "I know everything, you see, but I'm not giving any information out for free. That costs money."

Jumping up nimbly from the ground, she darts inside her house and reappears in a flash, clutching a supermarket tabloid called the *Sun*. The garish cover screams "Kirstie Alley Diet—Lose 20 Pounds," but she goes straight to an article crowned by an all-caps headline— "BLUEBLOOD MURDER,"—featuring three paragraphs of her quotes. "They paid me $500," she says with satisfaction. "They pay in cash, you know, so much for each question. I'm 80 years old, and I deserve a little something."

Then she looks up to the blue autumn sky and shares one final, free-of-charge comment about her former tenant, Roberto Villegas. "I know that he is a star up in heaven," she says. "And he is looking down on her, trying to show her the way." Then the old woman clams up and goes back to her digging.

—*Washington City Paper* | October 31, 1997

He began his teaching stint with idealism. And ended it in jail.

A pupil points a finger. A teacher is fired, his life rerouted. Now can they be buddies?

By Marc Fisher

Mr. Kaplowitz doesn't teach here anymore. Nor does Mr. Ehrmann. Teachers are forever leaving this place: One says she'll never teach again; another says this wasn't teaching, it was guard duty; still another never really knew how rewarding his profession could be until he got out of here and into a different system. The principal is gone—demoted, transferred—another name remembered with a grumble and a shake of the head, one of five principals who passed through Emery Elementary School in two years, a roller coaster of raised and dashed hopes. One mom says things are getting much better, but immediately asks for advice on how to get her child out—now.

It's not that this building just off North Capitol Street in Northeast Washington is the worst of the D.C. public schools. After all, this is a system that sees superintendents drift in and out, each savior bringing a new way to reform schools that have disappointed parents for decades. Rebuild from the bottom, create shining examples at the top, attack one school at a time, change the funding system, bring in new blood, restrain existing staff, erect new buildings, focus on the children. Save all the slogans—the two big questions about the District schools remain unchanged: Why are they so bad? And can they be improved?

Mr. Kaplowitz and Mr. Ehrmann believed they could make a difference. They were young and idealistic, bred to think of themselves as the best and the brightest. If tired bureaucrats couldn't press change on failing inner-city public schools, well, then these 22-year-olds from fancy colleges would just have to do it themselves.

Josh Kaplowitz, fresh out of Yale, and Nick Ehrmann, just arrived from Northwestern, stepped into Emery Elementary that fall of 2000 armed with the heady mix of confidence, curiosity and caring that their mentors at Teach for America had instilled in them over a six-week summer training program. Conceived in the late 1980s by a Princeton undergraduate, Teach for America encourages bright young people to give two years of their lives to classrooms, mainly in tough inner-city schools that have long failed to educate their students.

Kaplowitz and Ehrmann thought they knew what they were getting into: The rowhouses surrounding Emery's dead-end street were home to families that had hardly any money, little education, only the slightest connection to the school, and all manner of dysfunction. At many D.C. schools, most children are poor enough to get free or subsidized meals; at Emery, 100 percent qualified. Every single child.

What could a few kids straight out of college accomplish here? Wouldn't they hit the same wall of defensiveness, resistance and suspicion that has turned countless reformers, volunteers, news reporters, grantmakers and officials into sputtering testimonials to the impossibility of change? Or had some switch flipped in

Washington? Was there reason to believe that the housing boom and the influx of affluent residents eager to claim the city as their own would finally force the District to remake its schools? The District's renaissance, if it were ever to spread beyond a few chic sections within range of a Fresh Fields, required the presence not only of young singles but also of families who would demand decent schools before they'd consider life in the big city.

Even around Emery, you could sense something new coming. Just around the corner, contractors' pickups double-parked outside the freshly rehabbed rowhouses of new residents, some of whom had just gotten jobs at the burgeoning enterprises a couple of blocks away, at XM Satellite Radio, FedEx and other offices coming in at Florida and New York avenues—site of a future Metro station. Change was in the air, and if the D.C. schools weren't exactly the vanguard of the revolution, there were at least some signs of "transformation," as the new superintendent, Paul Vance, liked to put it. He was busy attacking the worst schools, pulling out their principals, their entire staffs, starting over, determined to create early and visible successes.

But inside Emery, a sad, sagging 1960s-era building with fading aqua-and-cream tiling in the lobby and overgrown weeds and shards of glass around its exterior, there was no sign of transformation that fall. When I asked people to describe what the school was like, three teachers, two mothers and an administrator each separately chose the same words: "The inmates ran the asylum."

In his senior year at Yale, Josh Kaplowitz ran for president of the student government. If elected, he promised to start a campus "escort" service and moon administrators who objected to his proposals. His campaign posters featured the endorsement of an adult video shop. No one expected a serious platform from Kaplowitz, who had been an editor of the Rumpus, the campus humor magazine, and host of a college radio station show that got pulled off the air after Kaplowitz and his co-host regaled their audience with descriptions of female genitalia read from a porn magazine.

Kaplowitz was a campus prankster, but he was also an excellent student: a graduate of the Governor's School, a public magnet school in Richmond where he led his "Battle of the Brains" team to the finals of the National Academic Championship. Son of two doctors, he interned on Capitol Hill with Sens. Chuck Robb and Joy Rockefeller. "I knew I wanted to end up in D.C.," he says.

As graduation loomed, Kaplowitz turned down job offers from a high-paying management consulting firm and Al Gore's polling firm. "I didn't want to devote my life to helping the rich get richer or crunching numbers to see what views were most popular for the vice president to adopt," he wrote later.

Tall, thin, with ruddy cheeks and the same backpack he carried around in college, Kaplowitz drove to Emery for the first time in his parents' old Volvo, intent on winning over students and parents. He would visit his kids' families in their homes, take the kids on trips, wow Emery with his smarts and creativity.

"My intuition was that these kids weren't learning because they didn't have teachers who got them excited," he says.

Nick Ehrmann's path to Teach for America was similar. He grew up in a leafy section of Indianapolis, son of two psychologists. After studying history and American studies at Northwestern, Nick was smitten with Potomac Fever. He wanted to do social policy. Teaching in Washington would give him a front-row seat on government. Like Kaplowitz, he loved the idea of Teach for America, the notion of growing while giving back.

That summer, along with 900 other college grads, Kaplowitz and Ehrmann headed to the University of Houston for an intensive training program where they would teach summer school for two hours a day and study pedagogy, child development and cultural sensitivity. The last was an essential part of the Teach for America curriculum because despite strenuous efforts to recruit "people of color" to the program, TFA consisted largely of affluent whites teaching poor blacks and Hispanics. In Washington the year Kaplowitz and Ehrmann started teaching, 50 of Teach for America's 62 corps members were white.

"We want to attract the best and brightest to D.C., and Teach for America has some of the brightest minds in the country coming from the greatest universities," says Steve Seleznow, who was the District system's chief of staff until earlier this year. "These kids have helped us assure that we have quality teachers who want to be here." The District has 133 Teach for America members this year among 5,000 teachers.

Both Kaplowitz and Ehrmann thought about living in Emery's Northeast neighborhood, but apartments were hard to find. Kaplowitz moved into a group house in Arlington, while Ehrmann rented an apartment in Dupont Circle. But they were each determined to make Emery their real home.

Yo, listen close, this is wakeup time.

This is Mr. K's class and we're laying down some rhymes.

See, there's so much more to education

Than filling in bubbles for test preparation.

The rap Josh Kaplowitz wrote for his 25 fifth-graders went on for four more stanzas.

When he heard about plans for an October "Parents, Children, Schools" assembly, Kaplowitz volunteered his class to perform his rap. It was a chance to demonstrate how he would close the gap between his life of privilege and the stresses of the inner city.

Getting his class ready for the show wasn't easy. Kids didn't want to rehearse. They didn't learn the words, and Kaplowitz reluctantly realized he would have to join the children onstage. He cringed at the vision of the white teacher leading his black students in a rap before an almost entirely black audience. But he felt he had no choice.

So he stepped up, turned his cap backward and launched into his rap.

Without the parents, we can't have the kids.

Without the kids, we can't have the schools.

The three have got to work together.

Or, we'll all end up a bunch of fools.

What Kaplowitz recalls is the ovation his kids won from the audience of 400, and his first compliment from Lisa Savoy, his principal.

"I actually had kids from other classes come up to me and say they want to be in my class," Kaplowitz says. "And a lot of teachers seemed to start respecting me, this white kid from Yale up on stage rapping. This is what I imagined Teach for America would be like, bridging the cultural divide."

But that's not how the show was perceived elsewhere. "As much as these children liked to dance and play, they stood up there doing nothing," remembers Patricia Vest, a third-grade teacher now in her fourth year at Emery and nearing three decades in the city schools. "It was awkward."

Several black teachers talked about the assembly afterward. They had to credit Kaplowitz's gumption, but there was something off about the spectacle of the white boy rapping up there. No one could quite put their finger on it, but some teachers would look back on that moment later and say it was the first time they thought Josh Kaplowitz was headed for trouble.

From his first day at Emery, Kaplowitz could see that most of his fifth-graders were ready and eager to learn. He could also see that at least half a dozen children in his class were hellbent on having a wild time.

He was in over his head from Minute One. Children threw crumpled paper, wrestled on the floor, punched each other. They challenged Kaplowitz to his face: "I'm not doing it. What are you gonna do about it?"

"Other kids would see them get away with it, and it would all go downhill," Kaplowitz recalls. "I lost half the class at the beginning of each lesson. I lost the class the first week."

A couple of doors away, in Room 312, Nick Ehrmann was struggling to command the attention of his 28 fourth-graders. One boy cursed Ehrmann out every time he walked by. Kids threw things, shouted, fought, wandered around. One kid brought a pocketknife to school.

"Every day for three months, I thought, 'This is not working,'" Ehrmann says. "They curse at you, and, at first, I played the game. I would raise my voice, send them to the office. And they'd be bounced right back to me.

"Our school was bereft of a discipline system—period."

At the summer institute, Ehrmann and Kaplowitz had been taught a color code: All students start at green, then move to various shades of yellow and red as they commit infractions. Each color brings consequences: timeout, no recess, call parents, go to office.

Kaplowitz moved through the rainbow with zero success. "He had beautiful charts, and he'd move your sticker if you misbehaved—stuff that works in a lot of environments, but not here," says Earl Wallace, who spent two years teaching at Emery before leaving for the Prince George's County schools, where "it's like Mayberry compared to D.C."

Kaplowitz learned that he couldn't threaten loss of recess because there was no recess detention. Lisa Savoy, Emery's third principal in less than a year, told Kaplowitz to quit sending children to her office or neighboring classrooms.

When he asked what he should do instead, she told him to redirect the children's attention and give them something exciting to work on.

Savoy, now an administrator at Mamie D. Lee special education school, declined repeated requests to be interviewed for this article and referred questions to the school system's press office, which in turn sent me to Assistant Superintendent Bill Wilhoyte, who couldn't answer questions about Savoy's tenure at Emery because he's new to the system. Steve Seleznow, then the system's No. 2 official, says Savoy had to leave before the school could improve.

That first week, Savoy announced over the public-address system that corporal punishment would not be tolerated; teachers were not to strike or even touch students. Her message, part of a citywide crackdown, was the result of an epidemic of allegations against teachers at Emery and many other D.C. schools.

Kaplowitz and Ehrmann figured they hardly needed Savoy's warnings. After all, they'd been brought up in homes where striking a child was considered criminal. And Teach for America's training drove the message home: Discipline is about winning respect by showing respect; screaming, threatening and physical force were evidence of failure.

Most of Emery's veteran teachers believed that, too. But Savoy's announcement, they say, came across as a passing of authority from teachers to children.

"She made it clear that the children were in charge," says Wallace, who estimates he spent 80 percent of his classroom time trying to maintain order.

"It was a nightmare year," agrees teacher Patricia Vest. "The children knew they could do anything. I was breaking up fights constantly."

Ted McGinn, one of the school's few white parents, says the new teachers who arrived that fall "were basically set adrift . . . You had parents roaming the halls and threatening teachers. In front of the children, even during school, parents would berate the teachers, loudly."

Emery, says Seleznow, was "reaching the level of being in real serious trouble. Of 146 schools, it was in that top 10 of schools in real conflict."

With four Teach for America teachers starting out that fall, parents and teachers were abuzz. "There's so much resentment about having them to come into the schools," says Vest, who is black. "We were always a divided faculty. People would say the same things about the Teach for America kids that they used to say about us: 'They need to go back where they came from, they need to stick to their own.'"

Some moms told me that the young white teachers were being paid big money and otherwise had no desire to be there. (In fact, TFA teachers got standard D.C. starting salaries of $32,000 a year.) Others fixated on the body piercings or casual demeanor of the new teachers. But within a few weeks, the parent gossip calmed, except when it came to Mr. Kaplowitz. Word was that he was bad news.

One mother, who worked in the school as a teacher's aide, was so suspicious of Kaplowitz that she would often walk into his room to check on her child; if she didn't like what she saw, she would berate the teacher—even using racial invective—in front of his class. Their run-ins grew so heated that the police were summoned, and the woman was finally formally barred from entering Kaplowitz's classroom.

"Mr. Kaplowitz was in a group of the first white teachers to come to the school in many years," explains Wendy Walcott, a black parent who serves as president of Emery's Parent Teacher Association. "Before that, we had one white teacher who had been there so long, he and we forgot he was white. People saw these young Teach for America kids as whites, not as teachers. They assumed he was this white, Jewish, rich kid, and how dare he come here with some idea that our kids could actually be taught.

"This neighborhood is predominantly black. They see these young white teachers come in, and they think it has to do with the neighborhood being revitalized and all these different people coming in and housing prices going up. They put all that together, and they're scared. They would rather have the black teacher who refuses to teach their children than this white teacher who's trying so hard.

"Mr. Kaplowitz was totally inexperienced," Walcott continues, "and he thought he could conquer the world. But at least he wanted to push our children. I appreciated that, even if it was threatening to some of our parents."

Kaplowitz had no idea how to allay their fears. One Saturday, he decided to try to "connect" with parents who weren't returning his calls or showing up for meetings. He headed into the neighborhood, knocked on Angela Brown's door and said, "Hi, I'm [your daughter's] teacher and I thought I'd drop by and talk about how she's doing." He told the mother that her child had "real promise," that she "can be a little sassy, but if we can work together on that, we can have a great year."

The mother, stunned and embarrassed by the unannounced visit, went straight to school the next week and complained that Kaplowitz was harassing her. Kaplowitz was summoned to a conference with Savoy and the mother, where he was informed that the girl had told her mom that Mr. Kaplowitz had threatened to take out his belt and whip the class.

"My jaw dropped," Kaplowitz recalls. He had never said anything of the kind, he's certain. That was his last home visit.

Kaplowitz's extra efforts didn't always backfire. One boy dominated the class with his disruptive behavior and regularly threatened to kill himself. Kaplowitz decided he had to win over the child. One day, he took him aside and asked what he liked to do. "Football," the boy said.

After school, Kaplowitz invited the boy out to the field and tossed the ball around. Then he walked the boy home, bought him raisins at a corner store and asked him if they could start fresh in class the next day.

That next morning, the boy came in like a new person. He behaved, listened to the teacher, quit disrupting lessons. The effect was only temporary, but Kaplowitz believes he could have made real progress "if there had been only one or two kids like him. But there were so many."

In class, Kaplowitz tried to be true to Teach for America's goal of high standards and expectations. He tested his students regularly and found almost all of them to be at least one and often two grades behind in basic skills. So when the first grading period came to a close, he submitted failing grades for 20 of his 28 students. That is simply not done, and Kaplowitz knew it. "I knew they had been passed along and I was, like, well, the buck stops here," he says. "These kids are going to learn, and if they don't, I'll take them back next year—it's my responsibility."

Savoy, Kaplowitz recalls, "had a cow." She told him that her policy allowed a teacher to fail no more than 10 percent of a class. Change the grades, she ordered. When Kaplowitz refused, she cited him for insubordination.

"I [have] had enough of your rude outbursts and your haranguing obsession with failing your class at-large," Savoy wrote. "I directed you not to fail your class as a whole or in the majority."

By then, his relationship with Savoy had deteriorated into formal memos of allegation and defense.

She peppered Kaplowitz with "official written reprimands." There were citations for using bad language—two for "ass" (Kaplowitz says he shouted, "Hey, Nick, get your ass down here" while waiting to give Ehrmann a ride) and one for "crap." ("If I cursed in that class two times in a whole year, give me a medal," Kaplowitz says.)

"Although this word 'crap' is not profanity," Savoy wrote, "it is most inappropriate for you to use this vulgar slang in the . . . school environment."

When pencils were vanishing from his room, Kaplowitz, on the advice of his Teach for America friends, asked his students to pay five cents for each pencil. The idea was to "build ownership." It worked beautifully—until Savoy sent a memo ordering Kaplowitz to cease the sales, a violation of system policy.

Kaplowitz turned elsewhere for help. He approached veteran teachers at Emery, fellow rookies around the city and his TFA supervisors. Some of them concluded that Kaplowitz was inviting problems by being arrogant; they urged him to try some humble pie. Others offered specific strategies for managing his class.

Nothing worked.

Meanwhile, two doors away, Nick Ehrmann stood frustrated and disappointed before a room full of children with similar troubles and behaviors. But one of those maddening moments pushed Ehrmann to a breakthrough.

It happened when his students were supposed to order copies of the class photograph and only three brought in the fee. Something pivoted in Room 312. "I just decided they were missing out on documenting their childhood," Ehrmann says. So he brought in his own camera and started taking pictures of his students. Every week, he would show the results to the children, and soon, he was encouraging them to make their own pictures.

Ehrmann collected the results into photo essays about the children and their dreams and realities. (Eventually, there was even a Web site, www.project312.org, where 10-year-old Xavier set his sights on becoming a comedian, 12-year-old Porshia declared she wanted to be a nurse, and 12-year-old Travis rhapsodized about following in the footsteps of rapper Snoop Dogg. "Mr. Ehrmann calls it a 'lyrical poet,'" Travis wrote in his "Meet the Students" autobiography, "but I couldn't spell that without his help.")

The photography Ehrmann and his students made together became the foundation of a new trust, and the teacher rewarded the improving behavior with Saturday outings to Washington's monuments and museums, where the children would make more pictures, which Ehrmann would blow up and collect in portfolios that made the students and their parents proud.

Word began to get around the building about what was happening in Room 312. Kids still fought and shouted sometimes, but the matter was resolved inside the room, and if parents resented Mr. Ehrmann for being a presumptuous young outsider, or for being a rich white kid slumming in the ghetto, there was precious little talk of that by midyear. Instead, Room 312 was taking on that magical aura that classrooms get when something's clicking.

One day, when Seleznow was visiting Emery to deal with yet another of the school's troubles, he dropped in on Ehrmann's class. Seleznow knew almost immediately that he was in the presence of a natural.

He sat down with Ehrmann, heard the rookie teacher talk about how photography had turned around his class, and embraced Ehrmann's nascent dream of Project 312, an effort to raise enough money to guarantee his children a path to college. Ehrmann audaciously asked the big boss from downtown whether he could grease the way for Ehrmann to keep these same kids the next academic year—a virtually unheard-of notion in the District schools.

Seleznow pledged to make it happen, and with approval and admiration from the very top, Ehrmann was now golden.

In January, Savoy switched Kaplowitz out of his problematic fifth-grade class and gave him a more manageable second-grade section. The trade was an immediate disaster. Parents rebelled against being saddled with a teacher who had already failed elsewhere.

And the new class was no walk in the park: Six of the 18 children were special education students, in need of extra services because of emotional or learning problems. One girl routinely charged other students, fists flying, because her father had told her that was the best way to handle teasing. A big boy who had already been held back once and was headed toward another retention wandered the room hitting kids. Another boy spent his days hurling boogers and pencils at others.

One day soon after taking over his new class, Kaplowitz came upon a girl on the floor pounding away on a boy. "I said, This can't happen. So I pulled her off him. I walked her to the classroom across the hall, wrote her up and sent her to the office." Two days later, the girl's father approached Kaplowitz on the playground and accused him of tying his daughter's hands behind her back.

Officers from the private company that handles the school system's security came around to interview the teacher, parents, students and other witnesses. Kaplowitz spent three weeks on administrative leave before being cleared of the charges.

"The violence just got worse," Kaplowitz says. "I should have just quit, but I wanted to get through the year and be able to succeed. And in those few moments when I could really teach, I thought I was pretty good."

Some parents didn't see any evidence of that. Connie Barnes, whose son clashed repeatedly with Kaplowitz, is quick to concede that Emery was a madhouse, and that Kaplowitz had more than his share of tough kids, including her son, who was suspended for 27 days that year. Barnes blames the principal and the system for failing to assert control: "I discipline [my son] at home—no toys, no GameBoy, just sit at the table and do work. Why can't they do it at school?" But above all, she blames Kaplowitz: "I don't think he was fit to be a teacher. Every time I came in that room, the kids were getting all wild, yelling and throwing paper and stuff."

Barnes's son eventually complained that his teacher jacked him up against a wall, and his mother believed him. Again, Kaplowitz was cleared of the charge.

Despite the official all-clears, Kaplowitz could never get out from under the cloud of suspicion.

"Josh's disciplinary methods were pretty much what I do," says Vest, "but I'm an African American woman in my mid-fifties, older than many of these children's grandmothers, and I get a different kind of respect. I'm sorry, but in many of those cases, there was nothing Josh could have done differently except be born a different color. We complain a lot about it when it's the reverse, but this was the same thing we face—racism. Children called the white teachers bitches and MFs, parents could threaten them, and it was okay."

Others don't see it that starkly. "Other white teachers were able to overcome the race issue," says Wallace, the teacher who left Emery for Prince George's County. "However, because Josh was having a tough time, race became an issue."

Seleznow, who is white, defends the District's decision to hire more teachers who "reflect the world that these kids are going into"; he contends that "white teachers are successful now all over the city."

But what Seleznow saw when he watched Kaplowitz while touring Emery one day "was a class out of control.

"That's not a function of the children, it's what the teacher brings. Poor teachers rely more on authority than good teachers do. A bad teacher is always telling kids what the rules are. Oppression leads to aggression."

At Emery, allegations against teachers were becoming almost as common as hall passes.

"At least six of us were accused that year, every male teacher," says Wallace, who was accused of hitting a child and withstood five months of investigation before the charges were dropped. "The kids knew they could get us in trouble by saying, 'Teacher touched me,' and that's what they did. In that school, you were presumed guilty just because you're a teacher."

Discussion of Savoy's no-touching policy dominated every faculty meeting. Wallace and Ehrmann, frustrated by the principal's failure to adopt a discipline policy, got one from another school and proposed that Emery use it. Savoy shot it down.

The combination of the no-touching policy, the lack of a discipline policy and the epidemic of corporal-punishment allegations drove many teachers to the edge. "There were many days I'd open my eyes, sit on the edge of my bed and I just hated the idea of going into Emery again," Wallace says. "There were a couple of days, I got to the parking lot, pulled out my cell phone and called in sick. I just couldn't go in there."

No one denies that Emery had had problems with teachers whupping on children. But the absolute ban on touching left teachers unable to hug a despondent 7-year-old, forbidden to pat a 10-year-old on the back when he made a breakthrough in math.

"We were told that even positive reinforcement through touch is considered corporal punishment because you could withhold that, and that is cruel," Wallace says. He says he was forbidden to order children to stand in the corner, copy words from the dictionary or write the classroom rules on the blackboard. "Those were all banned as corporal punishment," he says. "Miss Savoy said the only thing you could do is ask the child, 'Why are you angry, what made you feel like doing that?'"

Ehrmann assumed that Savoy's orders were the result of an over-reliance on lawyers: "I read straight through that no-touch, no-hug, no-pat policy as a way to limit school liability. Did I put my arm around a kid to praise and comfort? Absolutely."

Ehrmann sometimes felt obliged to do more. One day, he caught one of his students just as he was about to attack other children. "I had to restrain that child to prevent him from hitting others," Ehrmann says. A parent he had never met saw Ehrmann hold the child back. The school system's security office launched an investigation. For four months, Ehrmann heard nothing. Then, one day, an investigator came and told him he was cleared.

Kaplowitz dispensed hugs and pats, too, but he also had a temper, and when his frustration over his inability to attain order mounted, he on several occasions exploded. Children said Mr. Kaplowitz used profanity in front of them. A few times, he slammed his ever-present clipboard down hard and loud. And in several hotly disputed moments, he either shoved a child or he didn't.

Ehrmann initially told me that he had never seen Kaplowitz break the corporal-punishment rules, but in a letter he wrote just before this article went to press, he said he witnessed Kaplowitz losing it twice, including "placing his hands" on a student's shoulders "and shoving him against the wall while yelling in his face."

"I did not shove a kid against the wall," Kaplowitz says in response. "I'm sure I came into contact with him in the interest of restraining him. I never tried to hurt a child. I'm not sure of the motivation behind Nick's letter. The fact that Nick had a false corporal-punishment charge against him shows what was going on there."

Five times between February and June, Kaplowitz was accused of touching students, culminating in an incident that happened four days before the end of the school year. As Kaplowitz's class returned from recess, a boy named Raynard agitatedly told the teacher he had to go to the bathroom to get some water. Kaplowitz says he was unable to settle the child, who was preventing the class from watching a movie. "I just wanted him out," he says, "so I led him to the hall to go to the bathroom."

Kaplowitz says he did touch Raynard, but only to guide him out the door "with my hand on the small of his back," without any force.

As it turned out, Raynard's mother, Sharlene Ware, was in the building; she'd come to school to argue for her son to be placed in a special class for emotionally troubled kids. Raynard found his mother and told her that Mr. Kaplowitz had shoved him, causing him to fall and hurt his head and back. The mother called 911.

Within minutes, police, fire and ambulance arrived at Emery. Kaplowitz was questioned for two hours. He never returned to his class.

Two days later, Kaplowitz received a letter terminating him from his employment with D.C. Public Schools. Kaplowitz was devastated; he knew his year had been a disaster, but he believed he had connected with some children. He always felt he was on the verge of a breakthrough.

In August, he was charged with shoving 7-year-old Raynard to the ground, a misdemeanor count of simple assault.

Kaplowitz's lawyer arranged for him to turn himself in to police on the morning of September 11, 2001. A process that ordinarily takes a few hours fell victim to the terrorist attacks. Kaplowitz heard about the World Trade Center while he was handcuffed to a chair in an interrogation room. He saw one of the towers collapse while his mug shots were being taken. Amid that day's confusion, he didn't get out of his holding cell for 33 hours.

Days later, he learned that Sharlene Ware had filed a civil suit in federal court alleging that Kaplowitz and the school system had violated her child's civil rights. She said her boy suffered frequent migraine headaches and nightmares as a result of his fall. She wanted $20 million.

In March 2002, the criminal case went to trial.

Kaplowitz's defenders—including teachers, parents and students—said he often showed his frustration and sometimes yelled and even cursed, but never manhandled children. Some parents and students said Kaplowitz indeed touched students, but no one saw him hurt Raynard. Savoy did not testify; Kaplowitz has had no contact with her since his last day at Emery. Otis Lindsey, chief investigator for MVM Security, the company that handles school security, said he saw Raynard shortly after the alleged incident and found "no bruises, no knot on the head, no bleeding." He said the boy was not crying.

After six days of wildly contradictory testimony, with no evidence of injury to the boy, Kaplowitz was found not guilty. Superior Court Judge Frederick Dorsey said the criminal case was being driven by the Ware family's desire to win its civil suit. (Ware told me she would discuss the case, then did not return more than 30 phone messages over a two-month period.)

In December, over the objections of Kaplowitz and his lawyer, the D.C. school system settled Ware's civil suit; she got $90,000.

Seleznow sounds morose about the system's corporal-punishment policy, even though he supports its zero-tolerance approach. "You have to have human contact with kids," he says. "I know how I feel when the superintendent puts his hand on my shoulder, and I'm a 49-year-old adult. But out of fear of allegations, we have teachers who do not feel they can do that. It's very, very sad."

Especially sad, he says, is what Emery fell victim to that year: "When the climate is bad, there is a greater opportunity for allegations to be leveled. You have copycat sorts of things. It's very likely that that's what happened at Emery, and especially for the male teachers. It's often hysteria, and people's lives are ruined."

Who will push for change in the city's schools?

Many of Washington's most affluent and politically savvy citizens are childless. Many middle-class parents steer clear of the public schools—they move to the suburbs or send their kids to parochial or private schools. (Sixty-five percent of students in the District's Catholic schools are not Catholic; 89 percent are black.) Or parents pull strings, stand in icy air overnight or play the new lottery to get their children into the system's best schools.

At places like Emery, it's an eternal struggle to get parents involved in the school's daily life. Many parents hold two jobs, some barely function themselves. Who will agitate for change there?

A few activists push for reform because they see good schools as essential to the city's renaissance. A few reformers inside the system dedicate themselves to the belief that every child deserves a great school. But the overhaul of a large, defensive, beleaguered system with a reputation for incompetence, corruption and neglect rests in good part on energetic newcomers like Kaplowitz and Ehrmann.

Both young men stood out at Emery. Both were deeply dissatisfied with the way the system serves students and with the burnout they saw among veteran teachers. Both insisted on trying something different, even though they saw that this was a system that feared and resisted change.

"In many ways, Josh's and my stories were the opposite poles of the same experience," says Ehrmann, who is heading to graduate school for sociology. "I dealt with a lot of the same emotions and resistances that he did, but we had very different years."

They also had very different experiences with Teach for America. Kaplowitz says he was dismissed as a troublemaker when he sought help, while Ehrmann says his TFA mentors offered useful criticism. (Teach for America executives won't discuss Kaplowitz. The program's Washington director, Miwa Powell, says TFA regularly observes its teachers and sponsors discussions throughout their teaching stints. Powell was happy to talk about Ehrmann; his success, she says, is much more typical.)

As for Emery, it has a new crop of novice teachers this year, and Anne Jackson, the new principal, shows them off proudly. Four of them are young white women, and that goes unspoken as the principal touts their backgrounds.

"Emery still has a long way to go," Seleznow acknowledges, but he's hopeful that Jackson will find the right teachers and let them build their own little worlds. Jackson grew up near Emery; her younger sister attended the school. But she did not—she wasn't permitted to, because in segregated Washington, Emery was a white school.

PTA president Walcott says Jackson has restored order. But Walcott has sent two of her own children to Hyde charter school because "Hyde doesn't have to tolerate stuff like DCPS does. They don't have to just sit there if a child is continually disruptive. They don't just pass children along like they made Mr. Kaplowitz do. The children know what the rules and expectations are."

Despite Emery's difficulties, Ehrmann says he "found my life's work" there in 2001. He taught at Emery one more year, then devoted himself to Project 312. He raised money from philanthropists, arranged tutoring for his kids, took them on an overnight trip. Since leaving, Ehrmann has worked to get several of his students into charter schools, where he thinks they'll find the attention and high expectations they need.

But 18 of his students are still at Emery, and some are on their third teacher this school year. Ehrmann believes Emery is getting better, but he has no illusions that the D.C. schools have turned any corner. "You graduate 54 percent of your [high school] kids every year," he says, "that's a dead system."

Kaplowitz has not been back to Emery since he was fired; nonetheless, he is convinced that little has improved there: "Man, they ought to just bulldoze it. What a disaster."

Since leaving the schools, he has worked as a paralegal at the law firm that defended him in the Ware case, and he teaches SAT-prep courses in Arlington. He wrote an article for a New York policy journal about his star-crossed year at Emery, and he's trying to sell a book about his ordeal. He's looking for a TV network to buy his story. He still believes in Teach for America. Like Ehrmann, he wants to go to graduate school and devote himself to education reform.

"My biggest regret is that I failed the kids," Kaplowitz says. "I could have been a good teacher. The few moments I was in control, it was such a high to impart knowledge."

There is a mystery to the craft of the most effective teachers. Even amid a national obsession with finding concrete measures of teaching success, Steve Seleznow knows that great teaching is something "you sense and feel." Watching Kaplowitz and Ehrmann teach, he knew immediately that Kaplowitz's relationship with his students was "a series of very, very poor interactions," while "Nick Ehrmann was the kind of teacher who could just communicate with kids without talking to them, with just the glance of an eye. Josh, I guess, just didn't have a heart for the children. And to be fair, there aren't that many Nick Ehrmanns in the world."

Patricia Vest argues that Josh Kaplowitz did exactly what Teach for America is supposed to do—cling to high expectations and "refuse to accept that these children can't learn. In the D.C. schools, people are complacent, and Josh was really trying to take our children to a different level."

Jackson, Emery's new principal, says she is eager to hire more Teach for America teachers. She wants that energy, that confidence to do your own thing. Sometimes it will work out, and sometimes it won't. But they'll be trying, some like Kaplowitz and some like Ehrmann.

—*The Washington Post Magazine* | April 6, 2003

Part 2: A pupil points a finger. A teacher is fired, his life rerouted. Now can they be buddies?

T he friend request popped onto Josh Kaplowitz's Facebook page one afternoon. He was at his office at a top-shelf D.C. law firm, but the name on the screen transported him to a very different place, a decade earlier, to a time of humiliation and failure.

Just seeing Raynard Ware's name that January day in 2012 spiked the young lawyer's heart rate. His first thought: "You ruined my life." It had been only in the past few years that Kaplowitz had been able to live without The Incident looming over him—the assault allegation, the arrest, 33 hours in a detention cell, trial, acquittal, a $20 million lawsuit against him, the impossibility of knowing if he would ever really recover.

Even now, with a new career and a family, Kaplowitz had yet to tell his children about what 7-year-old Raynard had said he had done to him. Kaplowitz hadn't even told his kids that he had been a D.C. public school teacher—an idealist fresh out of Yale who thought he was going to help transform the lives of poor, inner-city children but who was instead besieged by unruly kids and, then, in a whirlwind of accusations and acrimony, was said to have pushed a 7-year-old to the floor.

Now, this friend request, from the very second-grader whose complaint had brought a rush of police to Emery Elementary School, a trauma compounded when Kaplowitz reported to a D.C. police station and found himself tossed into a cell and temporarily forgotten because it was Sept. 11, 2001, and terrorists were attacking the World Trade Center and the Pentagon.

What now? Click "Confirm" and maybe the kid is looking to vent a decade of anger, or seeking revenge, or pressing for money. Click "Delete Request" and never find out what happened to Raynard, something the former teacher had wondered unnervingly often.

Kaplowitz sought advice from his wife, whom he'd met just four days after The Incident. No, she said, leave it alone—hasn't he caused you enough grief? He asked his parents, who said, as ever, that they would support him whatever he decided. He reached out to old friends from that disastrous year in Teach for America and they said, Josh, you know you need to do this.

"Josh told me years ago that one of his frustrations was that there was no happy ending back then, and happy endings are important," says Wren Miller, a friend Kaplowitz met at the Teach for America training class in Houston the summer before they entered D.C. classrooms.

For days, Kaplowitz stared at the friend request. Finally, he clicked: "Confirm."

1/23/2012, 2:37 pm
From: Raynard Ware

Hey, Mr. Kaplowitz I'm Raynard as you can see. I just wanted to say I'm doing well. I graduated high school with a 3.6. I also had scholarship offers from Georgetown, Yale and Morehouse. I choose to attend Morehouse because I felt I wasn't prepared for Yale or Georgetown . . . I've re-evaluated the past incident and I just want to say I apologize for everything that happened. I would really appreciate it if I could hear back from you. ttyl!!

Six hundred and 40 miles away, on the bucolic campus of Morehouse College in Atlanta, the professor in Spanish 202 calls Raynard Ware to the blackboard. The assignment is to write a sentence using the present perfect tense to express your determination to achieve a specific goal by a certain age.

"Para los 30, yo habré tenido una grande casa," Ware writes. Before I am 30, I will have a big house. The exercise continues: By 24, he will have an MBA. By 35, he'll live as a business executive in San Francisco. (He has never been there, "just read about it on Forbes. com," he says.)

Ware is 21 now, a senior in college, a defensive back for the Morehouse Maroon Tigers with a knack for intercepting the football. He wants to work for JPMorgan. He will not return to the tough streets where he grew up; that much he knows for damned sure. His father, Joseph Ware, died when Raynard was 6, choked to death on pepper spray that police deployed against him in a robbery gone bad, or so the family story goes.

The father—a drug user and seller who spent years in prison, according to family and friends—was never really around when he was alive, but Ware keeps a pair of photos in his phone, showing himself and his father in similar poses. Their resemblance is striking. Ware wrote a caption: "Similar in stature, different grind. You're the reason why the level of focus."

On the football field, in school, among friends, Ware is quiet, but you can see him listening, deciding what matters. In his marketing class, Ware, spiffy in a maroon sport jacket with the college seal emblazoned on his chest, copies a list of "Eight Ways to Declutter Your Mind" that his professor is reading aloud. Three hit home: "Accept what is," "Be kind to yourself" and "Find what doesn't serve or interest you and let it go."

The past is motivation, Ware says. It's how he defines what he doesn't want. His mother had three children by three men; Ware is determined not to have any children until he is married, and to marry once and forever. His father wasn't there "to teach me to be a man"; Ware is on the hunt for male role models.

Mr. Kaplowitz knows the path to honest success, Ware found himself thinking in his dorm room. He started freshman year with doubts about whether he belonged on a campus where many other students had parents who were lawyers and doctors and executives, where students seemed to know they would do fine even if they didn't do the assigned readings.

Ware believed his doubts grew out of the years after The Incident, when, tagged as a troublemaker in need of special education, he was assigned to classes full of kids who had been labeled slow, disruptive, deficient.

"Raynard was a shy little thing when I met him," says Natalie Randolph, a science teacher at Alice Deal Middle School who was Raynard's football coach and environmental science teacher at Coolidge High School. "He was well-mannered and not that willing to come out of his comfort zone. But he was the hardest worker, and he always wanted to know why stuff happens. We called him the Little Philosopher."

Until late in high school, Raynard was still in special education, a label he and some of his teachers believed he needed to shed.

"Ever since I was a little kid, I misbehaved a lot," Ware says, "but I didn't think I needed to be in special ed. They had me riding the short yellow bus with people who couldn't function on their own. I was talked about. One of the drug guys next door where we lived saw me come off the short yellow bus one day, and he said, 'Ray, I didn't know you was retarded.' I went in my house and cried."

A couple of teachers in high school recognized his smarts and potential and worked to get him out of special ed and on a path to college. Coach Randolph's goal for Raynard was to enroll him at Morehouse. "I knew he would thrive there," she says.

It took a while, but he did. Alone in his room in the house he shares with three friends—Ware drives a 2002 BMW 325 he bought with the money he got from his mother's settlement with the D.C. public schools—he thinks about what he was just a few years ago and how to get where he wants to be.

"I always feel like I got to prove a point because people doubt me," he says. Now, when Ware goes home to the District, he sees that drug guy who called him names, "and I don't say anything. I say to myself, 'Look at me now.'"

On campus, after those rocky first few months in 2011, Ware came into his own. He got playing time on the gridiron. His academics started to click. He found his passion in finance and marketing. Guys on the team asked him for advice. Women admired him. Ware felt ready, and needy, and curious, all at once.

Look at me now: He Googled Mr. Kaplowitz, checked out his Facebook page, then, without consulting his mother or anyone else—"I just felt like I'm an adult now"—sent the message.

A clueless white knight

Mr. Kaplowitz's room was, by all accounts, a zoo. Even in a school where nearly every male teacher was accused of grabbing, pushing or hitting a child, Kaplowitz stood out: Six of his 18 students had emotional or learning problems, and teachers, administrators, parents and students knew he was unable to keep order.

"There was no control," Ware recalls. "Kids were throwing trash, not sitting down. I don't remember doing work. The homework would be handed out, and I'd just ball it up and throw it away."

Kaplowitz, the son of two doctors, chose Teach for America over a job he had been offered analyzing public opinion data for Al Gore's presidential campaign. At 22, he believed he could make a huge difference in his students' lives. He visited their parents at home, took kids on trips, even wrote raps for his students to perform: "Yo, listen close, this is wakeup time / This is Mr. K's class and we're laying down some rhymes / See, there's so much more to education / Than filling in bubbles for test preparation."

"I thought I was this white knight coming in and rescuing these kids," he says. "I was really clueless."

But by spring of his first year, Kaplowitz was ready to cry uncle. He had asked to be moved to another school or be given older students. Instead, he had been shifted from fifth grade to an even more challenging second-grade class.

On June 13, 2001, Raynard asked his teacher for permission to go to the bathroom to get some water, a ploy he had used before to get out of class. He asked and he asked—at least 30 times. Kaplowitz had decided not to fall for that ruse again.

"Lord, I was badgering him," Ware says. "'Can I use the bathroom? Can I use the bathroom?'"

Finally, Kaplowitz decided he needed to get Raynard out of the room to have any chance of restoring order, even if it meant giving in to an obvious ploy.

The teacher told Raynard to leave, stepped over to him and, he says, put his hand on Raynard's back to usher him out. The verbs Kaplowitz has used to describe his action are "guide," "lead" and "help."

The verb Raynard used a few moments later, when he showed up in the school office—where his mother was meeting with administrators about getting her son into a special ed class to get closer attention for his behavior issues—was "push."

He uses that word even all these years later: "I remember him pushing me out of the classroom. He slammed the door hard, and I heard it, and I was crying."

His mother, Sharlene Ware Mullings, recalls seeing her child crying, in pain, describing falling to the floor. "Raynard as a little kid had integrity," she says. "He would tell on himself. So I never questioned it when Raynard said he fell on the back of his head."

When school officials heard the boy say he had hit his head, they called an ambulance and the police. Kaplowitz was questioned for two hours. He would never return to his class. This was the fifth allegation that he had touched a student—a violation of a rule the school was strictly enforcing amid an epidemic of allegations against teachers. One father filed a report against Kaplowitz after the teacher had pulled the man's daughter off a boy she was sitting on and punching; the teacher was cleared in that case and others that were investigated. Still, two days after the incident with Raynard, Kaplowitz was fired.

That summer, he was charged with a misdemeanor count of simple assault. His lawyer arranged for him to turn himself in to police on Sept. 11, 2001. A booking that should have taken a few hours became 33 hours of detention as D.C. police shifted into emergency mode. Kaplowitz slept on a metal slab and ate bologna sandwiches.

After a six-day trial—including testimony from the school's chief security investigator that Raynard was not crying and showed no sign of injury after the incident—the judge found Kaplowitz not guilty, concluding that the criminal case was being driven by the $20 million civil suit Raynard's mother had filed.

That civil case never made it to trial. The school system settled for $90,000; after lawyers' fees and other costs, about $50,000 was set aside for Raynard. The entire ordeal became the subject of a Washington Post Magazine cover story I wrote in 2003.

"I never hurt a kid," Kaplowitz says. "But I was not a good teacher, and I yelled a lot. I was in the survival mind-set of getting through the day. If there's one thing I try to block out, it's what a lousy teacher I was most of the time."

1/31/2012, 10:05 pm
From: Joshua Kaplowitz

Raynard—it's a pleasant surprise to hear from you, and great to find out how well you are doing. . . . I have gained some perspective of my own over the last 10+ years, and I now have a son who is the same age as you were when you were in my class. While I deeply appreciate your apology, you should know that I don't blame you and never took anything that happened personally. The whole thing obviously had a big impact on my life, but I'm doing well now with a family and a new career as a Lawyer. . . . I'd be happy to meet you to catch up further.

'All about forgiveness'

"Guess what, Mom? I talked to Mr. Kaplowitz."

Ware's call to his mother, who now lives in Charlotte, where she works for a pharmaceutical company, stopped her cold.

"How did you do that?" she said. "What for? Why? Why would you open a can of worms?"

"It's all about forgiveness," Ware explained.

He has never backed away from his contention that Mr. Kaplowitz did something he shouldn't have: "You can't put your hands on kids in classrooms, so he was wrong."

But what jumped out at Kaplowitz as soon as he accepted the friend request was Ware's apology. Vague as it was—"I want to say I apologize for everything that happened"—Kaplowitz says, "I took it as 'I'm sorry I made up that accusation.'"

Elated, the lawyer assured his former student in their first phone conversation that "You don't need to apologize—you were 7, I have a 7-year-old now. Let's do lunch."

That first meeting, at the Austin Grill on E Street NW near Kaplowitz's office, was awkward. They didn't talk about The Incident. They talked mainly about Ware's remarkable progress.

Before the meal ended, Kaplowitz made a proposal: If this relationship worked out, if they really did build a friendship, maybe they could write a book together. In college, Kaplowitz had thought about going into journalism; he was editor of the campus humor magazine, and he wrote an article about his time at Emery Elementary. (The headline was "How I Joined Teach for America—and Got Sued for $20 Million.")

But as he walked back to the office from lunch, Kaplowitz told himself he had blundered, moved too quickly. "I just freaked him out," he thought.

He hadn't. Ware was indeed startled by the idea of a book, and puzzled that Kaplowitz would want to go public with their relationship before it had even really formed. But Ware liked the notion of letting the world know that he was moving on up, escaping a life of struggle and dysfunction.

"I know it sounds grandiose," Kaplowitz says, "but the idea that two people who had no reason to even speak to each other after a traumatic event could sit down and have a conversation—people might see some resonance in their own lives. I think of the Palestinians and the Israelis and 2,000 years of mutual hatred."

That's how Josh is, says his wife, Andrea. He puts the pain behind him and pushes forward. Through most of their 12 years of marriage, that moment with Raynard had rarely been far from consciousness.

When they started dating, Andrea recalls, she had the awkward duty of telling her parents, "I'm dating somebody, and he's been accused of hurting a child—betcha can't wait to meet him!"

She laughs now, but back then, some of their friends didn't believe Kaplowitz and withdrew from his life. For a time, Teach for America used Kaplowitz's story in their training program as an example of how a teacher can go wrong. A few years ago, after Kaplowitz finished law school at the University of Virginia, Andrea did part-time work watching other people's children, and she and her husband decided that they needed to disclose The Incident to potential clients, so there would be no surprises if the parents Googled them.

With dancing black eyes, rosy cheeks and a lean innocence, Kaplowitz looks unscathed by the trauma of a decade ago, but his friends say it hit him hard. "It took him four or five years to get out of that funk," says Wren Miller, Kaplowitz's Teach for America buddy, now a funeral director in Pennsylvania. "We all had accusations from kids, and the principal would tell us it was something kids do to get attention. Josh's case just went further than most others."

Connecting with Ware "was like a weight lifted from Josh this past year or so," Miller says. "There's a sense that things are now what he'd wished they could be all along, that he could finally have that close relationship with students."

But as therapeutic as the connection with Ware has been, Miller wonders whether it can truly flourish if the two men hold onto different stories about that June day.

"I would think, to move on together," Miller says, "they'd have to come to some common understanding of what happened."

Defending her child

If the first meeting between Ware and Kaplowitz three summers ago was awkward, bringing Sharlene Mullings into the circle promised to be much dicier. Kaplowitz had insisted that he could go no further with Ware unless he met with his mother. Kaplowitz needed to see if she still considered him the enemy.

He wanted to know if she still believed he had assaulted her son. "The hardest thing in all of this is for her to acknowledge that she brought this lawsuit based on something that didn't happen," he says.

What Sharlene Mullings, a Christian with a degree in theology, did instead was to forgive Kaplowitz—a religious act born of belief in redemption. What Kaplowitz, a secular Jew with reverence for the certainties of the law, wanted was a statement annulling the past.

Kaplowitz bristled when Mullings said she forgave him, but he decided to leave it at that because she didn't seem to have any lingering resentment. He had once accused Mullings of "fraudulently" winning the settlement money; now he says "there was less conniving than I assumed at the time. Now I look back and she's got three kids, in public housing—I certainly think she took advantage of the situation for financial gain, but I now think she genuinely thought something had happened. And the fact that Raynard is the person he is today is largely because of her."

Mullings has decided that whatever happened that day with Raynard and his teacher, Kaplowitz "was trying his best, and the kids in that school were off the chain. The school system failed the teacher as well as the child."

She makes no excuses for her aggressive defense of her child. She says she was aggressively protective of him because she was raped by a school janitor when she was in kindergarten. "So at Raynard's school, they always knew who Ms. Ware was," she says. "I was up in their face. I didn't trust nobody."

But she now credits Kaplowitz and The Incident for getting Raynard moved into a private school where his behavior issues were addressed. ("I used to have to punch him in his chest when he was little because he was off the chain," she says.)

Mullings had started pressing for help for her son a year before The Incident, when she applied to Social Security for disability payments because, she said, Raynard suffered from attention deficit hyperactivity disorder and a mood disorder. Her claim was denied, and she fought the ruling in the courts for four years, ultimately losing.

A federal judge ruled that although Raynard had been suspended from school six times, he "showed no signs of hyperactivity" when he was tested and worked well with adults and peers.

Mulling's pride in her son's transformation takes physical form in a room in her house that is a veritable shrine to his achievements—shelves full of trophies and certificates. Yet she still wonders why her son "feels the need to open up something I don't want to revisit. It was in the past—leave it there."

But she has come to believe that the bond between her son and his former teacher is true: "Two people coming back together after so many years, with no hostility? It's deep. Yeah, it's deep."

As a ninth-grader, Raynard wrote in a school essay that "without my Mom, I think I'll be in the streets. She disciplines me and tells me what's right and what's wrong."

When he turned 18 and got the settlement money, Ware gave $10,000 of it to his mother.

'Proud of who he's become'

Kaplowitz and Ware spoke or traded messages on 11 days in October. Sometimes it's just a few words, and sometimes it's a long conversation. They talk about what it's like to be a lawyer. They talk about politics and sports.

So what is this—a friendship? A building business partnership? A mentorship?

"I'm really reluctant to put a label on it," says Andrea Kaplowitz. "The two of them share something no one else does. Who else could they talk to about this?"

She hasn't met Ware, but she'd like to. Everyone realizes that the fact that Kaplowitz has not introduced his own family to his new friend means something.

"I don't know that we're there yet," Andrea says. "E-mail and text is a way to broach all these issues; it lets you choose your words carefully. I think they're past that now—they have open, casual conversations. But it's a process."

Kaplowitz isn't sure what to call his new relationship either. He thinks it may well be a real friendship.

"Every friendship is different," Kaplowitz says. "This is obviously different from my friends down the street who are complete peers. I certainly hope it's helpful to Raynard; I know I've learned a lot from him. I am very proud of who he's become. I don't know if he sees what he's doing, but it's very smart: He's trying to reverse the inequality he was born into by forming networks that he wasn't born with."

For Kaplowitz, Ware represents "a second chance, another bite at the apple of making a difference. I have no doubt some people will take the story the wrong way—that I'm only trying to redeem myself, or he's just using me for my networks. That's really not the motivation, and even if it is part of the motivation, so what? I have a new friend and some form of closure."

Ware sees his relationship with Kaplowitz as "an exchange of cultures. I know there's a stereotype that Caucasian people only have one black friend, but this is more than that."

He would like to meet Andrea and their children, though. "I'd like to see it move toward more of a friendship."

Whatever you call it, the relationship is valuable, Ware says: "He gets validation from me, knowing he wasn't as bad a teacher as he thought he was, that he made an impact in my life, that now we're both doing well. And I learn a lot from Josh. I pick up little things, certain lingo, being in corporate America like Josh is. I watch people really closely. I grew up very quiet, and people think I'm not listening, but I take it all in."

—*The Washington Post Magazine* | January 30, 2015

City Hall, and Step On It

Stumping for a D.C. Council Seat, Marion Barry Is Covering Familiar Ground. And in the Distance—Is That His Old Job?

By Wil Haygood

The little boys are pedaling as fast as they can, trying desperately to keep up with the whipped-cream-white SUV as it cuts through the sunshine. Marion Barry is in the back seat, wearing sunglasses, grinning.

"Mar'nbarry . . . Mar'nbarry . . . Mar'nbarry."

The little boys are yelling and shouting as loud as they can, their bicycles swooping through the streets of Southeast.

"Mar'nbarry . . . Mar'nbarry . . . Mar'nbarry."

He squints at them, into the morning. He hears them fine enough, and he's grinning the big country grin that served him so well over so many years as a riveting, polarizing and beguiling politician of the nation's capital.

These are hard and gritty streets, and sometimes it seems as if they're still in a slumber, from the '70s, from the '80s, from Mayor Marion Barry's glory years. Frozen in the amber that is Marion.

He bends out of the GMC Yukon as it comes to a stop. The grin's so wide, so churchy. Screen doors are being pushed open, and stout women and skinny men are coming out to offer greetings.

"Hi, baby." Barry has walked up to a comely woman. "How you doing? What's your name? Where you live? You married? Gimme kiss." Barry has an easy way with the language of the street and uses it to his advantage in a way that other politicians can only envy. He bends down and receives his kiss.

Barry is one of seven candidates running for the Ward 8 D.C. Council seat in Tuesday's Democratic primary. The winner is likely to sail to victory in November. Of course, Barry is an old story, a nostalgia act—like the Dells or the Stylistics singing groups, some say. A 68-year-old man with a mess of a history. Still, those who would author his political obituary have been fooled before. Both Barry and his main opponent, two-term incumbent Sandy Allen, predict the vote will be close.

The perpetual pol is wearing a white-and-blue sweat suit and a billed cap. There is a puppet's looseness to his movements, but sometimes, when he has to bend, a grimace will cross his face. And so here he stands, swallowing the pill that all aging and proud politicians have swallowed for years across the American landscape: time.

On this sunny day—"Mar'nbarry" ringing in his ears—it goes down just fine.

This is how he put it a couple of days earlier: "This guy in prison told me, he say, 'Marion, do the time. Don't let the time do you.'"

He started out the morning late—first it was 30 minutes, then an hour.

But then there he was, at campaign headquarters on Martin Luther King Jr. Avenue.

"Where my credit card?" he asks a staffer. Last night the campaign was running low on cash. Money was needed for gas and supplies.

His headquarters sits next door to Capitol Fried Chicken and across the street from ACE Cash Express. It's less than 30 yards from Allen's headquarters. Her forces are out this morning, too, preparing their own campaign caravan.

The first salvo, over the loudspeaker, comes from Barry's people. "Somebody's gonna be lookin for a job in 10 days!" bellows Muhammad Abdullah. He's a volunteer, visiting from Las Vegas, wearing a skull cap and a flowing shirt.

"Salaam alaykum," Barry says to Abdullah. Peace be upon you.

Abdullah's wife, Imani, is busy handing out leaflets. "Praise to Allah," Barry says to Imani.

Linda Greene is there. She once lived with Johnny Carter. He sang with the Dells. They've got a daughter together. Now she's Barry's spokeswoman and political adviser. Actually, she runs the ship. Greene's in a huff at the moment. She claims the Allen camp has been snatching Barry signs from yards and replacing them with Allen signs. She's holding a copy of a certified letter she sent to the Allen camp. "I'm filing a complaint with the board of elections," she hisses.

The sun is shining. She needs a cigarette.

"Okay, come on. Let's go," instructs Barry. "Linda, where you want me to sit? Huh. Just give me some direction. Tell me where to sit."

Barry is folding himself into the SUV's back seat, hooking his right hand beneath his knee, lifting the knee as he bends. The knee hurts. Soon he's talking about growing up in Mississippi and picking cotton. His head's rolling side to side like a balloon a few hours after the birthday party ends. "You could never see the end of the rows of cotton. You know, for a young boy, that's frustrating."

Then the former mayor says—he'll switch thoughts in mid-sentence like a rabbit changing direction—"There's no question I'm ahead in the race. The job is easy. Go to the committee meetings. Come out here and talk to the people."

He's waving out the window. "Hey, darling. Love you. Need your vote." He's unwinding, getting started, sipping coffee from a yellow mug.

Then the words come pouring from the loudspeaker: "Ladies and gentlemen, come on out and greet Marion Barry, the man who marched with Martin Luther King, the Muhammad Ali of politics, your champion!"

The SUV and a van roll to a stop, volunteers hop out, exchange quick words with some residents, then proceed to pound Barry signs into yards. Donald Sobokhan is one of those doing the hammering. He's 73 years old. The hammer hangs wobbly in his hand. He's wearing shorts and his socks are pulled up to his kneecaps, tight. The mayor is getting out now, opening the door. A second later he's deep in conversation with a woman, a potential voter. She's twenty-something, cute. She's smiling, he's leaning close.

"Bye, baby," Barry says, turning in his sneakers, having charmed the converted.

Several blocks onward, he's leaning out the window: "Awright now. Vote. Vote. Thank you, brother." The Bald Eagle Recreation Center is coming up on the right. "I built that. You know what I mean. My administration built it."

Around the corner—with the loudspeaker drawing the curious—a lady is running down off her front porch. She has a picture of Barry in her hands. Some people have pictures of Martin and Bobby and Jack in their homes. She has Marion. In the picture he's wearing an Afro. The Afro's gone now.

"Well, I'll be," Barry says. Then he turns slightly and spots a big guy. "You know you got my vote," says David Stewart, 30. "Ain't even gotta ask. When I was out there, in the nightclub world, Mr. Barry used to come to the nightclubs."

His Honor used to have a "Saturday Night Fever" penchant, which enthralled some city residents, while others were repulsed by stories of womanizing and drug use.

Stewart's a truck driver. He doesn't worry about Barry's past. "We all have had trials and tribulations. God gave him a second chance."

Barry hears it all, listening to the way people in living rooms listen to good music when the TV is off.

Ruby Bradley is suddenly in Barry's ear, talking about the past, good times, old times, time.

"How old you now?" Barry wants to know.

"I'm 60 now," she says.

"You're 60! No, you're not! Didn't you call me a couple weeks ago?"

"Yeah," says Bradley. "You know I follow you all the time."

"Gimme kiss. Bye, y'all. I gotta go now."

A knot of kids is across the street, staring, wide-eyed, as if they're watching something unfold on a movie screen.

Barry spots an elderly man standing behind a screen door. There's a "Barry Ward 8" sign in the man's front yard. "Hey, like that sign," Barry says, pointing. Barry waves, the man doesn't. Maybe he didn't hear him. Barry's voice is weak, like he's at the far end of a hallway. His communications with the elderly can be a painful pantomime of the hard-of-hearing and the weak-voiced.

Barry's riffing now about civil rights activist Fannie Lou Hamer and Hubert Humphrey, about Atlantic City and that 1964 Democratic convention. The rabbit is changing direction again. About his work for the Student Nonviolent Coordinating Committee in the '60s. "I was making $50 a week," he says. "Reginald Robinson was with me in Mississippi. I got him a job. He's still around D.C. I almost got killed in Mississippi."

Almost got killed?

"Yeah. I'll tell you about it in a minute."

Then he's talking about his diabetes and being sent "all over" to different doctors and insurance companies. And the medicine he takes. "That's why I lost all this weight," he says. In recent years, Barry's medical maladies have included anemia, high blood pressure and prostate cancer.

The price of "high livin'," he says, is costly. There's not an ounce of irony in his voice.

He's out of the SUV again. A woman is striding toward him. Already he's grinning.

"I was 17, 18 when he was mayor," says Vanessa Thigpen, now 36. "A friend of mine, Linda Moody, used to live on Oakwood Street SE. We lived in the house beside her. Well, she threw a party and the mayor came."

Barry cuts her off. No need for historical asides about partying.

"Where you working?" he wants to know.

"I'm not," she answers, hands on hips. "It's hard to find a job."

"Weren't you in my summer jobs institute?" Barry asks.

"No. Oh, wait a minute. Yes I was!"

He's got affirmation now. The jobs program. Those were the days. He puts the sunglasses back on. "Linda, let's go."

"When I was growing up," Barry continues, back in the SUV, "I went to segregated movie theaters. Whites downstairs, blacks upstairs. Actually, you got a better view upstairs. My mother gave me a quarter every Saturday."

The driver is pulling to the curb. Potential voters have been spotted.

"Hey, man. You vote?" Barry wants to know.

They seem a little surprised: Marion Barry, standing in their front yard, easy like Sunday morning. His eyes shift to the woman beside the man. "That your wife? How you get so lucky? Ha ha ha. I need your vote now. Bye."

He's rolling again. Back to Mississippi: "So with the quarter my momma give me, I'd spend 12 cents on the ticket, 5 cents for popcorn, and 3 cents for a long piece of black licorice. See, they'd show serials, cartoons, before the movie. And they'd show you just enough of the serial to make you come back the next week. Ain't that something? Ha. And when I'd get home, I'd listen to the radio. The Shadow. 'The Shadow knows!' Linda, you too young to remember that."

"Remember what?"

"Dick Tracy on radio."

"Oh, yes. Way too young," she says.

"Dick Tracy had a two-way radio," Barry says. "It wasn't worth a damn."

He leans out the window, nearly singing his words out. "Hey, beautiful, I want your vote. Hey now. Need your vote. Hey now. Awright."

Minutes later, a man approaches the SUV as it slows to round a curve. The man is clearly inebriated. Barry looks at him with sympathy.

"That's what we need! Somebody bring pride back into the city," the inebriated man says, peering inside the SUV.

"That's right," Barry says softly. "Pride."

Barry's cell phone rings—it's his son Christopher. The brief chat ends. "Christopher is deputy campaign manager," Barry says. A couple of staffers have looks on their faces as if that's news to them. "But he's in school now. Hard to catch up to him. He's in love now. It's the first love of his life. Sister Imani, we gotta hit it. Let's roll."

They come to a stop on Galveston Place. A woman stomps down to the van.

"Where Mr. Barry at?" she demands, looking right at the former mayor.

"Right here," Barry answers.

"Oh. Lord Jesus. You look so different," Veris McNeill, 42, says. It doesn't sound like a compliment.

Barry stays in the SUV, as if frozen by her tone.

She's arched her back and raised her voice. "We are homeowners. Right here. So I want you to represent homeowners! There are drugs on this block! After the election, people won't know nothing about Galveston Place. We got cars right here that have been burned up. Abandoned buildings where people go to have sex. I paid a lot of money to live in this building! And I love you Marion Barry. But I ain't supporting nobody. I been here 11 years and I have to sit in my window to watch and make sure nobody steals my car or bust my tires!"

This is not what Barry had planned on hearing. McNeill stares at him. "Okay, baby," he finally says, almost a whisper. "But don't blame me. I didn't do it." She's getting ready to launch another salvo but gets interrupted by her children.

Barry rolls down the street, smiling and waving. "I want your vote now. I need you."

Soon after, he's riding by a piece of vacant property, pointing. "All that, right over there, it's prime property. I tried to get the city to develop it when I was in office."

Back to Mississippi: "When I was out picking cotton, we'd take two baloney sandwiches to the field. That's all we had. And sometimes you'd have sardines and pork and beans. Let's go. I'm hungry."

They stop at a convenience store and Barry strides inside to buy some lunch. Back in the SUV, he tears open a package of turkey-ham, folding two slices and making himself a turkey-ham and cracker sandwich. The crumbs are flying everywhere. "I gotta send someone back to that store and ask for a campaign contribution," he says. The SUV is back on Martin Luther King. "In the 1960s, white people owned all this," he says, waving a hand with a piece of turkey-ham in it, pointing out the window. Then some apartment buildings come into view. "I got these built 15 to 20 years ago."

The driver's going too slow for Barry's taste. "Let's go." Looking out the window: "Hey now. Need your vote. Need your vote."

Boom and Busted

It's such a staggering political drama, goes back so many years, with so much darkness and moments of brilliant light. It crosses all the potent intersections of race and sex and crime. It's part blaxploitation movie and part civil rights history. It began in the Mississippi Delta and flowered in the nation's capital.

A newcomer to the District might not know the contours of Barry's rise and fall. A gawker on the streets of Southeast might wonder how he gets those children to race alongside him— "Mar'nbarry, Mar'nbarry"—and the elderly women to ask him to take a picture.

Maybe it's because of the transit boycott he led back in the '60s to protest an increase in bus fares. Maybe it's because of the Free D.C. movement he founded, when residents were saying the city was being held in a colonial grip by Congress. Maybe it's from his D.C. Council run in 1974 or from being shot by those Hanafi Muslim terrorists who had stormed the District Building in 1977. ("Almost got killed.") Maybe it's from his first term as mayor. Or maybe the second and third terms. Mayor of Chocolate City. The folks out in Phoenix and Brooklyn and San Diego knew Chocolate City, heard of its mayor. Tune the dial to Melvin Lindsay and Quiet Storm and you might not only hear sweet Al Green but Marion Barry also, lauding his city. He wasn't Gold Coast, he wasn't high-society. And when he got busted at what was then the Vista International Hotel in 1990 and went to prison for six months on a federal charge of drug possession—released in 1991—it only added to his aura, to the cult of Marion. It would have deep-sixed many a political career. But not Barry. He was back on the council in 1992 and won a fourth term as mayor in 1994.

'I Came Back Strong'

Days before he took that campaign outing through Southeast, he is sitting in the outdoor cafe of the Mandarin Oriental Hotel. He's dining on oysters, wearing a big Panama hat, wide-collared green shirt, gray slacks and lizard shoes.

When he first decided to run for the Ward 8 seat, he says, he phoned two people. His mother, in Memphis, and Greene. He and Greene go back many years, all the way to the '60s.

"She was fine as wine then," says Barry.

"And you were single then," says Greene, sitting at the table. "Very single."

Everyone, he knows, has wondered why he's running. Isn't there a book to write?

"Actually, I had a writer," Barry says. "He got me up to my first administration, then left on me. Anyway, I think I'd be better off with a fiction writer. Fiction writer can bring the dead parts of the story alive." He says this with a straight face.

Financially, Barry is not well off. "I'm a public servant," he says, alluding to his lack of savings. "I don't make no money. And I ain't gonna steal none."

So they launched a campaign on the cheap.

"For a normal candidate running a ward race, you'd need about $100,000 to $150,000," says Greene. "For Marion, it only takes about $50,000. He doesn't have to spend money on advertising. The people already know him." Greene goes on: "We gonna win. We were out in the rain a couple weeks ago. Folk came out in the rain, in pajamas. To shake this man's hand."

"Let me tell you a story," Barry begins again, sliding his big hand around an oyster, slurping it off the shell. "People in my neighborhood, when I was growing up, went to jail or to the cemetery. I knew nothing about college. My mother was a domestic. I was finally hoping I'd get a scholarship for college. I got accepted to Morehouse and Fisk. Morehouse wrote me. I finally went to LeMoyne College in Memphis. I was supposed to be commencement speaker at LeMoyne a couple years ago"—the rabbit's jumping around again—"somebody dropped the ball. Anyway, Morehouse told me to bring my work boots. Said I'd have to be working in some fields as part of work-study. I said 'Oh, no.' I'd had enough working in the fields. So I went to LeMoyne."

He's been married four times and now lives alone. There are all those physical ailments. Emerging from some hospital stays, he has looked gaunt, wounded. The past couple years have been slow. He was doing some consulting. "Some mornings I'd get up, go over to a school, and read to the kids," he says.

"I had retired in my own mind. Hadn't done much since '98 [when he left the mayor's office]. I was content trying to get through this divorce" from wife No. 4, Cora Masters Barry.

Then it started coming, those tugs at his elbow, whispers in his ear, complaints about the city's woes. Never mind that the city's economic woes and crime problems darkened under Barry's own watch.

"This whole thing started a year ago," Barry says. "I'd go to the Safeway on Alabama and Good Hope—I approved $10 million when I was in office to build that Safeway. Anyway, I'd go in there, trying to shop. I'm a pretty gregarious person. People would come up to me. I don't hear nothing but complaints about what Sandy's not doing, what the mayor's not doing. So I started looking around and talking to the people about Ward 8. Wasn't no sense of pride. I started praying on it. I do believe in prayer. For real. Instead of just listening to the complaints, I decided to run."

Oysters finished, he starts in on seasoned noodles.

"People are out of work, desperate," he says. "They feel down. God gave me a gift to uplift. I uplifted myself. We the worst ward in town. Dropout rate, cancer rate. Almost every area you name, I can do a thousand times better than Sandy. When I get in there, I'll get a bill going to renovate housing. Ward 8 has always been neglected. Except by me. When I was mayor."

The hurt souls walking around Southeast? ("We call it Soufeast," he instructs.) The problems with crack addiction and alcoholism? "I been there," he says. "I never been hopeless, but I been down. They saw me get up. Not let anybody break my spirit. I came back strong. When people see something like that, they get inspired. When you fall down, land on your back. With your head looking up. If you can see up, you can get up."

He orders dessert: strawberries and chocolate.

The Incumbent

Poor Sandy Allen.

The dutiful public servant, a bee of a government worker—Department of Public Works, D.C. Public Schools, D.C. Department of Corrections—for more than three decades. Now she's the two-term Ward 8 council member, and chairman of the Committee on Human Services. And she's fighting for her political life.

She's sitting in her Southeast office, elegantly dressed in a lime green suit, sipping a ginger ale.

Barry called her: "Sandy, let's have lunch." Greetings, hugs, the country grin turned right on her. Then down to business. He was going to run. For her seat. "Surprised was not the word," she says now, steam in her voice. "Four years earlier he had been talking about what a good job I had done."

She whips out an endorsement letter Barry wrote on her behalf in 2000.

When Barry came out of prison and ran for a council seat, she was his campaign manager. Now she feels double-crossed. "It gave me another insight into Marion," she says. "But this is politics." She goes on: "I asked Marion before I took the job as campaign manager if he was going to be truthful to my constituents in Ward 8." Two years later, Barry launched a run for mayor. "I should have learned from then," she says. "He used us to become mayor."

She predicts victory. But everyone in her camp worries about nostalgia, about the cult of Marion. "Mr. Barry had a name. People have been hearing it for 20 years. Like Elvis."

She turns to his personal troubles. "Mr. Barry's alleged drug use—this last time, well, there was no conviction. Maybe it's hearsay. I don't talk about hearsay."

She's referring to a March 2002 incident at Buzzard's Point, when Barry—sitting alone in a Jaguar in a no-parking zone—was questioned by police. Initial reports mentioned a white powdery substance that had allegedly been seen under Barry's nose. Police determined that whatever substance was in the car, there was too little to mount a prosecution. Just then, outside Allen's door, comes a voice from a loudspeaker: "Cast your vote for Marion Barry!"

"He has diabetes and hypertension," she says. "He says it will have no impact on the way he thinks. As lay people, we know those things have an impact on the way you think. Mr. Barry's just not as vigorous or articulate as he used to be. My biggest concern is why would he prey on the people who have the greatest need for counseling, for abuse treatment? My colleagues on the council follow me on these type of issues."

She's riled up. She takes a sip of her ginger ale to clear her throat. "The reason he picked this ward to live in is he thought the people were weak enough to fall for his game."

Smoke Jumper

You ask Marion Barry if he aims to run for mayor if he wins. Silence. Then: "No comment." Then the wide grin, spreading slow like maple syrup on a dinner plate.

Barry has hopped out of the SUV again. He sees smoke. Someone's barbecuing. "I wonder if it's ready," he says of these strangers' barbecue, a family reunion.

A man standing over a grill sees Barry coming, feels his privacy is being invaded. "No pictures," he says. "Yes, we got hamburgers almost ready."

"Okay," says Barry. "You got any bread?"

"Only wheat bread," the cook says. "We don't eat white bread."

The former mayor rips into a hamburger, his third helping of meat in five hours. He hasn't touched a piece of fruit or a vegetable all day.

Five minutes later, Barry's in a parking lot, about to appear in an anti-violence video that some rappers are shooting. An inebriated man comes over, wearing a black T-shirt and jeans.

"I love you, man," the man says, throwing his arms around Barry's neck.

Barry is bobbing as he makes his way to the stage, which is actually someone's balcony overlooking the parking lot. The music is loud and Barry is swaying with the kids. He glances to see what's hissing on the grill. Weiners and burgers.

"I love you, man," the inebriated man says again, keeping in lockstep with Barry.

"Love you too," Barry finally says.

Barry is on the stage-balcony. One of the singers hands him the microphone. Earth Wind & Fire's "Devotion" is playing. It was hot a long time ago, when Chocolate City was humming. When Marion Barry was the best known piece of chocolate.

"I been down, but I been up," Barry says, becoming a part of the video. "When you fall down, do like me, fall on your back. That way you can see up. If you can see up, you can get up. Now, I'm No. 4 on the ballot, got a good candidate in me. Good people around me. Thank you. God bless."

There's sweat on his neck and a bounce in his step as he strolls through the smoke of the grills into the parking lot, heading for the SUV.

A woman wants to offer her sentiments about Barry.

"When we had him in office, we got respect. I was raised right here in Anacostia," says Debra Harris, 40. Barry is standing inches away, listening to her endorsement.

"Debra," he says. "You cute. You married?"

"Yeah."

"Where your husband at?"

"Right here," she says, grabbing the arm of a man who has come up behind her.

"Oh," says Barry. "Hi, husband."

He's moving on now, having traveled the length of the parking lot, to get to the SUV.

He's rolling past Matthews Memorial Baptist Church. The Rev. John Henry Kearney preached there for years. "I spoke there not long ago," Barry begins. "Rev. Kearney said, 'I don't want you to run, Marion, but if you do, I'll run with you.' The place went wild. Four weeks later, he died. Now that's a powerful story."

Minutes later the former mayor has nodded off. But at Minnesota and 16th he snaps awake. "I'm going to double the schools' athletic budgets when I get in office," he says. "You know something? Baltimore does a great job with their school athletics."

A woman is walking up to the SUV.

"How you doing, baby?" Barry says.

"I finished a school training program and you sent me a certificate," she says, beaming. "I'll never forget it. Thank you."

"See," he says, rolling away, "it's the little things. People don't forget."

Here comes a girl with a tattoo on her arm. Cameo Ooten is 29, a student at U-D.C. She's right in Barry's face. "I didn't get pregnant. Didn't have no kids. Didn't do all that wild stuff. But I can't get free food or a free apartment. What you gonna do for me?"

Barry starts to raise his hand, to answer.

"You don't have to answer now," Ooten says. "Just think about it."

Minutes later, A.D. Marshall, the advance man who has been riding in the caravan, comes walking back to the SUV. He's found a block party, fire trucks blocking the street off. "Oh, I done told them about you, Marion. They waitin'."

"Let's go," Barry says.

Folks are coming up to him the moment he alights. A lady says he helped her get her nephew out of jail and on the right track. Another woman says he helped with a job. Another woman wants a picture. Barry is kissing cheeks, hugging children, walking like a wounded athlete.

"They try to hit him with everything they can," says Abdullah Muhammad, leaning on a fence, watching. "Call him a crack addict. All kinds of stuff. Well, there ain't no angels out here."

It's hot and the music is blaring. The politician doesn't wilt, but the advance man does. "My blood pressure," Marshall says, walking his wide body to a seat. A firefighter rushes to the truck and comes back with an oxygen mask.

Barry is leaning on a fence, chatting. A woman walks up to him, joining the cacophony.

"What's your name? Where you live? You married? I need your vote now."

Someone tugs him into the street where they're dancing the Electric Slide, one of those dances so popular a long time ago, when Marion Barry was bewitching the populace of his Soufeast, his Chocolate City.

Doing the time. Raising an arm, snapping his fingers. Grinning the country grin.

—*The Washington Post Magazine* | Sept. 11, 2004

When Washington Was Fun

The grand hostesses are history, the president would rather be in bed, and there's a price tag on every evening these days. Who killed Washington society? Ask a few of the local experts.

By Maureen Orth

R ed Fay, undersecretary of the navy under John F. Kennedy, was a charming bon vivant, a great pal of the president's, and the uncle of my roommate at Berkeley in the 60s. So it was my great good luck, on my very first trip to the capital, in May 1964, just six months after Kennedy's assassination, to have "Uncle Red" invite me to dinner on the presidential yacht, the *Sequoia*. A few minutes after we arrived on board, I was amazed to see not only Jackie Kennedy but also Bobby and Ethel Kennedy and Jean Kennedy Smith and her husband, Steve Smith, walking up the gangplank. They were followed by George Stevens Jr., the youthful head of the U.S. Information Agency's motion-picture division; the Peruvian ambassador and his wife; and my roommate's parents, Mr. and Mrs. Charles McGettigan, of San Francisco. This was one of Jackie's first nights out since the tragedy, but she greeted everyone graciously. She was in ethereal white and spoke little during dinner, except to the historian Arthur Schlesinger Jr., who was seated to her right.

What I remember most vividly about that evening was an exchange I had with Bobby Kennedy, the attorney general. "What are you going to be next, vice president or senator?," I asked rather impudently, because I did not want him to think I was a brainless bimbo. The question of how the Kennedy dynasty would proceed was very much in the air, for Lyndon Johnson had not yet announced a running mate. "What do you think I should be?," Kennedy shot back, his steel-blue eyes boring into me. "Well, I think you should be senator," I said, "because everyone remembers you trying to twist arms at the last convention, and I don't think Lyndon Johnson will let you be vice president." He then opened up a barrage of questions: "Who are you? What does your father do?" In the middle of one of my answers, he turned away and waved to a group of tourists on a boat at least a hundred yards from us across the Potomac. I was highly insulted, for I had been planning to enlist in the Peace Corps, whose director was his brother-in-law Sargent Shriver, and suddenly Bobby Kennedy seemed to me like just another pol. (In those days he was still closer to J. Edgar Hoover than to César Chávez or Martin Luther King Jr.)

The dinner was great fun, however, with lots of jokes and toasts, and the next day Uncle Red took me out to Hickory Hill, Bobby and Ethel's residence in McLean, Virginia. R.F.K., in cutoff jeans, was playing touch football on the front lawn. Ethel, wearing a two-piece bathing suit, was visibly pregnant. In the driveway, a limousine waiting to take the attorney general "up to New York" was sure proof, I felt, that he must be going for the Senate. (Like Hillary Clinton, R.F.K. became an instant resident of the state, and he went on to defeat incumbent Ken Keating.) "Bobby," Red Fay said, "I brought Maureen out here so you could give her some advice about her life." Bobby smiled. "Advise her?" he said. "Hell, last night she told me what to do!"

That trip to the capital allowed me to catch a glimpse of what I thought life in society must be like at the highest level, and to talk to the people who lived it. There was no agenda, no fund-raising, and a young woman like me could actually be allowed in close. In her three years in Washington, Jackie Kennedy set a standard against which social behavior here is still measured. Her White House was a locus of beauty, taste, and excellence. At the dinner the Kennedys gave for French author and cultural minister André Malraux in May 1962, for example, the guests included Tennessee Williams, Arthur Miller, Saul Bellow, Robert Penn Warren, Mark Rothko, Andrew Wyeth, Isaac Stern, George Balanchine, Leonard Bernstein, Robert Lowell, Elia Kazan, Charles Lindbergh, David Rockefeller, and Adam Clayton Powell, the outspoken Harlem congressman.

Just 12 days before that, they had given a dinner for 49 Nobel Prize winners, which the staff referred to as "the brains dinner." That evening Jack gave an often quoted toast: "I think this is the most extraordinary collection of talent, of human knowledge, that has ever been gathered together at the White House, with the possible exception of when Thomas Jefferson dined alone." And before those two momentous events, the First Couple had thrown a sumptuous state dinner for the Shah of Iran.

Today, people who remember those days never cease to lament how the capital has changed. The cost of running for office, the proliferation of lobbyists, the intense preoccupation with security since 9/11, the increase in careers for women, the deaths or withdrawals of ruling society figures, and an unpopular president and an unpopular war have all converged to kill much of the fun and excitement once unique to Washington social life. I spoke to a number of participants in, and close observers of, the Washington social scene then and now in order to hear what they have to say about how "the city of conversation," as Henry James called it, has become more partisan, less tolerant, and unabashedly focused on doing well rather than doing good.

Letitia Baldrige, social secretary to Jackie Kennedy and author of *Taste*: For the Kennedys, the criteria of a White House guest list were great minds, people of substance, doers, and the cultural scene—painters, composers, actors. We all contributed to the guest lists, because the Kennedys cared about it. Jackie and the president went over the lists very carefully. They knew there always had to be a few fat cats, but the majority of people were those who deserved to be there . . . It was the best in everything—and hold back the political paybacks so they don't take over the guest list. The Kennedys would ask, "Where are the interesting people who make the place go?" President Kennedy used to throw the whole list in the wastebasket, he'd be so mad when he saw a list of all the political paybacks that have to go in. The Kennedys would just say no and would throw it away.

Sally Quinn, author, co-founder of the blog On Faith, wife of former *Washington Post* editor Ben Bradlee, and Georgetown hostess: The biggest difference is that entertaining now is so much more partisan. When I first came here, you'd go to dinner and all different political persuasions were represented. You were all working for the same country, but you differed in what you thought was best for the country . . . The people who did the entertaining were women who today would have a career, and what they did for a living was to bring people together. At parties, a lot of news was made and deals were made. That rarely exists anymore.

Laurie Firestone, social secretary to George Herbert Walker Bush from 1988 to 1992 and author of *An Affair to Remember: State Dinners for Home Entertaining*: Everything today is about money and "I want it my way—I don't want to compromise, and, by the way, I want a lot of money too."

Last spring, George and Laura Bush's state dinner for Queen Elizabeth II raised eyebrows all over Washington, because the guest list was not only mediocre but also heavily sprinkled with people who had contributed hundreds of thousands of dollars to Bush or the Republican Party. The event was only the fifth state dinner the Bushes had had since he took office, almost seven years ago. "They do the bare minimum, and they do it glumly," one former member of Bush's staff told me.

At the White House luncheon for Chinese president Hu Jintao, in April 2006, which I attended with my husband, Tim Russert, of NBC News, there was one gaffe after another, starting on the South Lawn in a ceremony preceding the lunch, when a heckler interrupted and rattled Hu for several minutes before she was finally removed. A White House announcer referred to Hu's country as "the Republic of China," the official name of Taiwan, China's renegade province, and, later, when Hu started to exit the stage the wrong way, Bush grabbed him by the sleeve to turn him in the right direction.

At a formal reception at the White House last December, before the Kennedy Center Honors, three women showed up wearing the same red lace Oscar de la Renta gown the First Lady had chosen, causing her to flee upstairs and change. That sort of thing never would have happened to Jackie Kennedy or Nancy Reagan. For one thing, their designers would have protected them. For another, the invited ladies would have known one another well enough to discuss in advance what they were planning to wear.

With all the open, hostile criticism of the Iraq war, it is a struggle for this administration to fill the White House with the sort of glittering members of the cultural community that the Kennedys favored. Entertainment for the Hu luncheon, for example, was provided by the Nashville Bluegrass Band, which had been formed originally to accompany Minnie Pearl, the hillbilly comedienne of the Grand Ole Opry. Similarly, at the state dinner for the Queen, the two big names among the guests were Arnold Palmer, the golf champion, and Peyton Manning, the star quarterback of the Indianapolis Colts. During the welcoming ceremony, President Bush said that the 81-year-old sovereign "had helped our nation celebrate its bicentennial in 17—" Then he caught himself and concluded "in 1976."

Buffy Cafritz, member of the Kennedy Center board and noted Republican hostess: I have never seen a worse guest list than that of the state dinner for the Queen. Arnold Palmer? He won the British Open in 1962! Peyton Manning? And all the corporate people they had. Then someone said, "How dumb can you be, Buffy? It's the library. He has to fund the [George Bush presidential] library."

Liz Stevens, Democratic hostess married to George Stevens Jr., co-producer of the Kennedy Center Honors: Do you think the Queen had fun? I didn't know she was such a jock.

Letitia Baldrige: Now it is so much more of a payoff than it used to be. Now it's just payoff, payoff, payoff. It's still a great party, because it is still the White House, still the most fabulous place in the world for a party.

Elisabeth Hasselbeck, the pretty blonde Republican of ABC's *The View*, was a guest at the state dinner for the Queen. The next morning she gave her viewers the inside scoop, including the scary fact that wives were not allowed to sit next to their husbands. "When we first opened our place cards and saw we were at different tables, we had a semi-private panic attack," she confided, adding, "but I had Jeb Bush to my left. It was amazing to be able to sit with the Prince [Philip] and First Lady, who was so generous. This was such a meeting of the two nations, and I just thought, Gosh, it was such a peaceful moment." Dessert, she reported, had also rung alarm bells. "They had rose blossoms for dessert. They brought out a bowl of water that smelled like roses, and then something in the middle. And someone asked me what was for dessert, and I said, 'This is it.' But then I saw Secretary of State Condoleezza Rice—you dip your hands in it and you wash your fingers in it."

Lea Berman, former social secretary to George and Laura Bush and wife of lobbyist Wayne Berman: We stopped using finger bowls at all but the fanciest dinners, because people don't know what to do with them. Mrs. Bush said, "Don't use them."

Deeda Blair, biomedical-research advocate, international social figure, and wife of former ambassador William McCormick Blair Jr.: It's almost vanished, the finger bowl. I can remember, in Paris and in Washington, women who cultivated scented geraniums in pots to have a scented leaf in a finger bowl. Everything was very *raffiné*.

Many of the grandes dames who were so *raffiné* back then were of the World War II generation. They usually came from, or married into, old money, an illustrious family, or great wealth. They often had lived abroad and spoke more than one language. Susan Mary Alsop, for example, who had a leading role in the J.F.K. Georgetown set, was a descendant of Founding Father John Jay, and her platonic husband in her second marriage was syndicated columnist Joseph Alsop, a cousin of the Roosevelts and a flamboyant and irascible snob, who got behind Jack Kennedy almost from the start and took great pride in arranging artfully mixed dinners that were designed to produce elevated discourse as well as great gossip. Evangeline Bruce, another of the capital's doyennes, was the wife of millionaire David K. E. Bruce, who served as a leading diplomat in France, Britain, Germany, and China. British-born Pamela Harriman's first husband was the son of Winston Churchill, but she really gained fame for her long list of lovers, including Gianni Agnelli, Edward R. Murrow, and Averell Harriman. She eventually married Harriman, in 1971, became a fixture in Washington society, and created a fund-raising Democratic political-action committee known as "Pam pac." Seven years after Averell's death, she became Bill Clinton's ambassador to France. Katharine "Kay" Graham was the famous publisher of *The Washington Post*, which brought down Richard Nixon, but she was also a friend of another Republican president, Ronald Reagan, and his wife. Truman Capote gave his snobbish Black and White Ball in 1966 in Graham's honor. Her great pal was Meg Greenfield, *The Post's* editorial-page editor. All of these women have died within the last 15 years. The sole survivor, Oatsie Charles, has retired to Newport, Rhode Island. A bipartisan philanthropist, she told *W* magazine after George W. Bush's first term, "As far as I'm concerned, the Washington I knew is over."

Gahl Burt, social secretary to Nancy Reagan from 1983 to 1985: There were three spheres: the White House, the embassies, and Georgetown. The hostesses used to be Susan Mary Alsop, Oatsie Charles, Evangeline Bruce, Kay Graham, and Pamela Harriman.

They have all largely disappeared, and no one picked up the ball. No one has the embassy ball, and no one has the Georgetown or White House social scene either. They have all petered out.

Ann Jordan, board member, married to Vernon Jordan, attorney and power broker: It's very hard to become the new Pamela Harriman. Think about the life Pamela lived. That was a glamorous world. I don't see any Gianni Agnellis in this group. When you think about wars, it is a certain kind of experience. The Second World War brought out the best in people.

Deeda Blair: These were legendary women who would have hated to be called socialites, because what is a socialite? The late Lorraine Cooper, who was married to Kentucky senator John Sherman Cooper, was a cross between eccentric and exotic—profoundly intelligent. She did many dinners and lunches that were uniquely special. The Coopers had served in India, and she would have wonderful saris draped across a table. She knew how to combine people and really paid attention. She gave a famous garden party every June. It was an event that was really dazzling. The Senate and the Congress all turned out.

Entertaining then was more personal, and people had staff and wonderful cooks. During that time, there was a great party cook named Dora, and the dinners she provided were as homemade as you could get. Now people ring up caterers. That simply wasn't done by serious hostesses in the past. Pamela Harriman, who probably had more of a political agenda than the others, also had an elegant annual garden party that people yearned to be invited to. For those women, a major imperative was getting the right combination of people, not with the intent of accomplishing something—creating festivities with guest stars to raise money—but just to bring interesting and powerful individuals together in a catalytic way.

They were also concerned with looks and style. Women did their own flowers, and were proud of their pretty linens. Oatsie Charles, for instance, was known for her china and silver. Today, the Style section of *The Washington Post* virtually ignores social dinners. They'd rather write about what Lindsay Lohan is up to. In the old days, the hostess herself got on the telephone and followed up with a reminder. Today, you are apt to get invited by e-mail. Thank-you notes were once obligatory and personal. Today, you get an e-mail—"I had a great time."

Polly Kraft, painter, widow of syndicated columnist Joseph Kraft and power-broker attorney Lloyd Cutler: The Georgetown set was mostly about journalists—it really started because of Joe Alsop. Journalists didn't make a lot of money—it wasn't a big thing to be rich. It's all so polarized now, and pretty boring. They don't treat journalists very well. There is not that excitement, that same thrill you [used to] get.

Liz Stevens: Ethel Kennedy's parties were fabulous. There was a great mix, and you were there to have fun—the only purpose was to have fun. That doesn't seem to be the case now.

Letitia Baldrige: Jackie Kennedy introduced round plywood tables and cloths to the floor. Within four weeks Bloomingdale's was selling round cloths to the floor, and carpenters all over the country were making plywood tabletops. Jackie said conversation was best with 8 or 10—now 12 or 14 crowd around. We also had people like [Theodore Roosevelt's daughter] Alice Roosevelt Longworth, who was loved and cherished. There hasn't been another character like that since.

Andrea Mitchell, NBC correspondent and wife of former Federal Reserve chairman Alan Greenspan: My introduction to that world was pre meeting Kay Graham and Meg Greenfield. It was an introduction to Judith Huxley, a food columnist for *The Post*. She used to have table-for-eight dinner parties, with lots of conversation around a round table—New Dealers, artists, gardeners. She was married to Aldous Huxley's only child, Matthew. She had this salon going. . . . It was not about social climbing or social connections. It was about conversation. Meg Greenfield had one round table in a small house on R Street [in Georgetown]. She would have lots of bright Democrats and Republicans. The difference was that in the past people who entertained were old Georgetown grand ladies or journalists, and sometimes those two were the same. Now the younger generation is political types. This new generation that entertains a lot are lobbyists. Before, you would not willingly have a lobbyist to a party.

Sally Quinn: I find that, with both parties, the longer an administration goes on, the times get really bad no matter what. There are scandals in the second term. So they hunker down, circle the wagons, and disappear—there is no community at all.

Buffy Cafritz: We are in serious times, and this president is not a type to socialize—he likes to go to bed.

Gahl Burt: [George W. Bush] is not a social animal and not sociable . . . The Reagans had a state dinner every single month, with the exception of July and August. We scheduled them six months out. Every single month we were looking for a state dinner and actively perusing whom we should honor. There was a real reach out to foreign leaders. It helps you to start to know a world leader, instead of just meeting him in an office, and the wives get to know each other. If a real friendship develops—like Reagan and Thatcher—it gets you through the sticky times.

Laurie Firestone: George Bush Sr. worked at entertaining, in the sense he knew how important it was. We were entertaining the top six countries all the time [Great Britain, France, Germany, Canada, Japan, and Russia], not just at state dinners, but private receptions, lunches, and dinners. . . . He always told me that sitting at a dinner or a lunch and talking to people, and breaking bread at a meal together, [made] negotiations the next day much easier. . . . Every time Bush would lose a vote, he'd tell me to get on the phone and get the leaders over—at the time, they were all Democrats. We had a lot of bipartisan functions.

Buffy Cafritz: President Reagan used to have [Democratic Speaker of the House] Tip O'Neill over for a drink. Nancy had a little lunch here in May, and Bob Strauss [Democrat and former ambassador to Russia] sat right next to her in his wheelchair. He used to go in the back door and advise her. You don't see that in this administration.

Ken Duberstein, lobbyist and former chief of staff for Ronald Reagan: As much as our campaign was anti-Washington, the Reagans understood you had to be part of Washington, and they encouraged us to participate fully and go out. That meant embassies—where we chatted over dinner and did so much business.

Sally Quinn: Once Kay [Graham] died, that was the end of bipartisan entertaining.

When Jimmy Carter was elected, in 1976, he appeared deliberately to downplay White House opulence. He was heavily criticized for going on television in a cardigan sweater and telling Americans to turn down their thermostats to save energy.

Liz Stevens: Jimmy Carter started the downward trend. He did not serve drinks at the White House. After that, Reagan was the land of all-out. The wives [of the Reagan circle] got more involved than anyone. They went on boards.

Gahl Burt: Reagan's Kitchen Cabinet was so moneyed, a good chunk of the library got raised from 10 people. That makes a big difference. . . . Between the [Walter] Annenbergs, the [Alfred] Bloomingdales, and the [Charles] Wicks, those people didn't blink to have a major dinner at Blair House that cost a lot of money. Those were fabulous parties with glittering guest lists. . . . The de la Rentas, the Henry Kissingers, [socialite walker] Jerry Zipkin were together in New York before the Washington connection. For Zipkin it didn't hurt to have your best friend be the wife of the president. . . . If J.F.K.'s were the golden years for the Democrats, then Reagan's were the golden years for the G.O.P.

Letitia Baldrige: By the time the Reagans were in, the money started to matter a lot. California money and western money we were just not used to. That changed things a lot. The Annenbergs had a lot of money to throw around.

Lea Berman: I remember at the end of the Reagan years we got Democrats in Congress, and it really got ugly at dinner parties. We were just under siege the whole dinner. I told my husband, "I am not going to go through that again." People of different parties weren't really friends.

Buffy Cafritz: I remember Kay Graham had a lovely dinner in March of 2001—she died that summer. George W. Bush was there, and so was Laura, who was so adorable and outgoing and wanted to be part of the community. Everybody had high hopes *he* would be part of the community. Then we had 9/11.

Lea Berman: In the first term, September 11 threw them off. They did a lot of quiet diplomacy, based on the foreign country asking for a certain kind of visit; they asked for Crawford, Texas. Going to Crawford was considered intimate. Also, at the dinners, there are certainly people who are invited who choose not to come. For entertainers, the vehemence with which some said no, you could tell they were not supporters.

When the Clintons came to town, in 1992, there was tangible excitement that these two attractive young couples, the Clintons and the Gores, would somehow revive Camelot. Instead, the Clintons got off to a shaky start, with the issue of gays in the military, Nannygate, the suicide of Vince Foster, Travelgate, the failure of Hillary Clinton's health-care plan, and Whitewater. There were so many scandals that the White House came to see the press as the enemy, and the First Couple did not venture out much, but they sent loyalists such as Mack and Donna McLarty, who were Arkansas friends, and Vernon and Ann Jordan to cover Georgetown.

In the beginning, however, they also had a series of dinners in their private quarters. At one, which I attended with my husband, Bill Clinton gave a detailed tour of the Lincoln Bedroom. Later, that room would give rise to yet another scandal when it was revealed that wealthy donors were being invited to spend the night there. The Clintons did have a very lively, bipartisan engagement party early on for Bill's adviser James Carville and his very Republican fiancée, Mary Matalin; they also entertained at informal "movie nights"; and they significantly helped the cause of peace in Northern Ireland by beginning an annual White House St. Patrick's Day party, which both sides—who would never ordinarily venture into the same room together—attended. The Clintons, however, appeared in the end to view the White House not as a vibrant salon in which to host the best and the brightest, but as coveted real estate that could be used for fund-raising.

Dee Dee Myers, press secretary during Clinton's first term and *Vanity Fair* contributing editor: The Democratic National Committee controlled who was invited. They brought in Clinton people from all over the country. They called it "political-base building" and the white-hot center was the White House. Los Angeles was huge. When the film-production company DreamWorks was being launched, I remember walking out of the grand hallway during a state dinner, and on a bench, deeply engrossed, were David Geffen, Steven Spielberg, and Jeffrey Katzenberg [the founders of DreamWorks]. The Clintons expanded the size of state dinners and had them in a tent. They had two or three events and lined them up for a week in the tent. They had the Emperor of Japan in a tent. The thing about the Clintons is that more is always more. It loses intimacy and grace.

Liz Stevens: If some cause needed help, the Clintons were willing to have an event. The staff was exhausted. They were constantly feeding people.

Sally Quinn: In terms of entertaining being partisan, it started with Clinton. The people who were seen as "hostesses" were people who had money or were raising money. . . . When the stuff about Clinton and women started appearing, in the second term, things shut down. Everybody wanted to go hide in a cave. For people willing to defend him, it became intolerable for them to go out.

In 2000, after being elected to the Senate, Hillary Clinton bought a fashionable house near the British and Italian Embassies. Before her run for the presidency, she added on to the house in order to have more space for entertaining.

Sally Quinn: Since Hillary has been here in the Senate for the last eight years, I think I've seen her twice. Otherwise, she is at fundraisers. She entertains constantly, but it is all political. It is people who work for her or raise money for her.

The Clintons' second term was mired in the Monica Lewinsky scandal and ended with the president's shocking eleventh-hour pardon of the fugitive financier Marc Rich. Favored hostesses during the time were Clinton fund-raisers, who are now hoping a second Clinton presidency will provide a new opportunity to shine. One of the most aggressive contenders still vying to become a successor to the likes of Pamela Harriman is Beth Dozoretz, former Democratic National Committee finance chair.

Dozoretz, who constantly touted her close, personal relationship with Bill Clinton and pledged to raise $1 million for the Clinton library, is a onetime garment-industry executive married to Ron Dozoretz, a psychiatrist and the C.E.O. of a behavioral-health-care company that is heavily dependent on state contracts and that has been criticized in the past for providing substandard services. He contributes to both Republicans and Democrats. His wife first became known to the public when she took the Fifth Amendment before Congress in order not to have to answer questions about her role in the Marc Rich pardon. Last February, Clinton friends were taken aback when the Dozoretzes hosted a fund-raiser for

New Mexico governor Bill Richardson, a presidential candidate, but that should not have been surprising considering the contract for a reported $325 million that Ron Dozoretz's FHC Health Systems has in New Mexico. Beth Dozoretz is said to phone media outlets to tout her parties and ask to be included on "A-lists," and in the middle of dinners she allegedly confers with her husband to discuss whom they've spoken with and whom they should cultivate.

Lady Catherine Meyer, wife of the former British ambassador Sir Christopher Meyer: Poor Beth. She did try to invite us all the time.

Buffy Cafritz: Beth Dozoretz? Enough said.

The most controversial nouveau social figure on the scene is student-loan impresario Catherine Reynolds, whose tax-exempt nonprofit student-loan company, EduCap, is currently under investigation by Congress, the I.R.S., and the New York State attorney general's office. *The Washington Post* has reported that, with funds from EduCap, Reynolds has donated more than $100 million to cultural institutions, including $400,000 to her daughter's private school; has bought a $30 million Gulfstream IV private jet; and has given $9 million to her husband, Wayne, who runs the Academy of Achievement, another nonprofit organization, which stages an annual multi-million-dollar weekend extravaganza to bring global glitterati together with outstanding graduate students. After all the negative media attention, Reynolds's student-loan business, which was already being downsized, was severely curtailed, and dozens of employees were laid off.

In 2002, Reynolds made headlines when she pledged $100 million to the Kennedy Center, but the project in question was abandoned, so in the end she paid nothing. She still pledges $1 million a year for special performances, and stages a lavish annual dinner there. The $38 million she pledged to the Smithsonian Institution she took back, because scholars at the museum thought she wanted too much say in the contents of its exhibitions. After pushing to have Laura Bush host a White House dinner to benefit the Dance Theatre of Harlem, to which Reynolds had pledged $1 million, she brought in her own producers to stage the entertainment. The event later aired on PBS. In 2005, when she became chairman of the board, she promised that she would help the dance company for three years, but she severed ties after a year. Lady Catherine Meyer had a similar experience with Reynolds and PACT (Parents and Abducted Children Together), a nonprofit Meyer began because her ex-husband, in Germany, had refused to return their two sons to her, and the German courts sided with him.

Lea Berman: Catherine Reynolds is very persuasive and very determined. She had very fixed ideas of what she wanted the evening to be and who the entertainers should be for the White House dinner for the Dance Theatre of Harlem. It was an intense experience.

Lady Catherine Meyer: She immediately said, "I'll help you." She organized a dinner at the embassy. We invited 85 percent of the people, and she paid for it. It was completely free for us, and whatever money people paid for the tickets went towards the charity. At that time, around 2000, nobody had ever heard of Catherine Reynolds. I said, "Why don't you join the board?" Every time we had a dinner or a lunch, we invited her and her husband. I wasn't born yesterday; I knew why she cultivated me. She wanted to be invited. She stepped into the British Embassy, met people, and then she dropped me. . . . She made a pledge of $100,000 with the condition I would match it. I went out and raised the money, but lots didn't stack up for her, and she only gave $38,000, which of course was very disappointing. I never heard from her again. I was completely shocked.

Buffy Cafritz: Catherine Reynolds has left behind a trail of broken friendships. This I will never be able to understand. She has none of the old relationships. The [Tom] Daschles [former Democratic Senate majority leader from South Dakota and his wife, Linda] are now her best friends. I can go through seven people she's dumped. Nobody understands her. She goes to the ladies' room and her husband stands outside. Why not? She's the bank.

Thanks to the explosion of information technology and the billions appropriated for domestic security in the last several years, Washington today is flush as never before, and a whole group of people not associated with politics is coming to the fore. However, the city is so polarized that even the caterers are characterized as Republican or Democrat. Members of Congress rarely socialize across party lines. They vote on bills at night, so they don't really go out much, and as a rule they do not bring their families to live in Washington anymore, because it's too expensive and many of their spouses work.

With the spread of the 24-hour news cycle and the rise of the Internet, interviewers and their subjects are occupied more than ever before, so there is little time for politicians or journalists to socialize. Also, social affability and compromise do not play well with the increasingly powerful bloggers, who zealously patrol the Republican and Democratic bases.

Liz Stevens: The other night five new congressmen came to dinner. In the old days we used to see lots of senators and members of Congress. These members had never been asked by anyone. So they told us, "You are our new best friends! We haven't gone out at all." None has a family here. They are here for three days and then they go home and fund-raise. It seems to me it's a miserable life.

Ken Duberstein: The result of partisanship is gridlock—nothing gets done—and Washington and Capitol Hill have become the laughingstock of the nation. If you had a more nonpartisan social life, people would understand one another better as individuals, understand people's motives and integrity, and not see everything in terms of political one-upmanship. You also know that if they ever have to decide between being on a cable program and your dinner party, it's no contest.

Ted Kennedy, Democratic senator from Massachusetts: When my children were growing up and we had votes at night, the members' wives would bring picnics and we would watch our children play soccer on the lawn and listen to the various bands that would play on the Capitol steps. It was a way of getting to know the other members and their families, both Republican and Democrat.

Grega Daly, prominent hostess married to architect Leo Daly: Intimate, small dinners have always been the most intellectually stimulating, and still are, but they've changed over the past 10 or so years. It used to be that both Democrats and Republicans would attend, and interesting discussions would ensue, focused on the future of our country. Today the animosity between the two political parties is so great and so openly hostile that the blending of the guests at the dinners is no longer possible.

Letitia Baldrige: There is no question it is different here. The people who are giving the parties are the lobbyists. They eat lavishly all for a political reason. In the old days, 50 or 60 years ago, there was a real society here.

Bob Barnett, lawyer; book representative for Bill and Hillary Clinton, Bob Woodward, and Alan Greenspan; lawyer for my family; and husband of Rita Braver, of CBS News: Given the legal restrictions on lobbying, social occasions are used in a totally legal and proper way to advocate your client's position to a lawmaker or a regulator without having to spend money that is restricted. . . . Socializing is an important part of life for lobbyists and lawyers. A lot of old barriers have broken down. . . . The irony is, as more barriers are made official and written, the looser it is in the social realm.

Ken Duberstein: The pressure goes both ways. Everybody is getting leaned on, not just for presidential candidates but more importantly for Congress and the Senate. The fax machine just spews out these invitations for social events for fund-raising—for $500, for $1,000. I hear from people what kind of pressure they are under to contribute. Fund-raising has become insatiable.

One consequence of the fund-raising carnival is that embassies have been largely sidelined. The Bush White House barely socializes, so there is no one for embassies to honor in order to draw top guests. Embassies cannot contribute cash to members of Congress, so why should members bother to go to embassy parties? The British still make an effort to entertain, and from 1998 to 2005, when he was Colombia's ambassador to the United States, Luis Alberto Moreno was a highly visible social presence, gathering support for the $4 billion in U.S. aid under Plan Colombia. He became friends with Kay Graham by inviting her to a birthday dinner for Gabriel García Márquez, his country's Nobel Prize–winning author.

Luis Alberto Moreno, current head of the Inter-American Development Bank: Any ambassador has to influence 500 people [Congress and the White House], depending on the portfolio of his country. If you request a regular meeting, it takes two years. I would never say no, and I'd always try to go to big events. Nobody notices if you are late. I'd go into a room and say hello even if they were eating. Then I'd leave my little sound bite and get my feedback. You need to find ways to network and meet because Americans do business all the time.

Today, the only embassy making a big push is Kuwait—not the soft-spoken ambassador Salem Al-Sabah himself, but his intense, flamboyant wife, Rima, a former Lebanese journalist with platinum-blond hair down to the middle of her back, who in October gave birth to her fourth child, at age 45. Invitations to the first of four baby showers were mailed four months in advance, and 120 women attended. Rima Al-Sabah, who is known to call guests who have R.S.V.P.'d no to one of her dinners and plead with them to change their minds, draws Bush Cabinet members and top generals to her lavish evenings, which are always carefully photographed. Oil companies and their C.E.O.'s help sponsor her yearly benefit for various causes, where guests have included Angelina Jolie and Michael Douglas. About the only big private black-tie event last spring that both Republicans and Democrats attended was the Al-Sabahs' 60th-birthday party for Marvin Hamlisch, the principal pops conductor with the National Symphony.

Rima Al-Sabah: We came to Washington three weeks before September 11, and what happened was a shock. On September 12, I had a lunch invitation. I didn't think anyone would go, but the hostess said, "No, we want to show life goes on." The first question I was asked was "Did you see what you Arabs did?" I was horrified. So it is very important to change the stereotype. All countries have extremists. . . . After September 11 there became a need to be out there. I do big dinners for 120 or 140 and small dinners for 22 around a table. Entertaining is a crucial part of diplomatic work. I do four big dinners a year and small dinners twice a month and lunches. . . . A big dinner is a whole production. A successful party is not only a mix of beautiful setting and good food but who's on the chairs. The seating is very important. I always seat a guest next to one person they know and one they don't, but might be interested in. I didn't used to invite so much in advance, but then I started getting invitations two and three months ahead. You don't have to for small dinners as much, but for big dinners it's better.

Buffy Cafritz: Rima is the leading diplomatic hostess. She asks you to attend six months in advance. When my brother was asked to attend four months in advance, he said, "No, I'll be attending a funeral."

Washington is far more diverse today than it was when Wasps with pedigrees who went into journalism and government service constituted the Georgetown set. These days in the capital, journalists are far more adversarial toward politicians, often looking to play "gotcha," so the easy camaraderie between observers and participants no longer exists. And while Washington has always had plenty of policy wonks, the new influx to the D.C. area of high-tech companies that thrive on government research and contracts has created a whole class of fabulously wealthy entrepreneurs. Money lubricates this once sleepy southern town, which used to consider people first as human beings and second as Republicans or Democrats. Recently, the social broadsheet *Washington Life* ran a cover story on the richest people in the city, which would have been considered in very poor taste, if not altogether unheard of, just a few years earlier.

Even the prestigious press dinners that everyone used to look forward to, which the president and vice president attended in order to be able to joust with the capital's key journalists, have become embarrassing and dreaded. Several years ago, heavy-metal rocker and reality-TV star Ozzy Osbourne, who was one of the growing number of notorious invited guests present at the White House Correspondents' Dinner, stood up on his chair and shouted, "I am fucking more famous than all of you!" He wasn't quite correct, but until a new administration takes office, Washington as a social organism is essentially dead.

—*Vanity Fair* | December 2007

A Walk Through Congressional Cemetery

The 60,000 graves at Congressional Cemetery reveal stories about our past that you won't find anywhere else

By Josh Swiller

T ucked into a little-visited corner of the District up against the Anacostia River, a couple of blocks from RFK Stadium and across the street from the DC jail, Congressional Cemetery holds nearly 60,000 graves.

Come at dusk and the light is surreal, the sun setting over the city like a red-hot tear. Come at midday and you might be the only person here, walking the grounds as if it's your own private estate. It feels far away from the Washington power games.

Which is odd because it's Congressional Cemetery. It's just 18 blocks from the Capitol and is the resting place for scores of people from that more famous place.

But once they come here, they seem to disappear. There's a man named Stephen Pleasonton, buried near the main entrance, who rescued the Constitution and the Declaration of Independence from being captured and burned by the British in the War of 1812. He crammed the documents into coarse bags, commandeered a few rickety carts amid the general panic, and took off for Georgetown with minutes to spare. Had he not made it, how different would our history be?

When my girlfriend, Leah, first asked me to meet her at Congressional Cemetery, I was skeptical. To hang out at a graveyard seemed morbid and strange.

"There's nothing to do there," I said.

"There's history," she said.

"History? That's over by the Mall."

"Meet me at the entrance."

History. If Sarah Palin becomes the next female candidate for President, she should stop by the cemetery and pay homage to the first one. Belva Ann Lockwood—attorney, educator, author, suffragist— ran for President in 1884. Four thousand people (all male, of course, because women couldn't vote for another 36 years) voted for her.

Palin is polarizing, but she has nothing on Preston Brooks. A congressman from South Carolina, he was infuriated when, in 1856, Senator Charles Sumner of Massachusetts denigrated Brooks's cousin, Senator Andrew Pickens Butler, a supporter of slavery, on the Senate floor. Said Sumner of Pickens: "The senator touches nothing which he does not disfigure with error . . . He cannot open his mouth, but out there flies a blunder." Two days later, Brooks defended his cousin's honor by beating Sumner with a cane until the Massachusetts lawmaker was unconscious.

Cable news can give the impression that today's partisan fighting is more heated than ever, but there's solace in the fact that we have a long history of congressional insults. And that we're not caning each other anymore.

For Preston Brooks, Congressional Cemetery offers further solace: While 18 blocks away the incumbents may be thrown out every two years, at the cemetery they remain in office forever.

Legend has it that the night after John Wilkes Booth fired the shot that killed President Lincoln, one of his fellow conspirators,

Lewis Powell, hid in a vault at Congressional Cemetery before making his way across the river.

Seven people who were at Ford's Theatre that evening to see the play *Our American Cousin* are here as well, including the doorman who let the President inside.

As are two of the 16 doctors who worried and bled his body. Plus a policeman who helped carry the President from the theater to William Petersen's boardinghouse across the street.

The owner of the inn where Booth had a final drink for courage before leaving for the theater is buried here. And the businessman who rented Booth a horse that night.

So is Booth's co-conspirator David Herold, who fled with the broken-legged assassin for 12 days across Maryland and Virginia and was caught after the shootout on Garrett's Farm, tried, convicted, hung, and buried in an unmarked grave.

One lesson of the cemetery: The history of this city is not just of leading men but of small actors as well, even unmarked and unidentifiable ones. And all end up in the same place.

Leah and I walk the brick paths and take in the names and dates and inscriptions. The tombstones next to the cemetery chapel are lined up in crisp, soldierly rows. Down the hill, they huddle together like cold commuters at the nearby Potomac Avenue bus stop or they ride and tip over groundswells like surfers. Some graves are actually tables where you can rest and picnic. Some are crypts, half buried in the ground. Others stand alone in clear expanses—statues dropped from space.

The cemetery's stories illuminate a history that the museums on the Mall don't cover—for example, that brothels were legal in the District until 1914. Mary Ann Hall, DC's all-time finest madam, for decades had a brothel not far from the Capitol. She bought nine plots at the cemetery—one for her mother, one for her sister, and several others for men who are now nameless. Lovers? Customers?

In her time, she was famous for keeping a cellar stocked with $100 bottles of wine and Champagne—$100 in 19th-century dollars. She was worth the equivalent of millions when she died. A low stone coping surrounds her plot. WELCOME, it says. Even in death, 125 years on, a graceful host.

District native William H. Cross is buried here—most of him. In 1881, he was part of an expedition to the North Pole that got stranded. When rescue boats finally came, they noted that some of Mr. Cross was missing. "His friends had him over for lunch," explains Patrick Crowley, the chairman of the Cemetery Board.

Beau Hickman is buried here, but not his spirit. A gambler, carouser, and freeloader, Hickman never held a job and got by on his wits and charm. When he died in 1873, he was buried in a potter's field. By the time his friends learned of this, they were drunk and Hickman's remains were being dug up by grave robbers. Hickman's friends broke up the robbery, carried him to Congressional Cemetery, and put him in a shallow hole they dug themselves. Hickman's aggrieved ghost is said to haunt what used to be the site of the hotel where he lived, at Sixth Street and Pennsylvania Avenue in downtown DC.

Two or three times a month, a bus pulls up at the front gate and unloads a marching band in full dress regalia, and it troops in formation over to the grave of John Philip Sousa. There the musicians play a tune or two. Then they troop back, board their bus, and drive back to Indiana or New Jersey or South Carolina—wherever they've come from.

Sousa is buried here not because he's a national hero and the composer of "Stars and Stripes Forever" but because he was a local kid: Southeast DC-born, -raised, and -buried. That's also why J. Edgar Hoover is buried here, in a small family plot surrounded by iron fencing.

Alongside these graves celebrating local residents are rows of tombs for important people from distant places who are buried in those distant places. Called cenotaphs and shaped like squarish, half-buried dunce caps, these empty tombs commemorate, not at all artfully, the lives of national political leaders. Henry Clay and John C. Calhoun are here—detesting each other in life, they're together in death. But not really. Just their names. Tip O'Neill is here, too. Only his name. John Adams. His name. Empty graves.

Just when it seems the cemetery has crossed over into absurd symbolism, you come across the inscription on the headstone of

William Miller, age one year, four months: PARENTS, FOR ME DO NOT LAMENT. I WAS NOT YOURS, BUT ONLY LENT.

Tom Lantos, who died three years ago, is one of the most recent members of Congress to be buried at the cemetery.

Representing San Francisco, he was pro-choice, pro-gay rights, creator of human-rights committees, an advocate for international justice—he was also the only Holocaust survivor to serve in Congress.

Then there's Leonard Matlovich, the first openly gay serviceman, buried in a hollow beneath a cherry tree. When he came out of the closet in 1975, it was a national news story, covered by the networks, trumpeted on the cover of *Time*. He was discharged from the Air Force and later died of AIDS. Matlovich designed his tombstone, which reads: WHEN I WAS IN THE MILITARY THEY GAVE ME A MEDAL FOR KILLING TWO MEN AND A DISCHARGE FOR LOVING ONE.

Perhaps what's most striking about Matlovich's resting place is the gravestones nearby: They have dates of birth but not of death. These stones are placeholders for men and women young and healthy who want to spend their eternal rest next to their hero.

Also near Matlovich is the grave of Clyde Tolson, J. Edgar Hoover's longtime companion. Tolson's family didn't want him next to Hoover and insisted on a spot 30 yards down the hill from him. Matlovich took the one next to him.

Lieutenant Dan Choi, the outspoken gay serviceman who became the face of the push to end the military's "don't ask, don't tell" policy, came by early in the morning on Veterans Day last year to pay his respects. He spent the better part of an hour cleaning off Matlovich's grave. Then he went to the White House to get arrested. A month later, "don't ask, don't tell" was on its way to history.

Thirteen Native American tribes have members buried here, more than in any other place in the world.

"This one is beautiful. Taza, Cochise's son," says Terri Maxfield, the cemetery's office manager, when I visit Congressional again. Maxfield leads me to a grave fronted by a carved head with features reminiscent of a sphinx, elegant and lonely, near a towering evergreen.

We walk across a ridge. "And here is Push-Ma-Ta-Ha, a Choctaw Indian who came to Washington in the 1820s seeking the debt owed to his nation by the government," Maxfield says. The gravestone notes that Push-Ma-Ta-Ha's deathbed wish was that the "big guns be fired over me." The wish was granted. The debt was not paid.

Here is Scarlet Crow. Kidnapped and murdered.

Yellow Wolf—died a month after meeting Mary Lincoln.

Peter P. Pitchlynn, chief of the Choctaw nation, of whom Charles Dickens said in 1841: "He was a remarkably handsome man, as stately and complete a gentleman of nature's making as ever I beheld." Pitchlynn pressed for Choctaw claims for decades, with almost no success.

Maxfield tells me she moved to Washington a few years ago and was blindsided by the pace: "You get to thinking politics is the only thing that matters. And then you come here to the cemetery. And there's something . . . " She trails off. We're looking down the hill, over the grave of Push-Ma-Ta-Ha, and past him, at Matlovich's memorial under a cherry tree.

"Honor," Maxfield says. "That's what this place has. It honors people. Even those who had everything taken away from them."

The flat unbroken rows, the long planed fields, the burial ground as museum—with the same rules not to run, touch, or talk too loudly. Arlington National Cemetery changed everything, Maxfield says. Before it opened in 1864, cemeteries were places where families gathered to play and picnic and toast the departed. Death was a little less scary, a little more part of life.

Congressional Cemetery was built along this older, friendlier model. Burial plots are for sale, Maxfield adds, a thousand of them.

Congressional has no giant monuments. No 40-foot angels, cupids spewing water, multi-storied crypts here. This structural humility recalls the fact that DC wasn't a city built by powerful industrialists or old money but by a young government and by men working together. It's a nice thing to reflect on—in some ways, Washington is America's most democratic accomplishment, started from scratch by men dreaming of equality.

Except for the slaves, who did most of the work. Some are buried here. As are the men who designed their places of labor—William Thornton (the Capitol's first architect), George Hadfield (its second), Robert Mills (who designed the Washington Monument)—all here.

On a cold spring morning, Leah and I walk through the cemetery again. A light snow is falling, disappearing as it reaches the ground. We pass the empty graves, the slaves who built the Capitol, the first people who held office inside it.

We pass a white granite bench that reads poopsie and baby pie on one side and on the other one lifetime together was not enough. It stops us. What is enough? How many hours a day are enough at the office? What accomplishments are sufficient? What is it fair for us to ask of each other?

In the cemetery's public vault, where bodies were once stored as they awaited transportation to their final destination, William Henry Harrison, our ninth President, dead from a long speech on a cold day, spent three months. Three times longer than he spent in office.

Near the west gate is Mathew Brady, Civil War photographer, who did more than anyone else to popularize photography, the first and still most influential war photojournalist. He died in a New York poorhouse after being hit by a streetcar—having spent his fortune in the production of his work, mistakenly anticipating that the government would reimburse him—and was buried in a simple grave in a plot owned by his wife's family. In 1988, a group of 11 people from Ohio paid for and installed a more striking headstone.

Which is another lesson of this cemetery.

Great men are buried here. But so often greatness goes unnoticed, unrewarded, until long after death—if at all. Or, as in the case of President Harrison, it's met by a quick and undignified end.

"I think," Leah says as we pass a grave commemorating a Revolutionary War veteran who went on to serve in the House but whom no one has heard of now, "perspective is an important thing to remember. Follow the news too closely and it will seem that the fate of mankind hinges on whether a tax cut expires or not. But it doesn't."

"What does it depend on?" I ask.

She takes my hand. The snow is falling. We walk on.

—Washingtonian | May 19, 2011

Inside DC's Secret Covid Morgue

During the Covid Pandemic, the District built a secret disaster morgue, assembled an army of volunteers to staff it, and trained people who had never previously seen a dead body to care for the dead. This is the story of the Covid morgue—and the quiet force of civil servants tending to everyone lost to Covid.

By Luke Mullins

A pril 21, 2020—The clerics have been sworn to secrecy. On this warm morning, they've come to a vast and empty parking lot, instructed not to tell anyone of its location. The pitch of asphalt is unusually secure, hidden behind a 12-foot chain-link fence that's been swathed in sheets of black tarp to prevent anyone from peering through. At the front gate, armed soldiers stand guard.

Inside, large trailers are arranged behind tented canopies and banks of lights. Metal ramps are affixed to each trailer so that stretchers can be wheeled in. The interior walls of the trailers are lined with seven rows of metallic shelving, sturdy enough to support thousands of pounds. The temperature is 24 degrees.

The clergymen gather with a handful of city officials in front of the canopies. They form a circle, each six feet apart from the next.

Reverend Andre Towner of Covenant Baptist United Church of Christ.

Imam Talib Shareef of Nation's Mosque.

Rabbi Shmuel Herzfeld of Ohev Sholom—The National Synagogue.

Dr. Donell Harvin, a top official at DC's homeland-security department.

Kimberly Lassiter, a supervisor at the medical examiner's office. And Dr. Roger Mitchell, the chief medical examiner himself.

Wearing masks and rubber gloves, they bow their heads. Tomorrow, the first body will be sent here. Today, a blessing.

Yea, though I walk through the valley of the shadow of death, I will fear no evil: for thou art with me; thy rod and thy staff they comfort me.

One by one, the clerics offer prayers, solemn exhortations for strength and humility, courage and dignity, resonating above the grinding hum of the trailers. Imam Shareef invokes the victims—"Their deaths," he says, "are not to be in vain." Reverend Towner prays for the workers, that their bodies will be protected from the virus, that their minds stay healthy during the difficult days ahead. Rabbi Herzfeld stresses the righteousness of the mission. "In Judaism," he tells the group, "we believe that the greatest kindness is to care for the dead."

It's an ominous time in the nation's capital. Several miles away, federal officials are dismissing warnings about the deadly airborne pathogen that has exploded out of Asia. Their unwillingness to act has impelled local governments across the country to launch their own scattered efforts to prevent Covid-19 from decimating their communities. In the District of Columbia, where African Americans make up 46 percent of the population, the task is especially urgent, given the virus's disproportionately cruel impact on people of color.

Over the previous month, the city has been locked down as panicked residents watch their leaders navigate a 100-year crisis in real time. Mayor Muriel Bowser shuttered businesses. The DC Council pushed through legislation to extend unemployment benefits. Health-department officials opened testing sites and implored residents to wear masks and keep their distance. But away from public view, a weightier matter has come to preoccupy a little-known but essential corner of the bureaucracy: the caretakers of the dead.

It's a problem of space. As Drs. Mitchell and Harvin prepared for the pandemic, they realized that the city's morgue didn't have the capacity to handle the surge of fatalities that the virus would leave behind. And so, over the previous few weeks, they hustled to secure the land, equipment, and manpower necessary to build an additional facility.

The clergy who led prayers on the day the field morgue opened were there to make sure the space didn't violate the tenets of their three distinct faiths, and to consecrate the site as one. Then the work began. Over the next two and a half months, Harvin, who describes himself as the "general in charge of the death troops," and his top deputy, Lassiter, who has recovered bodies throughout DC for more than two decades, will oversee the makeshift mortuary. By the time the spring surge is through, 404 Covid victims will have passed through the site.

Still, through it all, almost no one in the city will have any idea the Covid morgue exists. The work is carried out in strict secrecy; staffers are instructed not to disclose the site's location or tell anyone what takes place there, not even their own family members. A mistake—such as a body being released to the wrong family—would be humiliating for the mayor and the city. News footage of workers moving the dead could upset victims' families, opening new wounds, or lure gawkers to the site. As much as anything else, though, the silence reflects the professional ethos of those who perform this work for a living. While they're dispatched to every hurricane and school shooting, their efforts take place entirely behind the scenes. They are the first responders you never see.

"There's not going to be a parade for you guys," Harvin tells each new set of workers to arrive at the Covid morgue. "You're not going to get discounts or big [thank-you] signs. The work we do, we do in silence. Not even the family members of the victims will know what we do. There's a pride in that. There's a silent pride in that," he says. "You're taking care of someone's grandmother, grandfather, husband, daughter, son, and that's a higher calling." When it's all over, they'll return to their previous jobs or assignments and no one will ever know what they've done here. "It's a heavy burden," Harvin says. "It's a very heavy burden.

"[But] the world is watching," he assures them, "whether they see us or not."

Donell Harvin is 48 years old, with a sturdy build and flecks of gray in his goatee. He's married to a physician and has four daughters. He lives in Howard County and spends most of the year looking forward to his annual scuba-diving trip.

Over the last 30 years, Harvin has been an eyewitness to some of America's darkest moments. As an EMT, he responded to the World Trade Center when it was bombed in 1993; after joining the New York Fire Department, he was there when the towers were destroyed in 2001. As a deputy director in New York's medical examiner's office, he led the effort to identify victims of Hurricane Sandy. And in 2012, at the request of Connecticut officials, Harvin assisted with forensics after the massacre at Sandy Hook Elementary.

His path from first responder to frontline bureaucrat began in the Bronx, where he spent his teenage years. After dropping out of high school, he got a GED and then a college scholarship from the Children's Aid Society, enlisting as a paramedic. Though he loved the work, as a young father he began to worry about his safety. He was caught in shootouts while tending to accident victims and lost colleagues in ambulance crashes. On 9/11, his wife and daughters saw him on TV, racing away from the rubble, and then didn't hear from him for 24 hours. Upon seeing their faces when he finally got home, he knew it was time for a change.

Harvin went back to school and earned a master's in emergency management. Landing a position with New York's chief medical examiner, he became an expert in mass-fatality management—the grim business of identifying and processing victims of large-scale tragedies. He also came to know Mitchell, and the two worked together on Sandy Hook. Two years later, when Mitchell was hired as DC's chief medical examiner, he recruited Harvin.

Their immediate task in the District was to turn around an office plagued by mismanagement. But an equally important project loomed. The previous year, Washington had been shaken by tragedy when a mentally disturbed government contractor gunned down 12 people at the Navy Yard. Although the medical examiner's office had properly managed those deaths, officials realized that a larger or more complex disaster would have overwhelmed its capabilities. The city needed a mass-fatality division robust enough to absorb the kind of tragedy that Harvin and Mitchell hoped Washington would never face. They went about building it—securing federal funds, adding staff, and running mass-casualty drills.

By early 2020, Harvin had been in Washington six years. He'd since left Mitchell's office and finished a PhD in public health. He was teaching at Georgetown and had become chief of homeland security and intelligence at DC's homeland-security agency. But the imminent arrival of Covid meant the District was facing the catastrophe he and Mitchell had trained for, the biggest mass-fatality event in the city's history.

On March 2, Harvin went to DC's Emergency Operations Center for the first day of formal briefings about how the city would navigate the pandemic. Halfway through the morning, he found a quiet spot in the hallway and placed a call to his mother. "This is going to be bad," he said.

The city morgue is located at 401 E Street, Southwest. In any given year, only a fraction of the fatalities that occur in DC pass through the facility. When a person dies of natural causes at a hospital, nursing home, or hospice, a physician will typically sign the death certificate and release the body to a funeral home. It's usually only those who die alone or in unnatural or suspicious circumstances whose bodies go to the morgue, where medical examiners determine the cause and manner of their death.

Initially, Harvin and Mitchell planned to use this same approach for the pandemic, relying on hospitals—where the bulk of virus-related deaths would take place—to serve as de facto Covid morgues. But they quickly revised their thinking. For one thing, little was known about how contagious the disease might be post-mortem. Would storing victims at hospitals risk infecting staff? At the same time, Harvin learned from former colleagues in New York—which was being ravaged by the virus—that hospitals were too overwhelmed to manage the bodies properly. The result was an appalling spectacle: forklifts carrying pallet-loads of bodies outside hospitals, decedents stacked on top of one another in trailers. At one point, police discovered nearly 100 rotting corpses in unrefrigerated U-Hauls parked by a Brooklyn funeral home. As the funeral home's owner told *The New York Times*, "I ran out of space."

The truth is that all mass-fatality events carry the potential for this type of disgrace. Amid the chaos of a calamity, victims get misidentified. Morgues fill up. "We saw that with Hurricane Katrina—bodies just left out there," Harvin says. "And that's a stain on our society."

So Harvin and Mitchell made a decision that would set them apart from most coroners and medical examiners in the country. Instead of depending on the hospital system, the chief medical examiner's office would assume responsibility. Every single person who dies of Covid in DC would be sent to Harvin and Mitchell's team—a protocol that remains in place today.

By studying the mortality rate and projecting infection levels for the city, the men estimated that as many as 3,500 residents could perish in the pandemic. Or one in every 200. Putting aside the magnitude of the suffering, the math presented a serious logistical problem: The city morgue had an official capacity of only 205. The solution was apparent—they would have to build the Covid morgue.

Harvin immediately began acquiring the materials he'd need. He ordered six refrigerated trailers. He borrowed mobile light towers for nighttime work and generators for power. He acquired PPE, Porta-Potties, drinking water, 500 gallons of hand sanitizer, and heavy-duty body bags specially designed for mass tragedies, 4,000 in all. For families who couldn't afford funerals, the District agreed to pay for cremations. And to prevent a backlog of fatalities, the city shortened the time it would hold unclaimed bodies before they could be cremated, from 30 to 15 days.

Meanwhile, Harvin combed the local and federal bureaucracy in search of an additional 30 workers—to volunteer. The Army agreed to detail members of its mortuary-affairs unit, which had operated similar morgues in combat zones. A trade association found out-of-state funeral directors who wanted to pitch in. DC's Medical Reserve Corps, a group of volunteers willing to assist in health-related emergencies, provided workers. The DC Guard and the Air National Guard sent personnel.

As he rushed to get things in place, the virus was already spreading through Washington. Harvin felt the same sense of foreboding he'd experienced six years earlier when he was waiting for Hurricane Sandy to make landfall. "It's like a slow-moving train," he says. "You know it's coming and you can't stop it."

While Harvin was acquiring equipment and manpower, his top lieutenant, Kim Lassiter, spent two days driving around the District, scouting possible sites for the morgue. At her last stop, she got out of her car and peered through the fence. The property had everything. It was city-owned land—a parking lot for DC employees, empty because staffers were now working from home. It was large enough for the trailers, and it could be secured with tarps and guards. Most important, the site was inconspicuous: You could drive right past it and not realize it was there. "This is perfect," Lassiter thought.

Lassiter, a 54-year-old grandmother with a soft smile, is the second-longest-tenured medical examiner's employee, with nearly a quarter century on the job. In the 1990s, she lifted the victims of gang wars off street corners and washed the blood from their wounds at the morgue. In 2002, she used x-rays to identify the remains of Chandra Levy, the 24-year-old intern whose murder had become the subject of national fascination when it was alleged she'd been dating a married congressman around the time of her disappearance. And in 2008, Lassiter carried the remains of four children—ages 5, 6, 11, and 17—from the house where they'd been decomposing for seven months, after their mother, Banita Jacks, became convinced they'd been possessed by demons and killed them.

Lassiter came to the work by way of her own personal tragedy. She grew up in a housing project in Prince George's County, with five brothers and sisters. Her father wasn't around, and her mother, who worked in healthcare, struggled to do it all on her own. She eventually fell victim to drug use. It was up to Lassiter—the eldest of the children—to run the household. She cut class three days a week to watch her siblings. At 12, she got a summer job to support the family. Even after she graduated from high school and entered the workforce, there were periods when she would drop everything to nurse her mother through the various chemical fogs and illnesses that encumber the life of an addict.

In 1987, when Lassiter was 21, her mother passed away. Lassiter was called to the hospital. A nurse escorted her to the elevator, and they rode down to the basement. There, in a frigid room, Lassiter found her mother lying motionless on a stretcher. Her eyes were still open. "I felt like," Lassiter remembers, "she was waiting for me to show up."

The nurse explained that her mother was being taken away for an autopsy. Lassiter didn't know anything about the process, and the news frightened her. "If I could have gone with her through that," she says, "I would have."

Following the funeral, Lassiter obtained custody of her siblings, whom she supported through her job as a clerk at the US Department of Health and Human Services. A few years later, her life took an unexpected turn when she spotted an alarming story in the newspaper: The DC chief medical examiner's office had released the wrong body to a grieving family. The incident sounded both outrageous and intriguing; more than anything, it reminded Lassiter—by then a mother herself—of when her mom had been sent to the morgue. She called the office, talked her way to a supervisor, and asked if she could help. She joined the office as a volunteer.

This was the late 1990s, and the agency was considerably smaller than it is today. Lassiter was quickly hired and eventually promoted, becoming one of seven technicians responsible for a full sweep of duties: fielding intake calls from police, snapping photographs at death scenes, transporting decedents to the morgue, and assisting with medical examinations and autopsies. She viewed the work not as some macabre responsibility but as an expression of love. While she hadn't been able to care for her own mother after her death, she now looked after the deceased loved ones of others.

When arriving at a place of death, Lassiter is vigilant about wearing a blank facial expression, to acknowledge the gravity of the circumstances. She offers condolences, then completes her tasks—attaching the toe tag, placing the deceased into the body bag—at a diligent pace so as not to prolong the trauma of those looking on. Once an autopsy is complete, she uses tight, neat sutures to close the incisions. She then washes the stains from the body and wraps it in a crisp white sheet.

Occasionally, when working alone, Lassiter has found herself speaking out loud to the bodies. If she hits a pothole while driving someone to the morgue, she'll apologize. *I'm sorry.* Upon entering the morgue's cold-storage facility, she sometimes greets the people being kept there. *Good morning.* When examining a crime victim's body—particularly when it's a child's—she often pledges to help get justice. *I'll do everything in my power to find the evidence needed to make whoever did this to you pay.*

The hardest days are the ones when she finds herself face to face with someone she knows. One morning, as Lassiter was preparing for autopsies, she checked the manifest and saw a familiar name. It was an older woman, a friend of her mother's who'd looked out for Lassiter as a child. She walked into the cold-storage room, slid the body out of its cabinet, and said goodbye. It was the only time she ever broke down crying at the morgue.

April 22, 2020—The day after the religious leaders consecrate the site, the Covid morgue begins to stir with workers in face shields, gloves, and white protective suits. It's been six weeks since DC recorded its first case of Covid, and the death toll has exceeded the city morgue's capacity. Now the first wave of bodies is arriving.

The process begins with a phone call. A hospital official, or sometimes a police officer, contacts the medical examiner's office. Lassiter, who is chief of the transport unit, dispatches her team to the scene. Two workers, in full PPE, arrive in a black, unmarked van. They present paperwork for the physician's signature. In the hospital's morgue, they take custody of the body. Opening the body bag, they attach identification. They zip the bag closed and spray the outside with disinfectant, then place it into a second, heavy-duty body bag. They disinfect it again. The workers lift the decedent onto a stretcher and paste an identification tag onto the bag. They slide the stretcher into the back of the unmarked van.

At the Covid morgue, the workers move the decedent onto a table in the intake tent. Here, they weigh the body, to help confirm identification, and enter the victim's name into a computer. They wheel the decedent across the blacktop and up into one of the refrigerated trailers. Next, the transfer. If the victim is heavy, the workers—at least two, sometimes four—lift the body onto one of the lower shelves. If the person is light, they place the body on a higher shelf. The staff use internal coding—6D, 2A—to record the exact location. They exit the trailer, remove their protective suits, and put on fresh ones.

A victim typically remains at the Covid morgue a few days, rarely longer than a week. During that time, a separate team calls family members to help them through the paperwork. Once burial arrangements are made, the funeral director schedules a pickup. The workers wheel the victim out of cold storage and into a second tented canopy—the release tent. They again wipe down the outside of the body bag. They again spray it with disinfectant. The funeral director pulls up. They load the dead into the hearse.

Though it was difficult to find volunteers, Harvin had assembled what he called "a coalition of the willing." The active-duty Army morticians and military reservists, the citizen volunteers, the funeral directors, along with medical-examiner staffers and UDC students. While many had backgrounds in mortuary services, others did not. "We had people," Harvin says, "who had never touched a dead body before—never seen a dead body."

When each new group of volunteers arrived, Harvin—"the general in charge of the death troops"—brought them together to discuss the effort. The victims had come to the Covid morgue after suffering lonely and terrifying deaths—hooked up to breathing tubes, surrounded by masked doctors and nurses. "These people often were dropped off at the hospital, and they couldn't see their loved ones for two or three or four weeks," he continued. "They expired around complete strangers." The staff's goal, Harvin told the troops, was to provide each person with a dignity in death that they didn't experience during their last days of life.

Then he turned it over to Lassiter, who ran the day-to-day operations. She instructed new volunteers how to implement the values Harvin had espoused. When carrying the deceased, move deliberately and with caution. Keep the body as horizontal as possible. Do not, under any circumstances, stack one on top of another. Check, double-check, and triple-check the manifest to make sure each victim is in the correct rack. And pay respect through your words. Lassiter never refers to the deceased as "corpses" or "cadavers" or "cases." Instead, she calls them "my people."

"That's the only way I can get [the workers] to treat them the way they would treat someone that they love," Lassiter says. "Because it makes them see how special these people are to me."

Gerald Slater, 86, was a television executive at PBS and WETA.

Richard Paul Thornell, 83, was a Howard law-school professor who helped establish the Peace Corps's first-ever program, in Ghana.

Jose Mardoqueo Reyes, 54, was a refugee of El Salvador's civil war and a beloved internet-radio broadcaster.

Luevella Jackson, 87, was among the first female bus drivers in DC's public-school system.

Samuel Shumaker III, 90, was an Army colonel who also taught English and creative writing at UDC.

Florence Gilkes, 97, was a loving wife and aunt, as well as a dedicated fan of the Washington Football Team.

Iraj Askarinam, 76, owned a restaurant in Adams Morgan, where he regularly provided free meals to the homeless. They called him "Mr. Spaghetti."

By May, the pandemic's bleakest days had arrived at the morgue. The daily influx of new decedents fluctuated—eight one day, 19 the next. As the volume swelled, the workers came face to face with the breadth of the city's suffering. They began recognizing the last names of victims they'd been dispatched to retrieve, and it dawned on them that these were additional members of already devastated families. Payton McFadden, a UDC premed grad, describes the crushing duty of traveling to a DC hospital to collect the body of a Covid-positive baby: "We had went and gotten one of the [baby's] family members one week prior. [Covid] was slowly but surely matriculating through the whole house." In a searing example of the District's racial inequality, 74 percent of the fatalities were Black. "I will never forget this as long as I live, ever," Lassiter says. "It just took so many people at one time, so suddenly."

A Chicago-area funeral director who asked to be identified only by her first name, Stacey, came to Washington to volunteer. She served in the medical examiner's main office, calling families and guiding them through the process of finalizing death certificates and retrieving loved ones. On one occasion, she spoke with a man whose father was in the Covid morgue, and he dissolved into tears. The man explained that they'd been estranged for years. It was only recently that they'd finally begun speaking again. "We do help carry that burden of grief," she says. "And it's hard." On another day, she had a series of conversations with a police officer whose mother was at the disaster morgue. When the officer suddenly stopped returning her calls, Stacey got hold of his wife, who told her he'd been hospitalized with Covid himself. Nearly a year later, she still wonders about him. "It is always in the back of my head," she says. "I don't know [if] he made it through."

As the morgue's lead official, Harvin was spending up to 12 hours a day at the site. "Everyone's talking about Covid and fatalities, and it's just numbers to them. We're actually dealing with them," he says.

"I have a PhD and I'm in there putting on gloves and a [protective] suit and I'm helping the crews move bodies in and out of trailers. It's visceral for us."

The staff feared for their own safety. "The scariest thing was [potentially being] exposed ourselves," says Denise Lyles, supervisor of the investigation unit. Lassiter grew terrified that she'd infect her family. "I have a husband that goes out and he works. I was concerned about him," she says. "Grandchildren that are asthmatic, concerned about them."

Routine tasks touched off bouts of anguish. While checking the manifest, a worker might spot a detail about a victim that resonated personally: a birthday shared with the worker's daughter, the same last name as a best friend. Harvin and Lassiter did what they could to look out for their staff's mental health. At the end of each day, Lassiter pulled people aside to see if anyone was experiencing symptoms of anxiety or depression, connecting them with counselors or chaplains. Over time, even veterans of the medical examiner's office began struggling with the weight of their mission.

After several weeks at the site, Harvin found that when he returned home from work, he would drift into a haze. He had no appetite. He stopped engaging his wife in conversation. He passed entire evenings staring blankly into the television. "I don't even know what I'm watching," he recalls. "I had no motivation."

Harvin, of course, had worked mass tragedy before. After hijackers flew the first plane into the World Trade Center, he approached the South Tower on foot. From two blocks away, he saw bodies falling from the sky and his entire body froze. He couldn't take another step forward. Minutes later, there was a deafening sound and the tower disappeared into a cloud of gray debris. Out of the rubble came a speeding ambulance. Harvin jumped into the back along with dozens of other firefighters and cops. As they neared the North Tower, Harvin turned to one of them. "Doesn't it look like this one's leaning?" he said.

He spent the next two days at Ground Zero searching for survivors and recovering the dead. The experience was so traumatizing that he vowed never to return to the site. But he found the work at the Covid morgue even more emotionally taxing. "I survived September 11," he says. "I didn't know if I was going to survive this."

While he was able to walk away from Ground Zero after the attack, the pandemic was taking new victims each day. Every time Harvin arrived at the Covid morgue, he confronted a fresh supply of misery, and there was no end in sight. "Your mind and your soul get worn down far long before your body [does]," he says. Recognizing that he was experiencing depression, he turned to colleagues at the homeland-security department and found solace in chatting with them virtually.

For Lassiter, the pain manifested not as psychological trauma but as profound sadness. The heartache was always there, growing more intense over time. May 9—Mother's Day—was the hardest. It had always been a tough one, the day her own mother's death was most painful. But there was an additional heaviness now; she couldn't stop thinking about everyone at the Covid morgue. "There were so many women," she says. "So many mothers there."

Though she was scheduled to be off, Lassiter didn't feel right staying home on that particular day. She left her house in Prince George's County and made the 25-minute drive to the site. Arriving at the morgue, she put on a protective suit and greeted the workers. "What are you doing here?" they asked. "It's Mother's Day."

"I know," she replied, "but I came down because I wanted to really thank you for what you're doing." She understood that some of them were mothers themselves, and she appreciated them for spending the day at the site.

Lassiter walked over to the cold-storage trailers and turned to face her people. "Happy Mother's Day to all the moms," she said. As she returned to the car, she noticed a lightness of spirit.

"It felt kind of like a sign of relief," she says. "Just to speak out. To let them know that someone cares."

June 2020—As summer approaches, the pace at the Covid morgue begins to slow. Fewer victims are arriving; the number of bodies in the trailers is declining. By the end of the month, the volume is thin enough that it can be handled at the city morgue. Washington's first wave of Covid has reached its conclusion.

It's time for Harvin to shut down the disaster morgue, at least for now. But before doing so, he organizes a final ritual. On July 7, 2020, Rabbi Herzfeld, Reverend Towner, and Imam Shareef return to the site. They were present at the beginning, and Harvin wants them here today, too.

The faith leaders gather by the intake tent as a group of three dozen workers form concentric circles around them. They offer prayers of thanksgiving that the work is coming to an end. "It is at death that the earth receives its treasures," says Imam Shareef. "And we want to honor the facility that now has allowed for individuals to be returned back to the earth."

After the ceremony, Lassiter assembles the men and women on her team to thank them for their two and a half months of service. When she finishes, a soldier who was assigned to the site pulls a patch off his flak jacket and approaches her. "This patch has been around the world," he tells Lassiter, "and I want you to have it."

Though the pandemic rages on, Harvin and Lassiter can't help but feel a certain triumph. They haven't misidentified any bodies. None of their team has contracted Covid. They know they may be back. But in a dark and painful year, this is a good day.

Months later, Lassiter will remember it, the special pride she felt that despite dozens of workers toiling and thousands of pounds of equipment rumbling, despite 404 fatalities passing through, word of the Covid morgue never reached the public. Her colleagues hadn't enlisted for accolades. They'd pressed through the fear and the grief in order to care for the innocent victims of a historic pandemic.

"It felt good," Lassiter says. "Even if no one would ever know about it."

It's been nearly a year since the pandemic struck Washington. In the first four months of lockdown, the city lost three times as many jobs as it did during the 2008 recession. By July, small business revenue had been cut in half. Metrorail ridership has plunged by as much as 90 percent. Over the coming four years, the District is anticipating a budget gap of roughly $800 million. All told, more than 933,514 people in DC, Maryland, and Virginia have contracted the virus, and 15,148 have died.

Today, Covid fatalities are being processed at the city morgue in Southwest DC; although the number of deaths is once again elevated, it's well below the peaks of last spring. At the disaster morgue, the light towers have been hauled away and the generators have gone silent. The trailers are resting on a deserted blacktop. Each day, thousands of cars pass right by the site, oblivious to what happened there. If they knew where to look, though, the drivers could see something that Harvin made sure to leave in place. The DC and US flags, rising above the fence.

—*Washingtonian* | February 22, 2021

Requiem for the Supreme Court

With the stroke of a pen, Justice Samuel Alito and four other justices, all chosen by Republican presidents running on successive party platforms committed to overturning Roe v. Wade, erased the constitutional right to reproductive autonomy that the Supreme Court recognized more than 49 years ago. The end of an era? Or the beginning of a new one?

By Linda Greenhouse

They did it because they could.

It was as simple as that.

With the stroke of a pen, Justice Samuel Alito and four other justices, all chosen by Republican presidents running on successive party platforms committed to overturning Roe v. Wade, erased the constitutional right to reproductive autonomy that the Supreme Court recognized more than 49 years ago. As the dissenting opinion—written by Justices Stephen Breyer, Sonia Sotomayor and

Elena Kagan—observed, never before had the court rescinded an individual right and left it up to the states whether to respect what had once been anchored in the Constitution.

The practical consequences of the decision, Dobbs v. Jackson Women's Health Organization, are enormous and severe. Abortion, now one of the most common medical procedures, will be banned or sharply limited in about half the country. Excluding miscarriages, nearly one in five pregnancies ends in abortion in the United States, and one American woman in four will terminate a pregnancy during her lifetime. Two generations of women in this country have come of age secure in the knowledge that an unintended pregnancy need not knock their lives off course. "After today," as the dissent pointed out, "young women will come of age with fewer rights than their mothers and grandmothers had."

What the court delivered on Friday is a requiem for the right to abortion. As Chief Justice John Roberts, who declined to join Justice Alito's opinion, may well suspect, it is also a requiem for the Supreme Court.

Consider the implication of Justice Alito's declaration that Roe v. Wade was "egregiously wrong" from the start. Five of the seven justices in the Roe majority—all except William O. Douglas and Thurgood Marshall—were appointed by Republican presidents. The votes necessary to preserve the right to abortion 19 years later in Planned Parenthood v. Casey, the Roe follow-up decision that the court also overturned on Friday, came from five Republican-appointed justices.

In asserting that these justices led the court into grave error from which it must now be rescued, Justice Alito and his majority are necessarily saying that these predecessors, joining the court over a period of four decades, didn't know enough, or care enough, to use the right methodology and reach the right decision. The arrogance and unapologetic nature of the opinion are breathtaking. (Of the justices who decided Casey in 1992, the only member of the court still serving is Justice Clarence Thomas, a dissenter then, who wrote in a concurring opinion on Friday that now that the court has overturned the right to abortion, it should also reconsider its precedents on contraception, L.G.B.T.Q. rights and same-sex marriage.)

The dissenting justices wrote on Friday, "The majority's refusal even to consider the life-altering consequences of reversing Roe and Casey is a stunning indictment of its decision." They observed, "The majority has overruled Roe and Casey for one and only one reason: because it has always despised them, and now it has the votes to discard them. The majority thereby substitutes a rule by judges for the rule of law."

Those sentences are as terrifying as they are obviously correct. Where do they leave the court, now having voluntarily shed the protection offered by its usual stance that it is simply the passive recipient of the disputes that the public brings to its door?

For several years, members of the new majority have been openly inviting opportunities to revisit Roe and Casey, just as the same justices, principally Justices Thomas and Alito, spent years inviting the gun lobby to bring cases affording an opportunity to expand on the Second Amendment analysis of the 2008 Heller decision; that campaign culminated on Thursday with the decision in the New York State gun-licensing case. That case, New York State Rifle & Pistol Association v. Bruen, of course, did not overturn an old right but expanded on a new one.

The court engaged in no such outreach at the time of Roe. To the contrary, the case reached the Supreme Court under a jurisdictional statute, since repealed, that required it to rule on the merits whenever a federal court had invoked federal constitutional grounds to invalidate a state law. A special three-judge Federal District Court, convened under that statute, had declared unconstitutional the Texas law that made abortion a crime except to save a pregnant woman's life.

For the court to take on Roe v. Wade, in other words, was the opposite of judicial activism. Friday's ruling, meanwhile, was judicial activism's epitome: A federal appeals court had blocked a Mississippi law on the ground that the law's ban on abortion after 15 weeks of pregnancy was obviously inconsistent with Roe and Casey. (Those decisions protected the right to abortion up until fetal viability, or about 24 weeks.) The state originally asked the justices to decide whether a ban on abortion before viability was always unconstitutional. Over Chief Justice Roberts's objection, the majority opinion went further, eliminating the right to abortion in its entirety.

In a concurrence, the chief justice underscored just how aggressive the majority opinion was, writing: "Surely we should adhere closely to principles of judicial restraint here, where the broader path the court chooses entails repudiating a constitutional right we have not only previously recognized, but also expressly reaffirmed applying the doctrine of stare decisis." He added that "its dramatic and consequential ruling is unnecessary to decide the case before us."

But Justice Alito declined that call for restraint. The chief justice's "quest for a middle way would only put off the day when we would be forced to confront the question we now decide," Justice Alito wrote. "The turmoil wrought by Roe and Casey would be prolonged. It is far better—for this court and the country—to face up to the real issue without further delay."

There will be turmoil now, for sure, as the country's highways fill with women desperate to regain control over their lives and running out of time, perhaps followed by vigilantes across state lines. But the only turmoil that was caused by Roe and Casey was due to the refusal of activists, politicians and Republican-appointed judges to accept the validity of the precedents. Justice Alito's reference to "turmoil" reminded me of nothing so much as Donald Trump's invocation of "carnage" in his inaugural address. There was no carnage then, but there was carnage to come.

Forty-nine years is a long time, but professional lives, including mine, are long as well. I was a freshly minted journalist at The Times in 1969 when I received an assignment to write about the growing controversy over abortion. I immersed myself in the issue, interviewing and learning from lawyers on both sides of the debate. On Jan. 25, 1970, The New York Times Magazine published my article under the headline "Constitutional Question: Is There a Right to Abortion?" It was, I believe, the first article in a general-interest publication to survey the nascent constitutional arguments, and it has been quite widely reprinted. When I finished reading Friday's decision in preparation for writing this essay, I realized that I will have chronicled this profound issue across its entire arc, a perspective I never could have anticipated.

Except, of course, that the story isn't over. Although Justice Brett Kavanaugh proclaimed with evident relief in his concurring opinion that the court was now bowing out of the picture and "will no longer decide how to evaluate the interests of the pregnant woman and the interests in protecting fetal life throughout pregnancy," that is not likely to be the case. Those pesky women will keep coming up with problems: What about pregnancy-related medical issues short of imminent death? Rape? Incest? Fetuses doomed to die in the womb or shortly after birth? Will young teens be forced to bear children? Will women who receive a prenatal diagnosis of a serious fetal anomaly be forced to bring a child into the world whom they can't care for adequately and in whom the state has little postnatal interest? What happens when states start prosecuting not only doctors but women?

Justice Alito has an answer to these questions: "rational basis." A law regulating abortion, he writes, "must be sustained if there is a rational basis on which the legislature could have thought that it would serve legitimate state interests." And what might be such an interest? The list of "legitimate interests" is frightening:

> Respect for and preservation of prenatal life at all stages of development . . . the protection of maternal health and safety; the elimination of particularly gruesome or barbaric medical procedures; the preservation of the integrity of the medical profession; the mitigation of fetal pain; and the prevention of discrimination on the basis of race, sex or disability.

With the exception of the first and second interests—the Casey decision itself recognized the state's interest in unborn life throughout pregnancy—these are anti-abortion dog whistles. The "particularly gruesome" procedures include a common method of second-trimester abortion that some states have tried to outlaw. The "integrity" of the medical profession is a slam on doctors whom Friday's majority refers to as "abortionists." The "fetal pain" issue is a canard, as fetuses lack the neural development to experience pain until late in pregnancy. And the discrimination issue refers, at least in part, to current state laws that would criminalize the abortion of fetuses with a Down syndrome diagnosis; currently, most such pregnancies are terminated.

And the dissenting opinion asks, "What about the morning-after pill? IUDs? In vitro fertilization?" Or medical management of miscarriage, often by the same methods used for abortion?

No, justices, your work isn't done. What you have finished off is the legitimacy of the court on which you are privileged to spend the rest of your lives.

—*The New York Times* | June 24/26 (digital/daily), 2022

Maya Lin's Vietnam memorial blazed a path in 1982, but no one followed.

Architects and designers have avoided grappling with Maya Lin's genius.

By Philip Kennicott

M aya Lin's Vietnam Veterans Memorial, which opened 40 years ago this month, changed everything and nothing about how we understand memorials.

Its list of soldiers lost in the war, more than 58,000 names carved into black granite, foregrounded not the valor of combat, but the toll of it. Its simplicity and abstraction, just two long walls set at an angle in the earth, broke with centuries of established memorial architecture. Its refusal to editorialize on a war that was deeply unpopular at home and destructive to millions of innocent people in Southeast Asia was a radical departure from the standard cant about noble causes that had defined war memorials for centuries.

It was the most consequential monument of the 20th century, and it reinvigorated the making of monuments and memorials in Washington. And yet, despite its groundbreaking power and enormous popularity, it has had a faltering influence on memorials ever since. New ones fail to equal its power, and most designers and architects avoid grappling with its basic premise. Lin's flame burns too brightly to be confronted directly, and the history of monuments and memorials in Washington has been a history of avoiding her real genius.

When the memorial was dedicated on Nov. 13, 1982, the highest-ranking member of Ronald Reagan's administration present was the deputy administrator of the Veterans Administration. Reagan declined to be keynote speaker at the ceremony, perhaps in deference to vitriolic right-wing opponents of the design, who likened it to a wall of shame or a gash in the landscape. The rancor of opposition to Lin's design was marked by anti-Asian racism and misogyny, and Lin's vision was decried as cynical and nihilistic because it refused to speak in the familiar language of classical columns, figurative sculpture and bathetic inscriptions.

Yet its construction brought to an end a period of relative inactivity in the core of Washington's memorial landscape. The flaming sword of the Second Division Memorial—like most war memorials at the time devoted to a military entity or the dead of some locality rather than the whole of a war—was dedicated near the White House in 1936. The Jefferson Memorial, a classical pavilion imitating Rome's Pantheon, opened in 1938. For almost a half century after that, Washington was focused more on modern infrastructure: roads, highways, urban renewal schemes and a new subway system which began construction in 1969. Memorial architecture was not part of that modernity.

Indeed, some critics argued that modernity and monument making were fundamentally opposed. In Lewis Mumford's 1937 essay "The Death of the Monument," the critic wrote an epitaph that seemed to hold true for decades: "The very notion of a modern monument is a contradiction in terms: if it is a monument, it cannot be modern, and if it is modern, it cannot be a monument." The modern spirit resisted the old impulse to squander creative energies on things that were moribund and reflective; it was better to live in the world, to make things anew, to create and push forward with useful additions to the city. The 1971 Kennedy Center for the Performing Arts, technically a memorial to the slain president, embodied that spirit, in contemporary architecture that provided a valuable service to the living.

The ultimate success of the Vietnam memorial proved Mumford wrong. But after four decades as one of the city's most popular tourist draws, it's easy to forget exactly what was new about Lin's design.

It wasn't the list of names. Earlier memorials had included names of the fallen, usually listed by some combination of their military rank and alphabetical priority. And the original competition brief for the Vietnam memorial mandated that the names be included.

Nor did Lin invent the language of abstraction in memorial architecture. Eero Saarinen's Gateway Arch in St. Louis, designed a decade after Mumford's essay and opened in 1965, is as spare as Lin's conjoined walls of dark stone. A 1950s competition to design a memorial to Franklin D. Roosevelt elicited some strikingly modern and abstract designs, though the drive to create a large, public memorial to the 32nd president languished for decades. The Washington Monument, stripped of the columns and folderol proposed by its original architect Robert Mills (decades before the Civil War) is also as austere and abstract as Lin's design.

Even the idea that the memorial should not take a stand on the war was dictated in the 1980 competition program published by the Vietnam Veterans Memorial Fund. The memorial should "make no political statement regarding the war or its conduct." Rather, it was to be contemplative, reflective and healing.

Like so many great works of art and architecture before, Lin's design succeeded not by inventing new things, but by balancing, emphasizing and underscoring preexisting or predetermined elements. She didn't just list the names of the dead, she made them the fundamental visual element, ordering them chronologically by the date of their death, not by rank. Her abstraction was more radical than that of Saarinen or Mills because it refused to refer to earlier architectural forms. It wasn't a stripped-down arch or a distended obelisk. It was just two walls meeting in a sunken patch of earth.

As for making "no political statement" about the war, she achieved that all too well. In the fevered climate after the United States lost the war and South Vietnam collapsed in 1975, a memorial that refused to comment on the war was seen as intrinsically pacifist, or critical of the war. After she won the competition, Lin would be forced to add inscriptions that trafficked in the usual banalities of memorial verbiage: "Our nation honors the courage, sacrifice and devotion to duty . . . "

The success of the memorial and its rapid embrace by the public helped inaugurate decades of new memorial building on or near the Mall. Every one of these designs steps back from Lin's severity of purpose and moral clarity. The 1995 Korean War Veterans Memorial is centered on figurative sculptures; the 2004 World War II Memorial regurgitates classical architectural banalities—arches, pylons and wreaths—on a scale worthy of Albert Speer. The 2011 Martin Luther King Jr. Memorial is a giant statue of the civil rights icon reminiscent of Soviet or Maoist visual hagiography.

None of these designs forces the visitor into the emotional space and isolated contemplation of the Vietnam memorial. And many of the new monuments come with what often read like a user's manual, instructing the visitor on what to feel, to think, even what to do. At the Japanese American Memorial to Patriotism During World War II, we are reminded at the edge of a pool of water, "Here we admit a wrong. Here we affirm our commitment as a nation to equal justice under the law." The National Park Service website for the American Veterans Disabled for Life Memorial guides visitors through a litany of symbolic elements: "The quiet flow of the water is intended to remind us of how disabled veterans can, with patience, overcome personal obstacles and find new meaning and purpose in their lives" and "the ceremonial flame is an eternal tribute to the strength and sacrifice of veterans."

The blunt symbolism of these memorials prompts us to worthy sentiments. But Lin offered no such prompts, and she resisted making connections between design and meaning. "What I really question is allegory," she said in a New York Times interview published in 1991. "This represents this because it says so in the guidebook. It's the difference between telling people what to think and enabling them— allowing them—to think."

She expected, or rather hoped, that people would experience the memorial as art—open-ended, ambiguous, dependent on the viewer to create meaning—rather than the curated sentimental experience that remains the standard for memorials and audiences today. Architects and designers have copied, imitated or been inspired by aspects of Lin's design for 40 years. But few if any have had the courage to push as far in the direction of minimalism.

And for good reason. The cost is simply too high. Lin's memorial was one of the opening battles in the culture wars that would rage in the 1990s. One residue of those debates about sex, gender and religion—some of which have abated—is a lingering anxiety about the tendency of artists to refuse explicit meaning. The suspicion that artists, intellectuals and academics are mocking us, cloaking subversion in obscure language, remains a vital form of paranoia in American cultural life. In the decades since the Vietnam memorial opened, Americans have become increasingly sophisticated in their anti-intellectualism, tenacious skeptics of ambiguity, adept at finding dark meaning in public art. Any space left open to interpretation becomes merely a vacuum, and conspiracy thinking quickly floods in.

That mind-set left its traces at the memorial early on. Even before it was inaugurated, opponents forced a fundamental design change that included the addition of a figurative statue of three soldiers by artist Frederick Hart. The conventional bronze sculpture was meant to redeem what Hart called a nihilistic memorial from being too elitist. "I don't like art that is contemptuous of life," he said.

When this desecration of Lin's original idea was unveiled in 1984, Reagan attended the ceremony, along with senior members of his cabinet. Unlike in 1982 when the memorial was opened, the president gave a dedication speech.

—*The Washington Post* | Nov. 16, 2022

The Golden Age of the White House Correspondents' Dinner (Yes, there was one.)

The annual gala had a great run of giddy, glamorous years—exactly 24 years, in fact. Let us explain.

By Amy Argetsinger; Roxanne Roberts

There was the time Ellen DeGeneres, just days out of the closet, canoodled with new girlfriend Anne Heche right in front of Bill Clinton. The time George W. Bush goofed around with a George W. Bush impersonator. The time

Barack Obama dunked on reality TV star Donald Trump to the rapturous shrieks of media elite.

What a time to be alive, and in attendance, at the White House Correspondents' Association dinner!

An event by that name is happening again this weekend. Many Washingtonians with entree to media-political circles will armor themselves in black tie or sequins in hopes of snuggling up to a "Vanderpump Rules" star for a selfie, and many more will surely gather the family around C-SPAN Saturday night to chortle over the comedy stylings of the current commander in chief and a guy from "The Daily Show."

But if any of those people think they're witnessing the White House correspondents' dinner—sorry, you already missed it. The pageantry is all just a pantomime at this point, a costumed reenactment paying homage to a golden age of Beltway excess and aspiration, defined by an unbroken quarter-century succession of (we're just going to come out and say it) cute presidents. Clinton. Bush. Obama.

Love them or hate them, it cannot be denied that this was a unique era in both Washington and popular culture, when the nation happened to be led by suave, quippy young boomers with low resting heart rates and fully intact natural hairlines, and who all looked great in a tux. And that era produced some pretty memorable parties.

Was the dinner bad for America? Did it amplify Washington's worst impulses—the chumminess, the insular tone-deafness, the willingness to let lobbyists pick up the tab? Perhaps! But for a while, it certainly gave us something to talk about.

May 1, 1993: Washington was emerging from a recession and a brutal winter, and on this night it was graced by something like royalty: the Honorable Barbra Streisand, EGOT. Fresh from financing the Democratic victories of the previous fall, she swanned through the shadowy expanses of the Washington Hilton ballroom as if key-lit from within, a vision in off-the-shoulder cream, pearls and diamonds—and the town's media heavyweights just about lost their damn minds.

"I've been a great fan of yours all my life," CNN's Wolf Blitzer informed the ambassador from Malibu, prying her away from Gen.

Colin Powell, with whom she had been conferring about gays in the military. Even loquacious professional cynic Christopher Hitchens, who in those days hosted a boozy cool-kids after-party at his Kalorama condo, was left dumbstruck.

"I ended up saying, 'I loved you in "The Way We Were,"'" Hitchens confided to a reporter later that night. "I was so embarrassed."

C-SPAN had decided to broadcast the spectacle for the first time and got way more than it bargained for. Blame or credit Elayne Boosler, the night's hired entertainer. Sliding into a gig traditionally worked by prime-time friendlies like Rich Little or Dick Cavett, the '70s nightclub veteran dutifully dabbled in political humor before settling into her wheelhouse: sex.

"This is the man you want in charge of the bombs!" she exclaimed about the late Sen. John Tower, only two years dead at the time, whose hard-partying reputation had scuttled his shot at running the Pentagon. "A guy who wants to live! He's smoking, he's drinking, he's trying to get laid. He just wants to make it to another Saturday night!" (Trust us: This was wild material, for that room, for that moment.)

But she was merely the opener for our pink-cheeked new prom king, William Jefferson Clinton, who chuckled and aw-shucksed his way through a riff about his first-100-days travails.

"I'm not doing so bad," he rasped. "I mean, at this point in his administration, William Henry Harrison had been dead 68 days!"

The correspondents' dinner predated the Clinton-Bush-Obama years, of course. But for seven decades, it had served simply as an annual hail-fellow-well-met interlude between Washington's press corps and the people it covered—not just the chief executive, but also the lower-level officials and politicians who made and implemented policy.

It was a low-key, inside-the-Beltway night, pleasant but unremarkable. Bob Hope sometimes hosted. Female correspondents weren't invited until the early 1960s.

Faint hints of disruption came in the waning years of the Reagan era. In 1987, Baltimore Sun reporter Michael Kelly famously threw a curve into the invite-a-newsmaker tradition by bringing Fawn Hall, the beautiful blond secretary at the center of the Iran-contra scandal. A year later, he jolted the room again by escorting Donna Rice, the Other Woman who sank Gary Hart's presidential hopes.

But the celebrity explosion began with Clinton, the first boomer president, who had an innate understanding of pop culture. He had braved the cringe to toodle a saxophone on "The Arsenio Hall Show." The hit-making producers of the sitcom "Designing Women" crafted his swooning biographical film for the campaign; Fleetwood Mac, only a few years removed from their chart-topping days, reunited to play his inauguration. So, yeah, you can imagine what those dinners were like.

"Clinton loved anything that was fun," said Ann Stock, a former White House social secretary. "And it was a fun night."

It was a fun time in general. Washington was beginning to enjoy an influx of money and cachet. Fourteenth Street, the city's erstwhile red-light district, begin to fill up with fashionable restaurants. No one was jaded about any of this, not yet. When the dinner rolled around, crowds of autograph seekers formed outside the Hilton, and the competition for the limited number of tickets surged.

The intersection of traditional Washington and Hollywood Washington was irresistible: After Michael Douglas starred in 1995's "An American President," he was greeted as something like the doppelganger in chief whenever he showed up for the White House correspondents' dinner weekend. By the time "The West Wing" debuted on NBC in 1999, the real White House and its fictional double had been melded into a fast-talking, liberal fever dream. The 2000 dinner opened with a seven-minute video starring the TV cast and the real White House press secretary, Joe Lockhart.

"The White House correspondents' dinner is meant to honor serious journalists," Lockhart told his fictional counterpart, actress Allison Janney, in the clip. "A lot of people are really uncomfortable with the Hollywood-izing of government."

Big laugh. All the cast members were at the dinner, of course, and treated as if they were actual administration officials. Weird, yes, but "shows like 'West Wing' became a civics course in why government matters," said Melissa Moss, a former finance director of the Democratic National Committee. And that was intoxicatingly flattering for a town like Washington.

The Hollywood ardor cooled a little with the advent, in 2001, of a Republican administration. But by then, the dinner was taking on its own momentum—and a whole new class of entertainment celebrities had emerged. They were reality TV stars—from "Survivor," from "American Idol"—happy to fill Streisand's empty seat if offered, and yet they were no less mesmerizing to their Washington banquet partners, at least during their moment of white-hotness.

Even the new Republican president was willing to play ball.

In 2002, Greta Van Susteren—at the time a hard-edge Fox News host who turned out to have extremely playful tastes in White House correspondents' dinner guests—brought Ozzy Osbourne and his wife, Sharon, at the height of their new fame as MTV reality stars. Ozzy, the perpetually dazed heavy-metal pioneer, flung himself into the spirit of things, making his way to the front of the room, where Bush was seated at the head table.

The two men gazed at each other across the Secret Service's 10-foot DMZ, reported our colleague David Montgomery. Ozzy made a prayerful gesture. Bush nodded.

And then Ozzy grabbed a hank of his shoulder-length brown-and-pink hair and shouted:

"You should wear your hair like mine!"

The president paused, flushed momentarily, then grinned.

"Second term, Ozzy!" he shouted back.

What started with cocktail receptions hosted by news organization exploded into a marathon of events piggybacking on the dinner. People magazine handed out groaning gift bags, but the undisputed A-list bash was Vanity Fair's, sometimes in partnership with Bloomberg—elegantly over the top, filled with stars, and almost impossible to crash. If you could get in, though, it could be beguilingly intimate. It was the place to see John F. Kennedy Jr. tenderly cuddling his wife, Carolyn Bessette-Kennedy—captured in an enduringly romantic photo that broke hearts after they were both killed in a plane crash months later.

"In the years before social media, when you had these cultural icons in town, there was a novelty and singular thrill of being in the room," said Juleanna Glover, a veteran public-affairs consultant.

The excitement over the election of the first Black president sent the correspondents' dinner into overdrive, the parties becoming a glut of A-listers: Demi and Ashton, and Affleck and Garner, and Kim Kardashian, and the Jonas Brothers, and Justin Bieber, strutting around as if he owned the joint. The dinner became an important stop on the promotional junket for any show or movie about politics— "Homeland" star Claire Danes, "Scandal" star Kerry Washington, "House of Cards" star Kevin Spacey, who brought down the house with his "House of Nerds" spoof video in 2013. (Co-starring presidential adviser Valerie Jarrett, Sen. John McCain, Rep. Kevin McCarthy, Mike Bloomberg and a number of Washington reporters.)

"Washington and Hollywood," intoned Spacey's Frank Underwood. "Some new faces, some old faces, some new faces on old faces."

Obama rose to the occasion, one year tag teaming with rising comedic powerhouse Keegan-Michael Key, who played Luther, the president's "anger translator," voicing the supposed rage simmering beneath Obama's cool demeanor.

Obama: "Despite our differences, we count on the press to shed light on the most important issues in our day . . . "

Luther: "We count on Fox News to terrify old white people with some nonsense! 'Sharia law is coming to Cleveland, run for the damn hills!' Y'all ridiculous!"

And then what happened? Well, Trump happened.

If you were the kind of person who hated Trump and hated the White House correspondents' dinner, you might have blamed the latter for the former—going back to the night in 2011, when both Obama and comedian Seth Meyers mocked Trump to his face in an electrifying pair of monologues excoriating him for his birther conspiracy theories. . . . and, supposedly, inspiring him to regroup and run for president.

So what would it be like if Trump came to the dinner as president? We never got to find out. He declined all invitations, but the celebrities and the party hosts had pulled out anyway. The White House Correspondents' Association struggled to find the right tone, balancing edgy comics with somber lectures on journalism and democracy by the likes of Ron Chernow and Woodward and Bernstein.

Then came the pandemic and two years of no dinner. Some greeted last year's first Biden-era dinner like a cathartic high school reunion, so glad were they to hit the cocktail circuit again . . . and then woke up the next week with a sore throat and fever.

President Biden's speech—well, it was fine, right? Everyone loves old Uncle Joe. Safe, decent, comfortable. No one died of horror. Trevor Noah did a routine, and he was probably good? We'll have to look it up on YouTube.

As for this year, there's always a chance something will surprise or delight us. But we're not holding our breath.

—*The Washington Post* | April 28, 2023

Acknowledgements

Special thanks to:

Anna Fiorino

Catherine Bruno

Maria Sheehan

Wendy Lovinger

Leorah Gavidor

Patsy Sims

Sherri Dalphonse at *Washingtonian*

Jennifer Rockwood at *The Washington Post*

Benjamin Shepard, Rights and Permissions Specialist at
Wright's Media for *The New York Times*

David Remnick at *The New Yorker*

And all the authors who have contributed their work.

Permissions

"The Saving of the President" by John Pekkanen, first published by *Washingtonian* in August 1981. Reprinted with permission of *Washingtonian* and of the author.

"L'Enfant Terrible" by Howard Means, first published by *Washingtonian* in January 1990. Reprinted with permission of *Washingtonian* and of the author.

"Gary Hart in Exile" by David Remnick, first published by *The New Yorker* on April 19, 1993. Reprinted with permission of the author.

"Maya Lin's Vietnam Memorial Blazed a Path in 1982, but No One Followed" by Philip Kennicott, first published by *The Washington Post* on November 16, 2022. Reprinted with permission of *The Washington Post*.

"When Washington Was Fun" by Maureen Orth, first published by *Vanity Fair*, December 2007. Reprinted with permission of the author.

"Prisoners of Overachievement" by Walt Harrington, first published by *The Washington Post Magazine*, November 12, 1988. Reprinted with permission of *The Washington Post* and of the author.

"City Hall and Step on it" by Wil Haygood, first published by *The Washington Post Magazine*, September 11, 2004. Reprinted with permission of *The Washington Post* and of the author.

"Street on the Hill" by David Finkel, first published by *The Washington Post Magazine*, February 27, 1993. Reprinted with permission of *The Washington Post* and of the author.

"He Began His Teaching Stint with Idealism. And Ended it in Jail." by Marc Fisher, first published by *The Washington Post Magazine*, April 6, 2003. Reprinted with permission of *The Washington Post* and of the author.

"A pupil points a finger. A teacher is fired, his life rerouted. Now can they be buddies?" by Marc Fisher, first published by *The Washington*

About the Editor

Susan Sheehan graduated from Wellesley College in 1958, worked as a fact checker for *Esquire* for a year and a half, started writing book reviews for *The New Republic* in 1959, and light pieces for *The New Yorker* in 1960. After contributing "casuals" and Talk of the Town stories to *The New Yorker*, she became a staff writer for the magazine in 1961 and wrote her first nonfiction series in 1963.

In 1965, Sheehan flew to Jakarta, Indonesia, to marry Neil Sheehan, a *New York Times* foreign correspondent she had met in New York City a few months earlier. In the summer of 1965, Neil was transferred to Saigon, where Sheehan wrote her first book, *Ten Vietnamese*, which was published in 1967. By then Neil had been transferred to the Washington bureau of the *Times*.

Sheehan commuted to New York for the next few decades. She continued to write Talk of the Town stories, and wrote occasionally for other publications, including the *Times*, *The Boston Globe*, and *Washingtonian*, but spent most of her time writing books, which were printed in their entirety in *The New Yorker*. *A Welfare Mother*, published in 1976, won a Sidney Hillman award. *A Prison and a Prisoner*, published in 1978, received the American Bar Association's gavel award. *Is There No Place on Earth for Me?*, published in 1982, won the Pulitzer Prize for general nonfiction in 1983. Sheehan's subsequent books are *Kate Quinton's Days*, *A Missing Plane*, *Life for Me Ain't Been No Crystal Stair*, and, with Howard Means, *The Banana Sculptor, the Purple Lady, and the All-Night Swimmer*.

Sheehan won the feature writing award from the New York Press Club in 1984, the Carroll Kowal Journalism Award from the National Association of Social Workers in 1993, the Public Awareness Award from the National Alliance for the Mentally Ill in 1995, and the Casey Medal for Meritorious Journalism in 1997.

She has received fellowships from the Guggenheim Foundation, the Woodrow Wilson Center for Scholars, and the Open Society Institute. She served as the chair of the Pulitzer Prize-nominating jury for general nonfiction in 1988 and 1994, and as a member of that jury in 1991. She was also a contributing writer for *Architectural Digest* for fifteen years. Most recently she reviewed books for the Outlook section of the *The Washington Post*.

About the Publisher

The Sager Group was founded in 1984. In 2012 it was chartered as a multimedia content brand, with the intent of empowering those who create art—an umbrella beneath which makers can pursue, and profit from, their craft directly, without gatekeepers. TSG publishes books; ministers to artists and provides modest grants; and produces documentary, feature, and commercial films. By harnessing the means of production, The Sager Group helps artists help themselves. For more information, please see TheSagerGroup.net.

More from The Sager Group

THE SAGER GROUP

Artifex Te Adiuva

www.ingramcontent.com/pod-product-compliance
Lightning Source LLC
Chambersburg PA
CBHW021703120626
46545CB00004B/1382